RELATIVE AUTHORITY OF JUDICIAL AND EXTRA-JUDICIAL REVIEW

Do independent boards of appeal set up in some EU agencies and the European Ombudsman compensate for the shortcomings of EU Courts?

This book examines the operation of EU judicial and extrajudicial review mechanisms. It confronts the formal legal rules with evolving practices, relying on rich statistical data and internal documents. It covers detailed institutional arrangements, the standard of review, the types of cases and litigants, and the activity of the parties in the process. It makes visible the diverse but complementary ways in which the mechanisms enhance the authority of EU legal acts and processes. It also reveals that scarce resources and imprecise rules restrict the scope of review and hinder independent empirical investigations. Finally, it casts light on how a differentiated system of judicial and extra-judicial review can accommodate various kinds of technical and political discretion exercised by EU institutions and bodies.

Volume 105 in the Series Modern Studies in European Law

Modern Studies in European Law

Recent titles in this series:

The EU as a Global Regulator for Environmental Protection:
A Legitimacy Perspective
Ioanna Hadjiyianni

Citizenship, Crime and Community in the European Union
Stephen Coutts

Critical Reflections on Constitutional Democracy in the European Union
Edited by Sacha Garben and Inge Govaere

Constitutional Law of the EU's Common Foreign and Security Policy:
Competence and Institutions in External Relations
Graham Butler

The Juridification of Individual Sanctions and the Politics of EU Law
Eva Nanopoulos

Sixty Years of European Integration and Global Power Shifts: Perceptions,
Interactions and Lessons
Edited by Julien Chaisse

Fundamental Rights and Mutual Recognition in the Area of Freedom,
Security and Justice: A Role for Proportionality?
Ermioni Xanthopoulou

Law and Judicial Dialogue on the Return of Irregular Migrants
from the European Union
Edited by Madalina Moraru, Galina Cornelisse and Philippe De Bruycker

Framing Convergence with the Global Legal Order: The EU and the World
Edited by Elaine Fahey

EU Citizenship at the Edges of Freedom of Movement
Katarina Hyltén-Cavallius

The Internal Market 2.0
Edited by Sacha Garben and Inge Govaere

New Directions in European Private Law
Edited by Mateja Durovic and Takis Tridimas

Standing to Enforce European Union Law before National Courts
Hilde Ellingsen

**For the complete list of titles in this series, see
'Modern Studies in European Law' link at
www.bloomsburyprofessional.com/uk/series/
modern-studies-in-european-law**

Relative Authority of Judicial and Extra-Judicial Review

EU Courts, Boards of Appeal, Ombudsman

Michał Krajewski

·HART·

OXFORD · LONDON · NEW YORK · NEW DELHI · SYDNEY

HART PUBLISHING

Bloomsbury Publishing Plc

Kemp House, Chawley Park, Cumnor Hill, Oxford, OX2 9PH, UK

1385 Broadway, New York, NY 10018, USA

29 Earlsfort Terrace, Dublin 2, Ireland

HART PUBLISHING, the Hart/Stag logo, BLOOMSBURY and the Diana logo are trademarks of Bloomsbury Publishing Plc

First published in Great Britain 2021

A catalogue record for this book is available from the British Library.

Library of Congress Cataloging-in-Publication data

Names: Krajewski, Michał (Writer of EU judicial review), author.

Title: Relative authority of judicial and extra-judicial review : EU courts, boards of appeal, ombudsman / Michał Krajewski.

Description: Oxford [UK] ; New York : Hart Publishing, an imprint Bloomsbury Publishing, 2021. | Series: Modern studies in European law ; vol 105 | Includes bibliographical references and index.

Identifiers: LCCN 2021013266 (print) | LCCN 2021013267 (ebook) | ISBN 9781509947294 (hardback) | ISBN 9781509947331 (paperback) | ISBN 9781509947317 (pdf) | ISBN 9781509947300 (Epub)

Subjects: LCSH: Judicial review—European Union countries. | Judicial review of administrative acts—European Union countries. | Ombudspersons—European Union countries. | Extraordinary remedies—European Union countries. | Justice, Administration of—European Union countries.

Classification: LCC KJE5053 .K73 2021 (print) | LCC KJE5053 (ebook) | DDC 347.24/012—dc23

LC record available at https://lccn.loc.gov/2021013266

LC ebook record available at https://lccn.loc.gov/2021013267

ISBN: HB: 978-1-50994-729-4
ePDF: 978-1-50994-731-7
ePub: 978-1-50994-730-0

Typeset by Compuscript Ltd, Shannon
Printed and bound in Great Britain

To find out more about our authors and books visit www.hartpublishing.co.uk. Here you will find extracts, author information, details of forthcoming events and the option to sign up for our newsletters.

ACKNOWLEDGEMENTS

This book is a substantially revised version of my doctoral thesis, defended at the European University Institute (Florence, Italy) on 10 January 2020. I wish to acknowledge that some of the chapters are based on other publications of mine. A part of chapter 4 appeared as 'The Many-Faced Court: The Value of Participation in Annulment Proceedings' (2019) 15 *European Constitutional Law Review* 220. Some of the research material underlying parts of chapters 4 and 5 was also used in 'Judicial and Extra-Judicial Review: The Quest for Epistemic Certainty' in Mariolina Eliantonio, Merijn Chamon, Annalisa Volpato (eds), *The Boards of Appeal of European Agencies: A New Paradigm of Legal Protection?* (forthcoming in Oxford University Press 2021).

I am indebted to many professors, colleagues and friends, as well as EU officials, for valuable data and feedback. First and foremost, I am grateful to Deirdre Curtin, the supervisor of my thesis, for her incredible patience and dedication, for inspiring feedback and for motivating me to always look for more data and sharpen my argument, for encouraging me to follow my judgment and intuition rather than instructions and, most importantly, for so much enriching the way I understand the purpose and opportunities offered by legal research. I am also indebted to Filipe Brito Bastos, a more senior EUI researcher and a wonderful friend, who has always let me benefit from his experience, making sure that my academic struggles are at least a little easier than his own.

In writing the thesis, I greatly benefited from discussions with professors and fellow PhD researchers at the EUI and elsewhere. There are too many to mention, but I wish to acknowledge the insights and exceptional support offered by Urška Šadl, Claire Kilpatrick, Gábor Halmai, Bruno de Witte, Lucia López Zurita, Janneke van Casteren, Michał Ziółkowski, Jan Komárek, Luca de Lucia, Sabine Mair, Rodrigo Vallejo, Rebecca Mignot-Mahdavi, Marcin Barański, Bartosz Marciniak, Przemek Pałka, Rían Derrig Hubert Bekisz and Stein Arne Brekke. I very much appreciate the feedback I received from Paola Chirulli and Joana Mendes, the members of my Examining Board from whose research I have always been drawing inspiration. My special thanks go to Nicola Hargreaves from the EUI Language Centre, who helped me realise that clear writing and in-depth understanding go hand-in-hand. I am also immensely grateful to the supervisor of my Master thesis at the University of Warsaw, Robert Grzeszczak, who has been offering colossal support ever since I told him about my plans to apply to the EUI. While transforming my thesis into this book, I greatly benefited from the support and influence of wonderfully inspiring colleagues at the *iCourts* Centre of Excellence for International Courts at the University of Copenhagen.

I also wish to thank Michal Bobek, Advocate General at the Court of Justice, for offering me a traineeship that made a large part of my research possible. I also wish to thank his incredibly inspiring team: François-Xavier Millet, Sara Iglesias Sánchez, Magdalena Ličkova, Donald Slater, Anjum Shabbir, Milla Tapionlinna and Monika Kotrhova. I was priviledged to meet so many dedicated public servants while working on my thesis: members, référendaires and staff of the EU Courts, the Ombudsman's Office, and the Board of Appeal of the European Chemical Agency. I am grateful to all of them for the time and effort they devoted to process my requests for access to documents and to respond to my questions.

I am grateful for the grant funded by the Polish Minister of Science and Higher Education that enabled my research and the completion of my thesis. I also thank the team of Hart Publishing for the remarkably smooth and helpful publishing process.

Finally, I wish to thank George for his constant and unconditional support, including sharing his incredible knowledge of interdisciplinary research. Also, I am indebted to my Mum, Dad (who helped me immensely with creating databases) and Brother. I dedicate this book to my family, thanking them for their love, dedication and support. Niniejszą książkę dedykuję mojej Rodzinie, dziękując za ich miłość, poświęcenie i wsparcie.

Florence – Copenhagen – Brwinów – Berevoiești
December 2020

CONTENTS

1

Introduction

I. Overview of the Book

This book investigates how extra-judicial review contributes to the authority of law-, rule- and decision-making by EU institutions and bodies. Extra-judicial review is performed at the EU level by boards of appeals, set up in certain agencies, and the European Ombudsman, as well as some other bodies and mechanisms. Most EU legal scholars and practitioners focus on the EU judicial review, which epitomises the ideal of the rule of law, despite its persistent shortcomings, such as fluctuating thoroughness and limited accessibility for private parties. This book casts light on extra-judicial review capacity to frame and constrain the discretion of EU institutions and bodies, and minimise the risk of arbitrariness, thereby supplementing the EU judicial review. It seeks to further the scholarly debate by embedding the judicial and extra-judicial review in the context of manifold institutional and procedural models for implementing the rule of law, and the empirical and normative epistemic uncertainty underlying contemporary EU law-, rule- and decision-making.

The EU Courts have been encountering difficulties in meeting elevated expectations voiced by scholars and litigators due to the expanding regulatory field of the EU and an ensuing increase in the scientific, technical and political intricacy of legal acts and decision-making processes. In reaction to that, extra-judicial review mechanisms – such as the Boards of Appeal (BoAs) and the Ombudsman – have emerged and proliferated. Over time, these mechanisms have improved their working methods and expanded their impact. However, we still know relatively little about their practical operation and their exact relation to judicial review. This book seeks to fill this gap. It collates sundry qualitative and quantitative data to confront the practical operation of EU judicial and extra-judicial review mechanisms, making visible the interplay of their legitimacy assets and weaknesses alike.

The book argues that the authority that the EU judicial and extra-judicial review mechanisms bestow upon law-, rule- or decision-making is relative to specific institutional and procedural features of these mechanisms, and their practical operation.[1] Although often idealised by lawyers, the EU judicial review's legitimacy assets are restricted by this mechanism's institutional and

[1] The authority of public institutions is partly due to how their audiences have assessed their output. However, their authority is continuously co-determined by the input side, ie institutional and

procedural design. Devised in the 1950s to ensure uniformity in the application of EU law and legal protection to a relatively narrow circle of economic operators, the EU judicial review nowadays faces growing challenges. Many scholars and practitioners argue that it should open up to claims by social actors and civil society, and that it should strive at comprehensive scrutiny of diverse, convoluted and disputable empirical and normative appraisals underlying EU legal acts. We should not overlook that extra-judicial review mechanisms can deliver surprisingly strong legitimacy assets, capable of filling some gaps in the EU judicial review. At the same time, they replicate some of the judicial review's weaknesses. Problems are due to under-determined competences, procedural frameworks and insufficient resources.

Nowadays, significant challenges constitute legal acts underpinned by epistemically uncertain empirical and normative appraisals in fields such as the regulation of chemicals, pharmaceuticals, food safety or financial supervision. In such cases, there is often no single correct or wrong answer to a scientific or technical question (empirical uncertainty). Moreover, the applicable law does not offer clear guidance regarding a priority or balance of clashing private or public interests (normative uncertainty). Legal acts and processes entailing different kinds of epistemic uncertainty may necessitate different models of review. A prior engagement of a specialist BoA equipped with tailor-made institutional resources or a more deliberative and persuasion-oriented inquiry led by an ombudsman might achieve goals beyond the capabilities of courts. An explicit articulation by the EU law-makers of the envisaged role of extra-judicial review mechanisms, attuned to their specific legitimacy assets which add to those offered by the EU Courts, may be a viable alternative to an expansion of the one-size-fits-all judicial review.

The book examines detailed and up-to-date qualitative and quantitative data relating to the practical operation of the Article 263(4) Treaty on the Functioning of the European Union (TFEU) action for annulment brought by private parties,[2] and two extra-judicial review mechanisms: the Board of Appeal of the European Chemical Agency (ECHA BoA) and the European Ombudsman. It specifically explores their independence safeguards and organisational resources, review techniques, case outcomes, litigation patterns and procedural tools for interaction with the parties. The book draws from a vast array of fragmentary sources, scattered across the respective review bodies, to explore and systematically compare their practices. In particular, the analysis relies on a unique dataset relating to the litigation before the different review bodies closed in the five-year period 2014–18. It also examines a wide range of public or internal documents, the latter obtained through

procedural assets such as independence, accessibility, the technique and process of review, and transparency (the input). The notion of authority used in this book is normative in nature as relating to reasoned arguments that can be formulated based on the institutional and procedural operation of specific institutions, and subsequently invoked to foster the rational acceptability of their decisions.

[2] Chapter 4 takes account of the indirect Article 267 TFEU validity references from domestic courts. Private parties are understood in this book broadly, as natural persons and legal persons, as well as any other profit-seeking entities and non-governmental organisations or associations acting in the public interest. This notion excludes governmental agencies, local governments, third countries and public international actors.

access-to-documents requests (preparatory works, reports, memoranda, procedural guidelines or case files). Moreover, the book draws from insights collected through a series of semi-structured in-depth interviews with EU judges and their référendaires, agency and Ombudsman staff, carried out in 2017–20 in order to enhance the author's understanding of the day-to-day operation of the respective mechanisms. Table 1.1 provides an overview of methods and sources employed in the book, on top of the doctrinal analysis of relevant legal provisions and case law, to reveal, compare and evaluate the examined mechanisms' practical operation.

Table 1.1 Overview of methods and sources regarding the practical operation of review mechanisms

Feature/ mechanism	**EU Courts**	**ECHA BoA**	**Ombudsman**
Independence		Internal documents regarding administrative arrangements	
Powers	Quantitative analysis of the rate of successful actions	Quantitative analysis of the rate of successful appeals	Quantitative analysis of the rate of settled cases and findings of maladministration
Accessibility	Quantitative analysis of the types of litigants and cases		
Procedural activity of the adjudicators and the parties	Internal procedural statistics and guidelines	Audio recordings of oral hearings, *travaux préparatoires* of procedural rules	Internal procedural guidelines, case files and documents from consultations of recent procedural reforms

The book is addressed to scholars and practitioners interested in the operation and challenges encountered by the EU judicial and extra-judicial review mechanism. It offers useful material for practitioners, facilitating a deeper understanding and critical evaluation of the institutional arrangements and procedural law of the EU Courts, BoAs and the Ombudsman. Institutional arrangements and procedural law are often conceived of as no more than technicalities aimed at efficient proceedings. However, this book makes visible that they play a crucial role in enhancing the authority of legal acts subject to review and, consequently, the authority of the whole EU governance structure. This way, the book adds a theory-laden and comparative layer of analysis to voluminous and practice-oriented guidebooks of EU procedural law.[3] Hopefully, its insights could prove

[3] Such as Koen Lenaerts, Ignace Maselis, Kathleen Gutman, *EU Procedural Law* (Oxford University Press 2014). René Barents, *EU Remedies and Procedures* (Wolters Kluwer 2016). Paul Lasok, *European Court Practice and Procedure* (Bloomsbury 2017).

relevant in ongoing discussions regarding the EU judicial and extra-judicial architecture.[4]

The book takes stock of the existing experiments with extra-judicial review mechanisms and provides a framework for analysing their future role. It joins an emerging scholarly discussion about the role of the BoAs,[5] the ongoing discussion regarding the added value of the Ombudsman,[6] and the long-standing discussion regarding the accessibility and thoroughness of EU judicial review. Thus, it seeks to further the debate on the legal protection of private parties at the EU level.[7] The current debate seems somewhat deadlocked, reiterating the well-known arguments of the 'rule of law' and 'effective judicial protection'. The postulated opening up of the EU Courts to social actors and civil society has never materialised. Inconsistencies in the intensified standard of judicial review stir doubts about the ability of generalist EU judges to review technically or scientifically complex legal acts. This book makes visible alternative ways to tackle the problems that have remained under-explored.

Finally, the book contributes to the recently revived debate in EU administrative law regarding the ability of law to frame and constrain discretionary power. This debate has been revived due to competence shifts between the Member States, the EU and other transnational bodies in the aftermath of the 2008 financial crisis, and the expanded EU regulation of risks to public health and the environment.[8]

[4] The recent enlargement of the General Court (EGC) will be assessed in the following months or years. At the same time, the role of the BoAs is now discussed in the context of them being a justification for limiting the right of appeal to the Court of Justice (ECJ) against certain rulings of the EGC. See Chapter 4, Section IV.D. A legislative debate on the Ombudsman's new Statute and some details of her mandate is also ongoing. See, Chapter 6, Section IV.A.

[5] See especially, Paola Chirulli and Luca de Lucia, *Rimedi amministrativi ed esecuzione diretta del diritto europeo* (Giappichelli Editore 2018). Barbara Marchetti (ed), *Administrative Remedies in the European Union. The Emergence of a Quasi-judicial Administration* (Giappichelli Editore 2017).

[6] See generally, Nikos Vogiatzis, *The European Ombudsman and Good Administration in the European Union* (Palgrave 2018). Jacques Ziller and Herwig Hofmann, *Accountability in the EU: The Role of the European Ombudsman* (Edward Elgar 2017). Maria Lee, 'Accountability and Co-production beyond Courts: The Role of the European Ombudsman' in Maria Weimer and Anniek de Ruijter (eds), *Regulating Risks in the European Union: The Co-production of Expert and Executive Power* (Hart Publishing 2017). Madalina Busuioc, 'Extra-judicial Accountability: The European Ombudsman and "Life Beyond Legality"' in *European Agencies: Law and Practices of Accountability* (Oxford University Press 2013). Paul Magnette, 'The European Ombudsman: Protecting Citizens' Rights and Strengthening Parliamentary Scrutiny' in N Diamandouros (ed), *The European Ombudsman: Origins, Establishment, Evolution* (Office for Official Publications of the European Communities 2005).

[7] This debate has hitherto been focused on the remedies and procedures before the EU Courts. One of the most comprehensive studies is Angela Ward, *Judicial Review and the Rights of Private Parties in EU Law* (Oxford University Press 2007). Regarding the accessibility of judicial review see, among many, Anthony Arnull, 'Judicial Review in the European Union' in Damian Chalmers and Anthony Arnull (eds), *The Oxford Handbook of European Union Law* (Oxford University Press 2015). Regarding the thoroughness of judicial review see, among many, Hans Peter Nehl, 'Judicial Review of Complex Socio-Economic, Technical and Scientific Assessments in the European Union' in Joana Mendes (ed), *EU Executive Discretion and the Limits of Law* (Oxford University Press 2019).

[8] Joana Mendes (ed), *EU Executive Discretion and the Limits of Law* (Oxford University Press 2019).

These shifts entail decision-making in the context of ineluctable socio-economic, scientific, technical and political uncertainty. A meaningful debate about EU law's capacity to constrain and orient political and administrative discretion cannot refrain from analysing the nitty-gritty of different institutional and procedural models of review mechanisms.

II. Beyond the Judicial Paradigm

For public law scholars, courts epitomise the rule of law, an idea which has to do mostly with constraining discretionary powers and minimising the risk of arbitrariness. Article 19(1) Treaty on European Union (TEU) ascribes the function of the ultimate arbiter of EU legality to the EU Courts: the Court of Justice (the 'ECJ') and the General Court (the 'EGC').[9] The ideal of the rule of law at the EU level has been equated with the right of court action against potentially unlawful legal acts of EU institutions and bodies. It is no surprise that one of the most popular themes in the EU constitutional and administrative law scholarship has been the EU Courts' legal and practical ability to supervise any typical or novel forms, instances and aspects of law-, rule- and decision-making.[10]

Scholars and practitioners have mostly been concerned about the inaccessibility of the Article 263(4) TFEU action for annulment.[11] Advocate General Kokott has proclaimed the interpretation of this article to be 'one of the most contentious issues in EU law'.[12] The annulment action is considered to lie at the core of the EU system of legal protection.[13] It enables private parties to trigger the judicial review of unfavourable and potentially unlawful EU legal acts.[14] This avenue has always been primarily accessible to individual economic operators, notwithstanding that EU legal acts may indirectly affect a variety of third parties and society in general. The Article 267 TFEU procedure for preliminary references by domestic courts regarding the validity of EU legal acts does not in practice seem to constitute a satisfactory alternative for industry associations, trade unions, public interest organisations and other social actors. Legislative and regulatory acts of general application, in particular, may consequently turn out to be immune to

[9] The EU Courts 'shall ensure that in the application and interpretation of the Treaties the law is observed'.

[10] Regarding the judicial review of soft law measures see most recently, Giulia Gentile, 'Ensuring Effective Judicial Review of EU Soft Law via the Action for Annulment before the EU Courts: A Plea for a Liberal-Constitutional Approach' (2020) 16 *European Constitutional Law Review* 466–92 and the earlier literature cited therein.

[11] Arnull (n 7).

[12] AG Kokott, Case C-583/11 P, *Inuit Tapiriit Kanatami v Parliament and Council*, ECLI:EU:C:2013:21, para 1.

[13] Lenaerts and others (n 3), 254.

[14] The action for annulment is therefore believed to provide an 'effective remedy' and a 'fair trial' before an 'impartial and independent tribunal' as required by Article 47 of the EU Charter of Fundamental Rights.

judicial control.[15] It is also argued that the inaccessibility of EU judicial review to social actors slows down or hinders development of common constitutional standards in certain areas, such as fundamental social rights.[16]

What is now Article 263(4) TFEU, governing private parties' access to the EU judicial review, was subject to several constitutional revisions. These revisions only insignificantly broadened the direct access of private parties to the EU judicial review, at least from the perspective of the kinds of interests represented by the litigants.[17] As this book will demonstrate, the EU Courts in the annulment procedure are most often requested to protect private interests of individual economic operators. They are unlikely to assume a more activist role of public interest watchdogs of EU institutions and bodies, despite the expectations of a part of legal scholarship and civil society.

Scholars and practitioners have also been concerned about the fluctuating thoroughness of EU judicial review. The generalist EU judges grapple with abstruse scientific and technical appraisals enmeshed with discretionary and controversial policy choices. The growing complexity of EU legal acts makes the judicial review an ever more effort-intensive and time-consuming endeavour. Following the *Gauweiler*[18] and *ESMA*[19] cases, it has become evident that complex factual appraisals requiring expert knowledge are inseparably enmeshed with genuinely political choices.[20] The EU judges – recruited from among legal generalists – deal at present with new intricate regulatory fields such as financial supervision, economic and monetary policy, the risk regulation of chemicals, food safety, pharmaceuticals, emission trading schemes and so on. Why should judicial review by a handful of legal generalists produce better outcomes than joint decision-making by dozens of EU and national experts representing democratically elected and accountable governments? What are the costs generated by judges acquainting themselves with areas of law requiring specialist knowledge? What is the risk that they will commit an error or overstep, even unwittingly, their judicial role?

The EU Courts have gone to great lengths to adjust the judicial review to novel challenges. However, if a thorough review standard was coupled with broad access for private parties, the EU Courts could quickly become overburdened with complex cases. The more accessible and rigorous judicial review is, the more power and responsibility for the substance of EU law-, rule- and decision-making shifts onto the EU Courts. Judicial review of legal acts unavoidably transmutates

[15] Claire Kilpatrick, 'On the Rule of Law and Economic Emergency: The Degradation of Basic Legal Values in Europe's Bailouts' (2015) 35 *Oxford Journal of Legal Studies* 325, 349–50.

[16] Claire Kilpatrick, 'Are the Bailouts Immune to EU Social Challenge Because They Are Not EU Law?' (2014) 10 *European Constitutional Law Review* 393.

[17] Ward (n 7). Importantly, the results of the last reform of the admissibility criteria brought about by the Lisbon Treaty proved disappointing to many.

[18] Case C-62/14, *Gauweiler and Others*, ECLI:EU:C:2015:400.

[19] Case C-270/12, *United Kingdom v Parliament and Council (ESMA)*, ECLI:EU:C:2014:18.

[20] Joana Mendes, 'Discretion, Care and Public Interest in the EU Administration: Probing the Limits of Law' (2016) 53 *Common Market Law Review* 419.

into their positive elaboration.[21] The discussion about the judicial review's accessibility and thoroughness does not concern only juristic technicalities and purely procedural or formal obstacles to effective litigation. It involves the separation of powers at the EU level and the EU Courts' authority vis-à-vis other institutions and bodies. A relaxation of the admissibility criteria or a further increase in the thoroughness of review would imply an accretion of EU judicial power and responsibility. In this scenario, the EU Courts could frequently be called upon to second-guess discretionary acts embodying difficult political compromises. Without robust institutional resources and procedural tools, the EU Courts could be exposed to a risk of erroneous rulings, protracted proceedings and, ultimately, loss of authority.

Alternative solutions to the access-to-justice problem, such as those offered by extra-judicial review, merit a careful study. For well over two decades, extra-judicial review mechanisms have been proliferating in the EU governance structure: internal and inter-administrative review, independent administrative review by BoAs and the like, and the right to petition the Parliament and complain to the Ombudsman. These alternative review bodies engage with, among other things, EU legal acts and decision-making processes. Nonetheless, they have hitherto attracted comparatively little scholarly attention.

The BoAs have been set up to limit the EU Courts' workload and ease some of the judicial review's shortcomings, primarily to provide more in-depth review of empirically problematic legal acts. They are quasi-judicial structures, endowed with some safeguards of decision-making independence, as well as relatively accessible and participation-oriented procedure leading to potentially far-reaching remedies. Until now, BoAs have been set up in the following agencies: the European Union Intellectual Property Office (EUIPO), the Community Plant Variety Office (CPVO), the European Chemical Agency (ECHA), the European Aviation Safety Agency (EASA), the Agency for Cooperation of Energy Regulators (ACER), the European Supervisory Authorities (a joint BoA for three agencies, ESAs) and the European Union Agency for Railways (ERA). The Appeal Panel of the Single Resolution Board (SRB) should be added to the list, as well as the Administrative Board of Review (ABoR) at the European Central Bank (ECB), although the latter is not equipped with binding powers. Similar bodies, dealing mostly with staff matters, operate within the Common Foreign and Security agencies.[22] Importantly, they are all governed by sectoral regulations, so their specific competences differ.[23]

[21] Christopher Zurn, *Deliberative Democracy and the Institutions of Judicial Review* (Cambridge University Press 2007), 256.

[22] Graham Butler, 'Hidden Administrative Review in EU Law: The Boards of Appeal of EU Agencies in the Common Foreign and Security Policy' in Merijn Chamon, Mariolina Eliantonio and Annalisa Volpato (eds), *Boards of Appeal of EU Agencies: A New Paradigm of Legal Protection?* (Oxford University Press, forthcoming 2021).

[23] Luca de Lucia, 'A Microphysics of European Administrative Law: Administrative Remedies in the EU after Lisbon' (2014) 20 *European Public Law* 277.

The Ombudsman's origins lie in the willingness to boost the EU's legitimacy assets by giving it a 'human face', to counter the rhetoric referring to the Brussels-based technocratic and democratically unaccountable bureaucracy, and to offer citizens a flexible and personalised form of redress in the fields outside the strict judicial remit.[24] The Ombudsman's task is to examine complaints from EU citizens and other private parties to identify 'instances of maladministration', a flexible concept akin to unlawfulness. She enjoys strong independence safeguards and offers widely accessible, deliberative, persuasion-oriented and potentially proactive inquiries.

Apart from significant differences,[25] what unites the EU judicial and extra-judicial review mechanisms is that they strive to frame and constrain EU institutions' and bodies' discretionary powers. They examine requests of adversely affected private parties. They operate in legally structured and participation-oriented procedural frameworks geared towards finding an adequate remedy or a form of redress. Moreover, a survey of these mechanisms' dockets has revealed that they frequently deal with EU legal acts or specific stages and recurrent practices in rule- or decision-making processes. An in-depth analysis of these mechanisms' practical operation is necessary to critically evaluate their potential to enhance the authority of the aspects of EU law-, rule- and decision-making remaining beyond the judicial remit.

The ECHA BoA has been chosen for in-depth analysis because its output is the most substantial among the BoAs, dealing with scientifically and technically complex and, at the same time, voluminous cases. Moreover, the ECHA BoA carries the burden of striking a balance between the economic interests of the powerful chemical industry and the protection of public health and the environment. The substantial experience of the ECHA BoA is likely to prove highly valuable in discussions about the resolution of a proliferating number of public law disputes involving advanced technical and scientific knowledge and inescapable empirical and normative uncertainty.[26]

III. Putting Formal Labels Aside

Domestic legal literature has offered various conceptual distinctions intended to elucidate the nature of judicial review, administrative review or ombuds-review. Domestic concepts have been used to uncover ideas behind the establishment and functions of EU extra-judicial review and its relation to judicial review.[27]

[24] Nikiforos Diamandouros, *The European Ombudsman: Origins, Establishment, Evolution* (Office for Official Publications of the European Communities 2005).

[25] The literature cited above (nn 5 and 6) underscores differences between 'legality' and 'good administration' to emphasise the unique role of the Ombudsman, or between the criteria of 'legality' and other scientific or technical criteria to stress the prospective added value of the BoAs.

[26] The analysis presented in Chapter 5 will also encompass challenges encountered in practice by other BoAs.

[27] Chirulli and Lucia (n 5).

However, the existing literature still contains diverging views regarding the nature and role of EU extra-judicial review, highlighting structural differences or functional similarities with the EU Courts.[28]

Rather than applying domestic concepts to the EU in a top-down manner, this book seeks to confront the practical operation of EU judicial and extra-judicial review with their deeper normative rationale. It offers a consistent analytical framework for a systemic and in-depth comparison and evaluation of different judicial and extra-judicial mechanisms. This framework grasps the distinctive features of different review mechanisms pertaining to their decision-making independence, powers, accessibility and procedure. Thus, the book aims to overcome preconceived ideas as to, supposedly, the entirely different or second-rate nature of specific mechanisms.[29] It uncovers the interplay of distinct legitimacy assets and the possible complementarity of the judicial and extra-judicial review. Contrary to clear-cut doctrinal distinctions between judicial, administrative and ombuds-review, the three mechanisms demonstrate some striking similarities concerning the review of EU legal acts and processes. Likewise, they share weaknesses.

This book applies and advances the 'relative authority' approach to the judicial and extra-judicial review of EU legal acts. According to this approach, the authority of a decision-making mechanism in the governance structure is relative primarily to this mechanism's institutional and procedural features. Relative authority deals with legitimacy in the allocation of decision-making powers. Why should a specific power and responsibility be conferred upon a given mechanism, such as a court, a board of appeal or an ombudsman? What institutional and procedural features make a mechanism particularly suitable to exercise a specific kind of power, such as the power to review legal acts of this or another kind? By dint of their specific features, the judicial and extra-judicial review mechanisms generate 'legitimacy assets', ie argumentative resources that can be rationally invoked to support the authority of decisions, including the legal acts subjected to review, regardless of the review's positive or negative outcome.[30] The legitimacy assets may pull affected parties towards consensual compliance.[31]

[28] Antonio Cassatella, 'Appeals Before the European Aviation Safety Agency' in Barbara Marchetti (ed), *Administrative Remedies in the European Union: The Emergence of a Quasi-judicial Administration* (Giappichelli Editore 2017), 45. See also interviews with EU judges, who tend to emphasise differences between the role of the Ombudsman and EU Courts, and interviews with the Ombudsman's legal officers, who tend to emphasise similarities, Milan Remáč, *Coordinating Ombudsmen and the Judiciary* (Intersentia 2014), 255–66. Paul Craig, 'Courts' in Paul Craig (ed), *EU Administrative Law* (Oxford University Press 2018) considers the BoAs to be a subset of the EU judicial bodies.

[29] Regarding the problems with applying domestic administrative law concepts to the EU-level institutions and legal arrangements, see Filipe Brito Bastos, 'Doctrinal Methodology in EU Administrative Law: Confronting the Touch of Stateness', (2021) *German Law Journal* 2021 (forthcoming).

[30] Joana Mendes and Ingo Venzke, 'The Idea of Relative Authority in European and International Law' (2018) 16 *International Journal of Constitutional Law* 75.

[31] This theoretical framework is normative in nature. It analyses moral arguments generated by decision-making bodies and procedures instead of predicting the actual behaviour of affected parties. It is akin to the theory of procedural justice/fairness, which analyses why reasonable persons *should*

It is argued in this book that review procedures produce primarily instrumental and deliberative legitimacy assets. They are instrumental in maximising the factual and legal correctness of legal acts, conceived of as either compliance with predetermined legal standards or as a right balance between different legally protected interests. The review procedures provide at the same time additional opportunities for deliberation and candid reconsideration of legal acts. It follows from theoretical and comparative literature that the institutional and procedural features of review mechanisms delivering instrumental and deliberative assets are: the *independence* of adjudicators (functional and organisational, including resources and expertise); the specific *powers* of adjudicators (the scope and criteria or technique of review, the type of remedies), the *accessibility* of the review mechanism to parties representing variegated interests, and the *activity* of the adjudicators and the parties during the review process.[32] These four features will guide the analysis in the main chapters of this book.

IV. The Book's Structure

Chapter 2 offers a survey of the discussion about the thoroughness and accessibility of EU judicial review for private parties. It summarises in which respects the EU judicial review falls short of the EU legal scholarship's expectations, why the implementation of suggested solutions poses difficulties, and what kind of risks this implementation may involve.

Chapter 3 advances the book's analytical framework. It proceeds in two steps. First, it identifies flaws in the dominant approach to the EU judicial review based on the under-determined ideals of the 'rule of law' and 'effective judicial protection'. What these ideals imply in terms of specific procedural solutions and practices may be subject to reasonable disagreement, especially in the context of the growing scientific, technical and discretionary nature of EU legal acts, the frequent indeterminacy of EU legal frameworks, and the institutional and procedural constraints of the EU Courts. Second, this chapter argues that the 'relative authority' approach helps discern a deeper normative rationale of judicial and

perceive themselves as morally obliged to follow decisions resulting from 'just/fair' procedures. See Lawrence Solum, 'Procedural Justice' (2004) 78 *Southern California Law Review* 181.

[32] Take a dispute regarding the scientific methodology underlying a legal act. Initial review by a specialist panel might, overall, generate stronger legitimacy assets than immediate judicial review by a generalist court, especially if both bodies are independent to a similar degree, have comparable powers, are equally accessible and offer meaningful participation opportunities. Some complex legal disputes should nonetheless end up before generalist courts, which benefit from a horizontal perspective and are, therefore, well placed to settle transversal legal issues. Also, take a case in which an EU legislative act does not specify substantive interests to be prioritised in its implementation through individual decisions, leaving to the administration a broad leeway in defining its policy. In such cases, deliberative and persuasion-oriented ombuds-review might offer more adequate legitimacy assets than peremptory judicial pronouncements.

extra-judicial review mechanisms, which should be confronted with their practical operation. This approach, relying on the four criteria of *independence*, *powers*, *accessibility* and *activity*, helps compare and critically evaluate the allocation of review powers to specific mechanisms.

The next chapter opens the book's central part, which examines the three review mechanisms. Chapter 4 complements and deepens the analysis of judicial review carried out in Chapter 2, relying on up-to-date quantitative and qualitative data. Chapter 5 examines the ECHA BoA and Chapter 6 examines the Ombudsman. The in-depth analysis of judicial review serves as a reference point for the analysis of the extra-judicial review mechanisms. The same analytical structure, based on the four institutional and procedural features, guides the three studies.

Chapter 7 presents conclusions. It stresses in what respects the extra-judicial review mechanisms supplement and in what respect they replicate the EU judicial review's assets and shortcomings. It calls for a careful reconsideration of legitimacy assets offered by the existing extra-judicial review models in a broader discussion concerning the EU judicial and extra-judicial review architecture. Concerns about the rule of law at the EU level result from the lack of consensus and a clear normative vision regarding the extent to which the EU Courts and supplementary mechanisms should bear the responsibility for the substance of EU law-, rule- and decision-making, especially in the context of normative and empirical uncertainty. The boundary between 'review' and simple second-guessing of the substance of law-, rule- or decision-making is persistently blurred.[33] Therefore, the rule of law's detailed meaning, along with institutional and procedural structures for its implementation at the EU level, should be hammered out in an open and political rather than exclusively juridical debate.

[33] Zurn (n 21).

2

The Shortcomings of EU Judicial Review

The scholarly debate about the legal protection of private parties against potentially unlawful acts of EU institutions and bodies has always revolved around the EU Courts.[34] The intensity and accessibility of judicial review, especially within the Article 263(4) TFEU annulment proceedings, have been among the most intensely debated topics in EU legal studies,[35] seen as intrinsically linked to the fundamental legal concepts of the 'rule of law' and 'effective judicial protection'.[36] The fundamental characteristics of the action for annulment were designed several decades ago. These characteristics include restrained accessibility, grounds for review relating to the idea of 'legality', and an adversarial procedure in which the judges can neither correct the parties' formal allegations nor obtain new evidence. However, this action is still considered 'to lie at the core of the complete system of EU judicial protection'.[37] This action's unique role relates to the Treaty mandate conferred upon the EU Courts to 'ensure that in the interpretation and application of the Treaties the law is observed'.[38] Therefore, the discussion about the structural characteristics and shortcomings of EU judicial review forms a crucial part of the broader discussion about the quality of the rule of law at the EU level.

The EU judicature has undergone profound institutional and procedural reforms to adapt to the evolving governance structure of the EU, as its competences

[34] The relationship between 'legal protection' and 'judicial protection' is unclear. The ECJ case law refers to 'effective *judicial* protection', whereas Article 19(1), second sentence, TEU, to 'effective *legal* protection'. However, in both provisions the French version of the Treaties use the same word: 'protection juridictionnelle'.

[35] The action for annulment is supplemented by the Article 277 TFEU objection of illegality, an incidental plea in law against an act of general application forming the basis of the directly challenged individual act, and by the Article 267 TFEU references from domestic courts regarding the validity of the EU acts these courts are to apply.

[36] See among many, Arnull (n 7), Kilpatrick (nn 15 and 16). For an argument that the narrow access might have been necessary to avoid *actio popularis*, see Laurent Pech, 'A Union Founded on the Rule of Law': Meaning and Reality of the Rule of Law as a Constitutional Principle of EU Law' (2010) 6 *European Constitutional Law Review* 359, 386–88.

[37] Lenaerts and others (n 3), 254.

[38] Article 19(1), first sentence, TEU.

have expanded in scope and complexity. In 1989 the EGC was established to deal with administrative law areas requiring intense fact-finding, such as public procurement, access to documents, competition, State aid or anti-dumping law. The EGC has improved the thoroughness of judicial review. Nowadays, the EU Courts operate, however, in an increasingly embroiled regulatory context. The EU institutions, supported by a growing number of committees, offices, agencies and the like, must look for the middle ground between 27 governments whose social, economic and cultural systems – and political interests and ideologies – are much further apart than those of the 15 governments 15 years ago. These difficult compromises are subsequently embodied in EU legal acts which may be subject to judicial review. Nonetheless, many controversial acts escape judicial review if none of the privileged applicants – the EU institutions or the Member States – have no political interest in challenging these acts. This is one of the reasons for the calls to expand the access of private parties, especially NGOs, to judicial review.

The EGC's docket includes ever more convoluted legal acts based on socio-economic, technical and scientific appraisals tightly intertwined with delicate choices between competing private and public interests, in areas such as the regulation of chemicals, pharmaceuticals, food safety, environmental protection or financial supervision. Such cases require specialist knowledge, and more time and resources to process voluminous case files.[39] The ongoing debate about the intensity and accessibility of judicial review demonstrates that the EU Courts are still not fully able to meet the elevated expectations of scholars and practitioners.[40]

This chapter summarises in which respects the EU judicial review falls short of the EU scholarship's expectations and why the implementation of suggested solutions poses difficulties. Section I discusses judicial review's limited thoroughness in cases raising complex scientific, technical and political appraisals. Section II discusses the limits of judicial expertise and why the EU judges are reluctant to engage in independent fact-finding and reach independent expertise. Section III discusses the everlasting dilemma of restrictive access to the EU judicial review for private parties. Section IV discusses risks relating to a possible relaxation of the access rules before the EU Courts. Section V presents conclusions.

[39] ECJ, 'Annual Report 2018: Judicial Activity', 161.

[40] Scholars point out more specific shortcomings of EU judicial review such as the EU Courts' refusal to control the legality of domestic acts underpinning subsequent EU acts (Filipe Brito Bastos, 'Derivative Illegality in European Composite Administrative Procedures' (2018) 55 *Common Market Law Review* 101), the exclusion of the judicial review of soft law measures that may nevertheless produce tangible effects (Mariolina Eliantonio and Oana Stefan, 'Soft Law Before the European Court: Discovering a "Common Pattern"?' (2018) 37 *Yearbook of European Law* 457) or the exclusion of the judicial review of data transfers (Mariolina Eliantonio, 'Information Exchange in European Administrative Law: A Threat to Effective Judicial Protection?' (2016) 3 *Maastricht Journal of Comparative and European Law* 531).

I. Limited Review of Uncertainty

The action for annulment was initially designed to serve only a limited group of international companies affected by legal acts of emerging supranational institutions.[41] The authors of the European Coal and Steel Community Treaty of 1951 acknowledged the limited epistemic capacity of generalist EU judges. They explicitly ruled out the judicial review of economic appraisals underpinning impugned legal acts.[42] Nowadays, the Treaties do not contain a similar caveat. Instead, they specify that the EU Courts can only review breaches of competence, essential procedural requirements, applicable substantive legal norms, and misuse of power.[43] However, these four grounds of review give the EU Courts significant leeway in customising the intensity of review for a specific type of case.

The EU judicature initially set up a limited review of the determinations of relevant facts and their legal qualification in cases requiring specialist, mostly socio-economic knowledge.[44] Faced with allegations of leaving potentially incorrect empirical determinations and arbitrary legal qualifications unverified, the EU judicature elaborated a process-oriented review technique in factually 'complex' cases. According to the usual formula, 'the EU judicature must not substitute its own assessment for that of the challenged body'. Instead, it must verify 'whether the relevant procedural rules have been complied with, whether the statement of reasons for the decision is adequate, whether the facts have been accurately stated and whether there has been any manifest error of appraisal or misuse of powers'.[45]

There is a consensus in the literature that, starting from the early 1990s, the EU Courts intensified the standard of review. This change was arguably possible thanks to the setting up of the EGC, an additional layer of the EU judicial branch intended for direct actions and cases involving complex factual assessments.[46] In the seminal *Technische Universität München* case, the ECJ asserted the EU

[41] Morten Rassmussen, 'The Origins of a Legal Revolution – The Early History of the European Court of Justice' (2008) 2 *Journal of European Integration History* 77, 83–84. Anne Boerger de Smedt, 'La Cour de Justice dans les négociations du traité de Paris instituant la CECA' (2008) 14 *Journal of European Integration History* 7, 17.

[42] Article 33(1) ECSC Treaty: 'The Court may not, however, examine the evaluation of the situation, resulting from economic facts or circumstances, in the light of which the High Authority took its decisions or made its recommendations, save where the High Authority is alleged to have misused its powers or to have manifestly failed to observe the provisions of this Treaty or any rule of law relating to its application'.

[43] Article 263(2) TFEU.

[44] Joined Cases 56/64 and 58/64, *Consten and Grundig v Commission*, ECLI:EU:C:1966:41, 347. Case 55/75 *Balkan Import-Export*, ECLI:EU:C:1976:8, para 8. Mirko Prek and Silvère Lefèvre, '"Administrative Discretion", "Power of Appraisal" and "Margin of Appraisal" in Judicial Review Proceedings Before the General Court' (2019) 56 *Common Market Law Review* 339.

[45] Case 42/84, *Remia v Commission*, ECLI:EU:C:1985:327, para 34.

[46] Alexander Fritzsche, 'Discretion, Scope of Judicial Review and Institutional Balance in European Law' (2010) 47 *Common Market Law Review* 361, 378.

judicature's duty to review whether the competent institution has examined carefully and impartially all the relevant aspects of the case, has enabled the interested person to make her views known and has adequately reasoned its decisions.[47] In *Tetra Laval*, the ECJ added that, faced with complex cases,

> not only must the Community Courts, inter alia, establish whether the evidence relied on is factually accurate, reliable and consistent but also whether that evidence contains all the information which must be taken into account in order to assess a complex situation and whether it is capable of substantiating the conclusions drawn from it.[48]

Moreover, in cases in which different rights, legally protected interests or principles are at stake, the EU Courts began to reach for proportionality analysis.[49]

The intensification of the review was mostly a response to criticism voiced by competition law scholars and practitioners. They were concerned about the accuracy of economic appraisals leading to fines imposed by the Commission on individual undertakings for violations of competition law.[50] 'Comprehensive' judicial review was to encompass both legal questions and factual determinations.[51] In an oft-quoted piece, the EGC President argued that the intensified judicial review standard in competition law cases ensures a 'thorough, meticulous and precise review'.[52]

The *Tetra Laval* process-oriented technique, developed in the context of competition law,[53] has permeated other areas such as State aid,[54] anti-dumping,[55] restrictive measures,[56] and the regulation of risks to public health and the

[47] Case C-269/90, *Technische Universität München*, ECLI:EU:C:1991:438, para 14.

[48] Case C-12/13 P, *Commission v Tetra Laval*, ECLI:EU:C:2014:2284, para 39.

[49] For instance Case C-62/14, *Gauweiler*, ECLI:EU:C:2015:400, paras 74–80.

[50] Among many, Wouter Wils, 'The Compatibility with Fundamental Rights of the EU Antitrust Enforcement System in Which the European Commission Acts Both as Investigator and as First-Instance Decision Maker' (2014) 37 *World Competition: Law and Economics Review* 5. Denis Waelbroeck and Donald Slater, '"Marginal Review" by the European Court of Justice in Competition Cases and its Compatibility with Fundamental Rights' in Massimo Merola and Jacques Derenne (eds), *The Role of the Court of Justice of the European Union in Competition Law Cases* (Bruylant 2012). Ian Forrester, 'A Bush in Need of Pruning: The Luxuriant Growth of "Light Judicial Review"' in Claus-Dieter Ehlermann and Mel Marquis (eds), *European Competition Law Annual: The Evaluation of Evidence and its Judicial Review in Competition Cases* (Hart Publishing 2009).

[51] Comprehensive judicial review thus understood is different from the ECtHR's concept of 'full jurisdiction'. ECtHR, Joined Cases 32181/04 and 35122/05, *Sigma Radio Television v Cyprus*, ECLI: CE:ECHR:2011:0721JUD003218104, paras 151–57. It is also different from the Article 261 TFEU concept of 'unlimited jurisdiction'.

[52] Marc Jaeger, 'The Standard of Review in Competition Cases Involving Complex Economic Assessments: Towards the Marginalisation of the Marginal Review' (2011) 2 *Journal of European Competition Law & Practice* 295, 301. Georgios Gryllos, 'Discretion and Judicial Review in EU Competition Law: A Technical Analysis on Sources of Discretion, Judicial Review and Implications for the Litigants' (2016) 4 *Concurrences* 1.

[53] Case C-413/06 P, *Bertelsmann and Sony v Impala*, ECLI:EU:C:2008:392, paras 144–50.

[54] Case C-525/04 P, *Spain v Commission and Lenzing*, ECLI:EU:C:2007:698, paras 56–57.

[55] Case T-528/09, *Hubei Xinyegang Steel v Council*, ECLI:EU:T:2014:35, para 53.

[56] Joined Cases C-584/10 P, C-593/10 P and C-595/10 P, *Commission and Others v Kadi*, ECLI:EU:C:2013:518, paras 97, 119 and 124.

environment.[57] It has been applied with regard to both individual administrative decisions and general regulatory acts.[58] It has been developed further in the regulation of risks and hazards to public health and the environment. This area is characterised by a high level of epistemic empirical uncertainty, pertaining to the science and technical appraisals underlying the impugned legal acts, and the impossibility of obtaining conclusive evidence.[59] In other words, in cases marked by empirical uncertainty, it is impossible to obtain unambiguous technical or scientific data, so the decision-making consists of weighing discrepant evidence and incompatible arguments. Scientific or technical appraisals underlying EU legal acts tend to be convoluted and permeated with tentative generalisations, approximations and conjectures unavoidable in view of the need to fill data gaps and determine a course of action to handle potential risks.

The precautionary principle addresses the problem of empirical uncertainty. According to this principle, EU institutions and bodies may adopt measures aimed at protecting public health and the environment even in the face of persisting uncertainty as to the existence of risk or adequacy of the measure. As a result, the precautionary principle lowers the burden of proof for the EU institutions and bodies when they need to limit the rights of, for instance, economic operators in the name of public health or the environment.[60] Balancing between values such as public health and business rights is still an onerous and, ultimately, discretionary exercise, which crucially depends on the adjudicators' epistemic ability to interpret and weigh the competing evidence. Entirely exhaustive and 'objective' review of this type of appraisals may turn out to be nigh on impossible.

The problem is aggravated by normative uncertainty as to which substantive values, or private or public interest goals have been prioritised under the applicable EU legislation. EU legislation incorporates burdensome intergovernmental and inter-institutional trade-offs between conflicting interests. Hence, its crucial provisions may be phrased in highly open-ended terms. Normative epistemic uncertainty may relate, for instance, to the level of risk to public health and the environment deemed acceptable for society. Under what circumstances or faced with what level of potential risk is it appropriate to take preventive measures despite the persisting empirical uncertainty? Preventive measures may consist in withdrawing from the market certain chemical substances or pharmaceutical products, thereby restricting the business rights of relevant industries.

The EU judicature usually uses the notion of 'complexity' as a shorthand for a mixture of epistemic empirical and normative uncertainty, ie the need to

[57] Case T-475/07, *Dow AgroSciences v Commission*, ECLI:EU:T:2011:445, paras 150–53.

[58] Dominique Ritleng, 'Judicial Review of EU Administative Discretion: How Far Does the Separation of Powers Matter' in Joana Mendes and Ingo Ventzke (eds), *Allocating Authority: Who Should Do What in European and International Law?* (Hart Publishing 2017), 205–08.

[59] Case T-13/99, *Pfizer Animal Health v Council*, ECLI:EU:T:2002:209.

[60] Paul Craig, 'The Precautionary Principle' in Paul Craig (ed), *EU Administrative Law* (Oxford University Press 2018). See, for instance, Case T-115/15, *Deza v ECHA*, ECLI:EU:T:2017:329, paras 172–74.

undertake a decision balancing a combination of various factors: socio-economic, technical or scientific evaluations, prognoses, interests and rights.[61] On the one hand, it holds that the responsibility for determining the level of acceptable risks and hazards lies with competent institutions and bodies.[62] On the other hand, it must verify whether the scientific risk assessment has been based on the best scientific data and carried out in an independent, objective and transparent manner.[63] In other words, the EU judicature should verify if the empirical epistemic uncertainty has been reduced to the greatest possible extent.

A satisfactory comprehension of rambling empirical data and legal frameworks stuffed with scientific or technical standards, even to perform the process-oriented review, clearly requires more time and effort from the judges and their supporting staff.[64] The intensified process-oriented review also poses a new kind of problems. Advocate General (AG) Mengozzi argued that the intensified review standard might neutralise administrative discretion, the boundary between process-oriented and substantive review being fluid.[65] Courts and other review mechanisms can undoubtedly help exercise discretion more responsively and transparently, but – considering the 'transmutation thesis'[66] – they risk imposing their own arbitrary vision of substantive values upon the challenged institutions and bodies, even unwittingly.

The EU Courts have recently been criticised for their rulings in *Bilbaína* case.[67] They quashed the Commission's and the ECHA's precautionary approach to assessing the aquatic toxicity of a chemical substance used in industrial production. By formally applying process-oriented review, the EU Courts indicated a 'relevant' scientific factor which the Commission and the ECHA had not sufficiently considered. However, the inclusion of this specific factor might have the effect of completely changing the methodological approach to the risk assessment from one that had overestimated the risk, being more protective of public health and the environment, to one that would underestimate the risk, being more protective of the industry's economic interests. The problem was that any middle ground between the two approaches might have been impossible from the

[61] Herwig CH Hofmann, 'Interdependencies between Delegation, Discretion and the Duty of Care Regarding Facts' in Joana Mendes (ed), *EU Executive Discretion and the Limits of Law* (Oxford University Press 2019), 225.

[62] Case T-31/07, *Du Pont de Nemours (France) and Others v Commission*, ECLI:EU:T:2013:167, paras 133ff and 155ff, Case T-475/07; *Dow AgroSciences v Commission*, paras 144ff.

[63] *Dow AgroSciences v Commission*, ECLI:EU:T:2011:445, para 141.

[64] A judge of the EGC, writing extra-judicially, admitted that the Commission's more 'economic approach' to competition law enforcement, introduced from the late 1990s, represented a new challenge for the EU judges, who since then have been obliged to delve into purely economic appraisals. Nicholas Forwood, 'The Commission's More Economic Approach – Implications for the Role of the EU Courts, the Treatment of Economic Evidence and the Scope of Judicial Review', *European Competition Law Annual: Evaluation of Evidence and Its Judicial Review in Competition Cases* (2009).

[65] AG Mengozzi, Case C-382/12 P, *MasterCard v Commission*, ECLI:EU:C:2014:42, para 119.

[66] According to which the boundary between the review of 'legality' or 'constitutionality' and a simple second-guessing of the merits of legal acts is persistently blurred. Zurn (n 21).

[67] Case C-691/15 P, *European Commission v Bilbaína*, ECLI:EU:C:2017:882.

scientific point of view. The defendants might not properly have explained this specific feature of the risk assessment in question. Consequently, the EU Courts might have neglected it.[68] At the same time, it would not seem fair to simply accuse the EU Courts of favouritism towards the economic interests. On other occasions, the EU Courts have been criticised for excessive reliance on the precautionary principle to fill gaps in the regulation of new technologies, to the detriment of industry and innovation.[69]

Notably, the action for annulment operates within an adversarial procedural framework. The EU judicature relies solely on the evidence and arguments provided by the parties. A mistake by one of the parties may lead to a substantively questionable ruling. The EU Courts will identify a '*manifest* error of assessment', only if 'the evidence adduced *by the applicant* [is] sufficient to make the factual assessments used in that measure implausible'.[70] Therefore, it has been argued that references to the 'manifest error test' often make a purely semantic difference[71] and 'serve as a pretext for the judges not to engage in a more intense scrutiny of the facts although it might be warranted'.[72] Simultaneously, the '*manifest* error' formula emphasises the paramount role of the applicants' active participation in the judicial review proceedings and imposes on them the burden of providing the evidence and elucidating its meaning to the judges.[73] It is doubtful whether, without the applicants' initiative and adequate resources to prepare the litigation carefully, the EU Courts will be able to effectively verify whether the challenged administration has examined 'carefully and impartially all the relevant elements of the individual case', as they declare,[74] beyond the review of the superficial appearance of coherence and comprehensiveness of the statement of reasons. Applicants who provide only general arguments against the scientific or technical findings underpinning the contested measures, expecting the EU judicature to independently confirm or refute these findings using its own procedural tools and resources, may end up disappointed.[75]

[68] Giulia C Leonelli, 'The Fine Line Between Procedural and Substantive Review in Cases Involving Complex Technical-scientific Evaluations: Bilbaína' (2018) 55 *Common Market Law Review* 1217, 1234–35.

[69] Han Somsen, 'Scientists Edit Genes, Courts Edit Directives. Is the Court of Justice Fighting Uncertain Scientific Risk with Certain Constitutional Risk?' (2018) 9 *European Journal of Risk Regulation* 701.

[70] Case T-584/13, *BASF v Commission*, ECLI:EU:T:2018:279, para 94 (emphasis added).

[71] Fernando Castillo de la Torre and Eric Gippini Fournier, *Evidence, Proof and Judicial Review in EU Competition Law* (Edward Elgar 2017), 268 and 284.

[72] Nehl (n 7), 90.

[73] The EU judges do not even have ex officio access to the documents produced by the EU bodies relevant to the case at hand. Case T-100/15, *Dextro Energy v Commission*, ECLI:EU:T:2016:150, paras 42–43. Sometimes, the applicants may resort to different kinds of auxiliary materials during the oral hearings (such as printed schemes, illustrations) which could help them elucidate their complex point. See, for instance, AG Mengozzi, Case C-680/16 P, *Dr. August Wolff v Commission*, ECLI:EU:C:2018:819, para 163.

[74] Case C-269/90, *Technische Universität München*, ECLI:EU:C:1991:438, para 14; recently Case T-584/13, *BASF v Commission*, para 95.

[75] Case T-177/13, *TestBioTech and Others v Commission*, ECLI:EU:T:2016:736, para 224.

The EU judicature has availed itself of the process-oriented review also with regard to acts of general application, including legislative acts.[76] The review of the legal bases of legislative acts or their compliance with the subsidiarity or proportionality principles requires consideration of complex political, economic and social issues, something that EU co-legislators are better equipped to do.[77] Therefore, the EU judicature has relied on the analysis of background documents such as impact assessments and explanatory memoranda.[78] However, it has been observed that the EU judicature is generally reluctant to inquire into the substantive content of such documents, invoking them usually to support the EU legislature's choice rather than scrutinise it.[79] Deference to substantive legislative choices may be advocated due to the reinforcement of the Parliament's position in the legislative procedure brought about by the Treaty of Lisbon. The EU legislative acts may now be considered to enjoy a higher degree of democratic legitimacy in representative and deliberative dimensions. It is nonetheless argued that the EU judicature does not distinguish in practice between legislative and administrative discretion.[80] Moreover, the increased intensity of the judicial review of legislative acts may be observed in cases involving fundamental right issues.[81]

The intensity of EU judicial review seems to be fluctuating. At any rate, the EU judicial review has undoubtedly become a time-, cost- and effort-intensive endeavour. It generates costs for EU judges (who need time to acquaint themselves with complex case files and areas of decision-making), for litigants (who often need both lawyers and scientific or technical specialists to prepare litigation strategy) and for EU institutions and bodies (which need more resources and time to prepare their defence).

II. Deficient Judicial Expertise and Procedural Tools

Domestic systems of administrative law employ the concept of administrative 'technical discretion', according to which certain complex empirical assessments

[76] Dorota Leczykiewicz, '"Constitutional Justice" and Judicial Review of EU Legislative Acts' in Dimitry Kochenov, Gráinne de Búrca and Andrew Williams (eds), *Europe's Justice Deficit?* (Hart Publishing 2015), 102–03.

[77] Jacob Öberg, 'The Rise of the Procedural Paradigm: Judicial Review of EU Legislation in Vertical Competence Disputes' (2017) 13 *European Constitutional Law Review* 248, 252.

[78] Nehl (n 7), 189. Koen Lenaerts, 'The European Court of Justice and Process-Oriented Review' (2012) 31 *Yearbook of European Law* 3.

[79] Andrew Woodhouse, 'Process Review as Panacea: A Critique of Process Review Advocacy in the European Union' (2020) 45 *European Law Review* 373, 387–88.

[80] Ritleng (n 58), 198.

[81] Leczykiewicz (n 76), 104–05. Marie-Pierre Granger and Kristina Irion, 'The Court of Justice and the Data Retention Directive in Digital Rights Ireland: Telling Off the EU Legislator and Teaching a Lesson in Privacy and Data Protection' (2014) 39 *European Law Review* 835.

belong naturally to administration, due to their expertise and organisational assets. Courts should not interfere with the merits of these assessments. Legislative provisions may explicitly reserve certain decisions for administration. In the EU legal scholarship, it is sometimes argued that judicial review should aim to be comprehensive regarding empirical questions in the name of the rule of law and effective judicial protection.[82] Hofmann claims that 'the fact that a matter contains economically or technically complex considerations should not necessarily put it beyond the intellectual reach of a court'.[83] Other authors contend that the EU judicature should step back only from second-guessing politically discretionary choices reserved for EU institutions and bodies through unequivocal higher-order legal provisions.[84]

Conversely, Mendes argues that the conceptual distinction between 'technical' and 'political' discretion – related to empirical and normative epistemic uncertainty, respectively – reinforces the false impression of scientific or technical 'objectivity'. This distinction conceals the fact that technical and scientific appraisals are tightly intertwined with public interest choices. Consequently, it excessively confines the role of law in structuring the exercise of discretion. Mendes believes that judicial review can be seen as the second step in a complex governance process. This second step helps orient the exercise of discretion, following the applicable legal norms, rather than constraining the administration's prerogatives. Instead of calling out the EU Courts to second-guess substantive public interest choices of EU institutions and bodies, Mendes proposes to enrich the understanding of the general duty of care and reason-giving, which could be used to pressure EU institutions and bodies to 'self-reflect' and clearly articulate their political choices. In other words, she advocates for more *process*-oriented review of political appraisals, with concomitant advantages for the process-oriented review of closely related empirical appraisals. She also mentions that the Ombudsman or administrative mechanisms might achieve better results in this respect.[85]

Other authors have also observed that the entanglement between legal rules and scientific or technical assessments goes very deep. Legal rules may provide criteria for the selection or prioritisation of scientific and technical studies. They also determine the form and content of scientific studies, delineating the epistemic basis for scientific conclusions. Finally, they determine the composition of expert bodies – including scientists, industry and civil society representatives – and, consequently, the type of expertise and *political* interests which such

[82] AG Jacobs, Case C-269/90, *Technische Universität München*, ECLI:EU:C:1991:317, paras 10–16.

[83] Hofmann (n 61), 225.

[84] Prek and Lefèvre (n 44).

[85] Joana Mendes, 'Discretion, Care and Public Interest in the EU Administration: Probing the Limits of Law' (2016) 53 *Common Market Law Review* 419.

bodies consider.[86] A considerable intellectual effort is needed to disentangle scientific, political and legal issues as they are intertwined at every level. This exercise is very prone to errors.[87] Crucially and paradoxically, a judge trying to filter out legal issues from a melting pot of empirical problems would have to possess relevant specialist expertise to fully and correctly separate the legal from the scientific and from the political.

Where the dividing lines between science, politics and law become increasingly blurred, and where normative and empirical epistemic uncertainty increases, questions about the institutional and procedural confines of the EU Courts come to the fore. Judicial review is confined by limited judicial expertise and resources; by hurdles resulting from the largely adversarial nature of judicial proceedings and the reliance on partisan evidence; by the binary nature of judicial rulings which either uphold or annul the contested legal acts; a solution which is not necessarily conducive to the 'self-reflection' by the defendant institutions and bodies.

Moreover, it has been argued that litigators calling for comprehensive review in competition and other cases are interest driven. Perfectly aware of generalist judges' limited expertise, they hope to 'stand a greater chance of convincing the (on the whole) non-specialist judges on the General Court, who do not possess the expertise and the institutional back-up of the European Commission'.[88] A similar problem relates to the regulation of risks to public health and the environment. 'The science underlying decision-making has become of ever-increasing importance', as noted by Vos, whereas the EU judges visibly struggle with reviewing uncertain empirical issues such as risks to public health and the environment in a uniform way.[89] The traditional deferential approach of the EU Courts is not suitable for reviewing legal acts involving empirically uncertain appraisals. However, 'judges should remain judges. They should not become amateur scientists'.[90] As noted by Nehl, where there is no right or wrong answer to an empirically complex question, the crucial issue becomes the cognitive capacities of judges and the adequacy of their institutional back-up and procedural framework. Arguably, a judge is always at a comparative disadvantage. Primary law-, rule- and decision-makers typically possess appropriate human resources, technical equipment,

[86] Vesco Pascalev, 'The Clash of Scientific Assessors: What the Conflict over Glyphosate Carcinogenicity Tells Us About the Relationship between Law and Science' (2020) 11 *European Journal of Risk Regulation* 520, 531.

[87] ibid, 532.

[88] Paul Mahoney, 'Flogging a Dead Horse: The Appropriate Human Rights Policy for Judicial Treatment of Competition Fines' in David Edward, Jacquelyn MacLennan and Assimakis Komninos (eds), *A Scot Without Borders – Liber Amicorum Ian S Forrester*, vol I (Concurrences 2015).

[89] Ellen Vos, 'The European Court of Justice in the Face of Scientific Uncertainty and Complexity' in Mark Dawson, Bruno de Witte and Elise Muir (eds), *Judicial Activism at the European Court of Justice* (Edward Elgar 2013), 161. See also, Anne-May JP Janssen and Nele F Rosenstock, 'Handling Uncertain Risks: An Inconsistent Application of Standards?' (2016) 7 *European Journal of Risk Regulation* 144 and the earlier literature cited therein.

[90] ibid, 164.

infrastructure, suitable processes (including scientifically recognised methods or tests), advisory committees, delegated national experts, internal quality panels and the like, to perform complex appraisals. Generalist administrative courts are not equipped with the same resources and procedures. Their methods, investigatory and fact-finding powers are not suited for replicating primary law-, rule- and decision-making processes.[91] The judicial review of legal acts underpinned by complex factual appraisals and political judgments is therefore prone to errors and, in any event, may be disproportionately time and effort intensive.[92]

AG Jacobs proposed that EU Courts be assisted more often by court-appointed experts and apply measures of inquiry more readily, instead of relying solely on the parties' material.[93] The EU Courts have always been reluctant to accept this idea, arguably for fear of relinquishing their power, allowing 'battles of experts' in the courtroom, or increasing the length and costs of proceedings. It has been argued that even court-appointed experts could not bring the judge onto an equal footing with the administrator. The EU judicature lacks the means to control the quality of technical or scientific studies. Due to the imprecision of both social and hard science, difficult to comprehend for a layperson, it is doubtful whether studies by court-appointed experts could convincingly confirm or deny the appraisals of the challenged EU institutions and bodies.[94]

The stream of litigation regarding complex technical or scientific assessments is likely to increase in the future. This factor only intensifies the question about EU judicial review's sufficiency in its current form to provide private parties with a meaningful degree of legal protection. There is perhaps a growing need for specialised courts or specialised chambers at the EGC.[95] However, both solutions have recently been rejected, including by the EU Courts' leadership, mainly due to concerns about potential divergences in case law. Instead of setting up specialised courts, the ECJ and the co-legislators opted to double the number of judges at the EGC. Subsequently, the EGC adopted a decision laying down the rules for allocating the cases that do not allow for a comprehensive specialisation of court chambers.[96] In this context, the forms of legal protection offered by non-judicial remedies, such as the BoAs and the Ombudsman, merit in-depth analysis.

[91] Nehl (n 7), 175–76.

[92] See the concerns of an English judge in this respect in Oliver Bartlett and Angus Macculloch, 'Evidence and Proportionality in Free Movement Cases: The Impact of the Scotch Whisky Case' (2020) 11 *European Journal of Risk Regulation* 109.

[93] AG Jacobs, Case C-269/90, *Technische Universität München*, ECLI:EU:C:1991:317, para 13.

[94] Fritzsche (n 46), 398.

[95] Vos (n 89), 165. Graham Butler, 'An Interim Post-mortem: Specialised Courts in the EU Judicial Architecture after the Civil Service Tribunal' (2019) 17 *International Organizations Law Review* 586. Eric Barbier de la Serre and Anne-Lise Sibony, 'Expert Evidence Before the EC Courts' (2008) 45 *Common Market Law Review* 941.

[96] EGC, 'Criteria for the assignment of cases to Chambers' [2016] OJ C296/4. In its most recent decision, the EGC decided that its different chambers will examine cases regarding civil service and intellectual property. This is, however, far from the specialisation that competition or intellectual property litigators and scholars have in mind.

III. Restrictive Access

A. The Origins of Narrow Standing Rights

EU judicial review has also been subject to criticism because of its limited accessibility for interested private parties. AG Kokott has proclaimed the restrictive admissibility criteria of private annulment actions as 'one of the most contentious issues in EU law'.[97] Enshrined in Article 263(4) TFEU, these criteria authorise only a narrow category of private parties to directly challenge EU legal acts. Private parties litigating in Luxembourg are predominantly individual economic operators, and the challenged acts are individual administrative decisions formally addressed to the applicants rather than third parties.

By contrast, the action for annulment is practically unavailable, as far as legal acts implementing EU internal policies are concerned, to social actors such as trade unions, consumer associations or environmental organisations. Moreover, the action for annulment is unavailable to private parties, with few exceptions, against regulatory and legislative acts of general application. Based on a traditional conceptual distinction between individual and general acts, these access rules are seen as restrictive and unsuited to the practical effects of many EU legal acts. Such acts, due to their subject matter, frequently affect not only their formal addressees (economic operators) but also different categories of third parties (workers, consumers, economic competitors) and raise public interest issues (for instance, the protection of public health and the environment).

The origin of restrictive admissibility criteria lay in concerns expressed by the founding Member States about the decision-making autonomy of fledgling supranational institutions. This autonomy might have been impaired if frequent legal challenges by private parties were allowed.[98] The Member States modelled the admissibility criteria of private annulment actions on the narrow access rules applied at that time by the German administrative courts. The admissibility criteria contrasted with the remaining Treaty provisions governing the Court's powers and procedures, which were modelled on the French Conseil d'Etat.[99]

[97] AG Kokott, Case C-583/11 P, *Inuit Tapiriit Kanatami et al v Parliament and Council*, ECLI:EU:C:2013:21.

[98] Christopher Harding, 'The Private Interest in Challenging Community Action' (1980) 5 *European Law Review* 354. Hjalte Rasmussen, *The European Court of Justice* (GadJura 1998). Jurgen Schwarze, 'The Legal Protection of the Individual against Regulations in European Union Law' (2004) 10 *European Public Law* 285, 289. See also AG Mayras, Case C-43/72, *Merkur v Commission*, ECLI:EU:C:1973:74, 1078–79. AG Duthelillet de Lamothe, Case C-9/71, *Compagnie d'approvisionnement v Commission*, ECLI:EU:C:1972:43.

[99] Michel Fromont, 'L'influence du droit français et du droit allemand sur les conditions de recevabilité du recours en annulation devant la Cour de justice des Communautés européennes' (1966) *Revue Trimestrielle de Droit Européen* 47. Gérard Rasquin and Roger-Michel Chevallier, 'L'article 173, alinéa 2 du traité CEE' (1966) *Revue Trimestrielle de Droit Européen* 31.

B. Standing for Individual Economic Operators

The admissibility criteria of annulment actions were subsequently revised, somewhat broadening access to justice for new categories of economic operators, but the changes did not relate to the basic restrictive model. According to what is today Article 263(4) TFEU, in a nutshell, legal acts adopted by EU bodies can be directly challenged in *three scenarios*: (1) if the contested act is addressed to the applicant; (2) if the contested act is of 'direct and individual concern' to the applicant; and (3) if the contested act is a 'regulatory act' of 'direct concern' to the applicant and requires no further implementing acts.

The EU bodies adopt a variety of administrative decisions concerning the rights and obligations of individual economic operators (in fields such as competition law, State aid, anti-dumping, the regulation of risks to public health and the environment, the authorisation of medicinal products, the supervision of banks and financial institutions and so on). These operators may challenge such decisions under the first scenario.[100]

The second scenario – 'direct and individual concern' – is supposed to prevent the EU bodies from ruling out judicial review by manipulating the act's form. Its proper interpretation has been the subject of fervent controversy. According to well-established case law, for the requirement of *direct* concern to be met the challenged act must modify the applicant's personal *rights or obligations*,[101] ie those belonging to the applicant in her individual capacity and serving her private interest.[102] Thus, the condition of 'direct concern' largely excludes public interest litigation before the EU Courts.[103] Civil society members or public interest organisations cannot rely on their statutory goals to claim being directly concerned by EU legal acts relating to EU internal policies. This interpretation has been met with strong objections from scholars and practitioners, who have seen it as a missed chance to strengthen the social legitimacy of the EU through broader access to justice.[104]

Moreover, the mere fact that a measure only indirectly affects an applicant's interests does not yet qualify her as 'directly concerned'.[105] As already mentioned,

[100] Also, the EU bodies adopt a variety of decisions relating to institutional (access to documents, public tenders and contracts) and other matters (Common Foreign and Security Policy (CFSP) restrictive measures) that may also be challenged by their addressees.

[101] Case T-541/10, *ADEDY et al v Council*, ECLI:EU:T:2012:626, para 64.

[102] Ludwig Krämer, 'Access to Environmental Justice: the Double Standards of the ECJ' (2017) 14 *Journal for European Environmental & Planning Law* 159, 169.

[103] Public interest litigation is moreover precluded by the judge-made condition of *legal interest*, according to which the potential annulment of the contested act must bring 'a *personal* and *actual* benefit to the applicant' or 'procure an advantage to the applicant', whether of legal or merely factual nature. Case C-682/13 P, *Scheitz v Commission*, ECLI:EU:C:2015:356, paras 25–27. Case T-177/04, *EasyJet v Commission*, ECLI:EU:T:2006:187, para 41.

[104] Among many, Laurence Gormley, 'Access to Justice and Public Interest Litigation: Getting Nowhere Quickly?' in Kai Purnhagen and Peter Rott (eds), *Varieties of European Economic Law and Regulation: Liber Amicorum for Hans Micklitz* (Springer 2014).

[105] Case T-669/15, *Lysoform v ECHA*, ECLI:EU:T:2016:610, paras 36–37.

a significant number of EU legal acts affect vital interests of third parties. A potentially unlawful Commission merger decision formally addressed to the merging companies may alert their market competitors or social actors such as trade unions.[106] However, such decisions are not seen by the EU judicature as modifying the rights or obligations of said competitors or trade unions.[107]

The condition of 'direct concern' is reinforced by that of 'individual concern'. For the requirement of individual concern to be met, the challenged act must affect the applicant 'by reason of certain attributes which are peculiar to [her] or by reason of circumstances in which [she is] differentiated from all other persons … just as in the case of the person addressed by such a decision'. In other words, the applicant must belong to a 'closed group', membership of which should be considered as 'fixed' at the moment when the act was adopted.[108] If this is the case, the EU judicature assumes that the decision-makers have or should have examined the individual situations of the act's de facto addressees (as in the case of individual administrative decisions).

Hence, it is not excluded that an act which, from the formal point of view, is of general application – for instance, an implementing regulation – would turn out to be of individual application to certain private parties. The conceptual distinction between (executive) rule-making acts of general application and (administrative) decision-making acts of individual application breaks down in the EU context. The EU institutions adopt a variety of 'hybrid acts' – having the form of generally applicable regulation and producing general effects but also individually addressing a specific operator just as an administrative decision does. For instance, regulations authorising health claims on food products or the use of risky chemical substances or pesticides are adopted at the request or with the involvement of an individual operator. Moreover, individual administrative decisions may raise public interest issues. For instance, registration of a chemical substance or a decision requiring chemical tests on animals could raise public health or animal welfare concerns. Individually concerned economic operators are entitled to challenge 'hybrid acts' or decisions,[109] unlike public interest organisations,[110] consumer associations,[111] or informal associations of individuals acting in the common interest and invoking their statutory goals.[112]

[106] Case T-96/92, *CCE de la Société générale des grandes sources v Commission*, ECLI:EU:T:1995:77, paras 38–35. Case T-12/93, *CCE Vittel v Commission*, ECLI:EU:T:1995:78, paras 50–58.

[107] See also cases regarding State aid decisions affecting the employees of concerned companies, Case T-156/10, *ADEAS v Commission*, ECLI:EU:T:2014:41. Case T-2/13, *CFE-CGC France Télécom-Orange v Commission*, ECLI:EU:T:2014:226.

[108] Case 25/62, *Plaumann v Commission*, ECLI:EU:C:1963:17, para 107. Case T-629/13, *Molda v Commission*, ECLI:EU:T:2014:834, paras 26–36.

[109] For instance, Case T-326/07, *Cheminova et al v Commission*, ECLI:EU:T:2009:299, para 66. Case T-483/11, *Sepro Europe v Commission*, ECLI:EU:T:2013:407, para 30. Case T-269/11, *Xeda International v Commission*, ECLI:EU:T:2014:1069, para 33. Case T-17/12, *Hagenmeyer & Hahn v Commission*, ECLI:EU:T:2014:234.

[110] Case T-673/13, *European Coalition to End Animal Experiments v ECHA*, ECLI:EU:T:2015:167.

[111] Case T-224/10, *Association belge de la consommateurs*, ECLI:EU:T:2011:588, paras 31–64.

[112] Case T-224/12, *Alessandro Accorinti et al v ECB*, ECLI:EU:T:2014:611.

The EU Courts may depart from the strict understanding of direct and individual concern, mostly dealing with competition law, State aid and anti-dumping cases. The exceptions tend, however, to serve exclusively economic operators whose market position or economic interests have been impaired to a high degree by decisions conferring significant benefits upon their competitors,[113] and who have also participated in the administrative proceedings leading to the adoption of the contested act.[114] The standing criteria may also be fulfilled in other areas by the economic competitors of administrative decisions' beneficiaries, especially if these decisions deprive them of an advantage they have enjoyed under EU law.[115] Moreover, the standing may also be granted to a shareholder[116] or business partner[117] of the operator who is concerned by the contested act, if it is certain that the execution of the contested act entails automatic consequences for the applicant.[118]

The notion of direct and individual concern, on the contrary, precludes actions by social actors such as trade unions. For instance, that Commission State aid decisions could lead to massive layoffs from affected companies was insufficient to establish the individual concern of the trade unions representing the affected companies' workers. In the ECJ's view, social rights invoked by the trade unions had only 'a tenuous link' with the subject matter of the contested State aid decisions.[119] Only exceptionally could social actors such as trade unions and consumer organisations challenge decisions addressed to economic operators, if they managed to derive a procedural right from a legislative or Treaty provision to be consulted in the administrative proceedings. However, in such a case they might only raise a plea in law relating to the breach of this procedural right

[113] For instance, Case T-57/11, *Castelnou Energia v Commission*, ECLI:EU:T:2014:1021, 33 and 43. Case T-125/12, *Viasat Broadcasting v Commission*, ECLI:EU:T:2015:687, paras 34–35.

[114] For instance, Case T-394/15, *KPN BV v Commission*, ECLI:EU:T:2017:756. Case T-162/10, *Niki Luftfahrt GmbH v Commission*, ECLI:EU:T:2015:283. Case T-89/09, *Pollmeier Massivholz v Commission*, ECLI:EU:T:2015:153. Case T-57/15, *Trajektna luka v Commission*, ECLI:EU:T:2016:470. Case T-162/13, *Kletterhallenverband Klever et al v Commission*, ECLI:EU:T:2016:341, para 39. Standing of non-addressees of some decisions in State aid or competition cases can be recognised on account of enforcing these parties' procedural rights conferred by binding EU measures. For instance, Case T-79/14, *Secop v Commission*, ECLI:EU:T:2016:118. Case T-693/14, *Hamr Sport v Commission*, ECLI:EU:T:2016:292.

[115] For instance, Case T-452/14, *Laboratoires CTRS v Commission*, ECLI:EU:T:2015:373.

[116] Case T-499/12, *HSH Investment Holdings Coinvest-C et al v Commission*, ECLI:EU:T:2015:840, paras 10, 12 and 34.

[117] Case T-170/06, *Alrosa v Commission*, ECLI:EU:T:2007:220, paras 36–40. Case T-76/14, *Morningstar v Commission*, ECLI:EU:T:2016:481, paras 30–31.

[118] The exception to the traditional approach seems to be justified by a recognition of the specificity of State aid and competition law. Economic operators act on relevant markets within complex economic interactions with each other. If a Commission decision confers rights or imposes obligations on one operator, it is likely that exercising these rights or complying with these obligations by their addressee will somehow affect other operators.

[119] Case C-106/98 P, *Comité d'entreprise de la Société française de production*, ECLI:EU:C:2000:277, paras 51–54. Case T-2/13, *France Télécom v Commission*, ECLI:EU:T:2014:226. Case T-7/13, *ADEAS v Commission*, ECLI:EU:T:2014:221.

but not the substance of the contested act.[120] Likewise, the direct and individual concern is an insurmountable obstacle to public interest organisations who do not stand to protect their own rights.[121] Therefore, the EU judicature has been accused of double standards and a bias in favour of individual economic rights.[122]

Some authors see these access rules as simply incompatible with the nature of certain fields of law, such as environmental law, data protection, consumer protection, or the regulation of risks to public health and the environment. These branches of law protect values which are of a general as opposed to individual interest.[123] Social actors and public interest organisations are therefore naturally interested and well placed to directly challenge EU legal acts dealing with these matters.[124] The criticism of the EU judicature in this respect could be exacerbated by a line of case law liberalising the rules for access to national judicial review courts in environmental matters according to the Aarhus Convention's requirements, which the EU has ratified.[125] In what may seem like a moment of downright hypocrisy, the ECJ recently imposed a liberalisation of access rules applied by the German administrative courts.[126] At the same time, it refused to bring its access rules into line with the Aarhus Convention requirements.[127] It regularly holds, which one could find to be a convenient excuse, that the Treaty authors have

[120] Case T-96/62, *CCE*, ECLI:EU:T:1995:77, para 37. Case T-12/93, *CCE Vittel*, ECLI:EU:T:1995:78, para 48. Case T-224/10, *Association belge de la consommateurs*, ECLI:EU:T:2011:588, paras 31–64. Case C-319/07 P, *3F v Commission*, ECLI:EU:T:2015:373. Case T-140/13, *Netherlands Maritime Technology Association v Commission*, ECLI:EU:T:2014:1029, and (on appeal) Case C-100/15 P, *Netherlands Maritime Technology Association v Commission*, ECLI:EU:C:2016:254.

[121] Case T-585/93, *Greenpeace v Commission*, ECLI:EU:T:1995:147, para 50. Case T-673/13, *European Coalition to End Animal Experiments v ECHA*, ECLI:EU:T:2015:167. Public interest organisations could fulfil the standing requirements on condition that they perform some economic activity, Case C-640/16 P, *Greenpeace Energy v Commission*. They could also fulfil the standing requirements if they invoked procedural rights, Case C-384/16 P, *European Union Copper Task Force v Commission*, ECLI:EU:C:2018:176, para 88. Case T-125/18, *Associazione GranoSalus v Commission*, ECLI:EU:T:2019:92.

[122] Krämer (n 102). See also Giulia C Leonelli, 'A Threefold Blow to Environmental Public Interest Litigation: The Urgent Need to Reform the Aarhus Regulation' (2020) 45 *European Law Review* 324.

[123] Krämer (n 102), 169.

[124] Case T-673/13, *European Coalition to End Animal Experiments v ECHA*, ECLI:EU:T:2015:167, para 23.

[125] Council Decision of 17 February 2005 on the conclusion, on behalf of the European Community, of the Convention on access to information, public participation in decision-making and access to justice in environmental matters [2005] OJ L124/1.

[126] Case C-115/09, *Bund für Umwelt und Naturschutz Deutschland, Landesverband Nordrhein Westfalen*, ECLI:EU:C:2011:289. See a robust controversy in German scholarship mentioned in Catherine Warin, 'Individual Rights and Collective Interests in EU Law: Three Approaches to a Still Volatile Relationship' (2019) 56 *Common Market Law Review* 463, 466–69. Eva Julia Lohse, 'Surprise? Surprise! – Case C-115/09 (Kohlekraftwerk Lünen) – A Victory for the Environment and a Loss for Procedural Autonomy of the Member States?' (2012) 18 *European Public Law* 249.

[127] Joined Cases C-401/12 P to C-403/12 P, *Council v Vereniging Milieudefensie*, ECLI:EU:C:2015:4, para 60. Matthijs van Wolferen and Mariolina Eliantonio, 'Access to Justice in Environmental Matters in the EU: The EU's Difficult Road towards Non-Compliance with the Aarhus Convention' in Marjan Peeters and Mariolina Eliantonio (eds), *Research Handbook on EU Environmental Law* (Edward Elgar 2020).

explicitly opted for the restrictive access rules for private parties, as regards the action for annulment.[128]

C. Decentralised Access to Justice Against General Acts

In addition, in order for the requirement of *direct* concern to be met, the challenged act cannot require further implementing measures. The contested act must contain complete legal norms, leaving no discretion to the authorities entrusted with their execution, such execution being purely automatic and resulting from the contested legal norms without the application of other intermediate norms.[129] This condition makes it possible to establish a causal link between the contested act and the alleged breach of higher-order law.[130] Otherwise, it could turn out that the breach of law results from implementing measures or that the breach is still hypothetical. Interested parties should therefore await implementing measures, usually taken at the national level, to challenge these measures before national courts and request a preliminary reference regarding the validity of the basic EU act.[131]

Likewise, the 'individual concern' rules out direct legality challenges by private parties against the EU acts of general application, whether regulatory or legislative, and those addressed to individual Member States.[132] Usually, the EU judicature finds that applicants are affected by the said acts by reason of objective criteria, just like any other parties, and not particular circumstances required by the condition of individual concern.[133] The fact that multiple economic operators such as local farmers or small entrepreneurs form associations to challenge, by a 'class action', regulatory acts or those addressed to Member States that affect their vital business interests does not raise their chances of proving individual concern.[134]

[128] For instance, Case T-825/14, *IREPA Onlus v Commission & Court of Auditors*, ECLI:EU:T:2016:345, paras 47–51. This formula is regularly repeated.

[129] Case T-541/10, *ADEDY et al v Council*, ECLI:EU:T:2012:626, para 64. Exceptionally, this condition is met if the contested act requires an implementing measure, but the implementing authority has no real discretion in deciding on its substance, Case T-337/13, *CSF v Commission*, ECLI:EU:T:2015:502, paras 30ff. Joined Cases T-346/02 and T-347/02, *Cableuropa v Commission*, ECLI:EU:T:2003:256, para 53.

[130] Case T-150/05, *Sahlstedt v Commission*, ECLI:EU:T:2006:172, para 53.

[131] Case T-541/10, *ADEDY et al v Council*, paras 71, 84–85.

[132] For instance, Joined Cases C-408/15 P and C-409/15 P, *Ackermann Saatzucht et al v Parliament and Council*, ECLI:EU:C:2016:893. The exclusion of private challenges to general acts does not concern the CFSP restrictive measures. See for instance, Joined Cases T-4/11 and T-5/11, *Export Development Bank or Iran v Council*, ECLI:EU:T:2013:400, para 37. The same obstacle may be posed by the criterion of direct concern as it requires the lack of implementing measures, which often must be adopted at the national level. In practice, the EU judicature may reject the action on the basis of either direct or individual concern.

[133] See exceptional cases, Case C-309/89, *Codorniu v Commission*, ECLI:EU:C:1994:197. Case C-358/89, *Extramet Industrie*, ECLI:EU:C:1992:257, para 17.

[134] Case T-312/14, *Federcoopesca et al v Council*, ECLI:EU:T:2015:472. Case T-153/16, *Acerga v Council*, ECLI:EU:T:2017:73. Case T-180/13, *Pesquerias Riveirenses and Others v Council*, ECLI:EU:T:2014:78.

Exceptionally, the EU judicature declares admissible actions by certain economic operators against Commission decisions concerning general (sectoral) State aid regimes, on account of their specific factual and legal situation,[135] especially if the Commission has ordered the recovery of the aid the applicants have already received[136] or if the applicants have had legitimate expectations of receiving this aid.[137]

In this way, the ECJ advances a conception of the decentralised judicial system, according to which private parties should seek judicial protection from EU acts of general application or those addressed to the Member States before national courts. Private parties should challenge implementing measures before national courts and, if needed, convince the judge to make a preliminary reference regarding the validity of the basic EU act.[138]

In the early 2000s, AG Jacobs called this conception into question. He pointed out multiple obstacles that may impede access to justice at the national level, such as major differences between national access rules and the lack of an enforceable right to a preliminary reference. As a result of these obstacles, certain acts of general application may practically turn out to be immune from judicial review. In his view, moreover, in the EU legal order at that time acts of general application did not enjoy a higher democratic legitimacy that would justify the ECJ's conception of indirect challenges.[139] The ECJ finally upheld the restrictive interpretation of individual concern.[140] Jacobs' opinion has nevertheless resulted in a revision of

Case T-560/14, *ABZ Aardbeien Uit Zaad Holdingv v Parliament and Council*, ECLI:EU:T:2015:314. Case C-455/13 P, C-457/13 P and C-460/13 P, *Confederazione Cooperative Italiane et al*, ECLI:EU:C:2015:616 (in which the CJ rejected the GC's more lenient approach). In highly exceptional cases, private applicants could challenge an act of general application on procedural grounds as a hierarchically superior legal norm conferred upon them a procedural right (to be heard). Case T-456/14, *Association des fonctionnaires indépendants pour la défense de la fonction publique européenne v Parliament and Council*, ECLI:EU:T:2016:493, paras 144–45. It may also happen that a higher-order provision imposes on the law- or rule-making body a duty to take a specific substantive interest into account. The beneficiaries of such a guarantee may claim individual concern. Case C-152/88, *Sofrimport*, ECLI:EU:C:1990:259, paras 12–13. Case T-264/03, *Schmoldt v Commission*, ECLI:EU:T:2004:157, paras 116–17.

[135] For instance, Case C-203/16 P, *Dirk Andres v Commission*, ECLI:EU:C:2018:505, paras 53–59. Under the third admissibility scenario (see below), direct actions by the competitors of the beneficiaries of State aid may also turn out to be admissible. Joined Cases C-622/16 P to C-624/16 P, *Montessori & Ferraci v Commission*, ECLI:EU:C:2018:873 (thanks to a combination of a liberal interpretation of direct concern – see paras 43 and 50 – with the concept of a regulatory act not entailing implementing measures at the national level).

[136] Case C-15/98, *Sardegna Lines v Commission*, ECLI:EU:C:2000:570, para 34.

[137] Case C-133/12 P, *Stichting Woonline v Commission*, ECLI:EU:C:2014:105. Case C-132/12 P, *Stichting Woonpunt et al v Commission*, ECLI:EU:C:2014:100.

[138] Koen Lenaerts, 'The Basic Constitutional Charter of a Community Based on the Rule of Law' in Miguel Maduro and Loic Azoulai (eds), *The Past and Future of EU Law: The Classics of EU Law Revisited on the 50th Anniversary of the Rome Treaty* (Hart Publishing 2010).

[139] AG Jacobs, Case C-50/00 P, *Unión de Pequeños Agricultores v Council*, ECLI:EU:C:2002:197, paras 43–48 and 86. Similar arguments had been earlier raised in the literature: Paul Nihoul, 'La recevabilité des recours en annulation introduits par un particulier à l'encontre d'un acte communautaire de portée générale' (1994) *Revue Trimestrielle de Droit Européen* 171.

[140] Case C-263/02 P, *Commission v Jégo-Quéré*, ECLI:EU:C:2004:210. Case C-50/00 P, *Unión de Pequeños Agricultores v Council*, ECLI:EU:C:2002:462.

what is today Article 263(4) TFEU. The Treaty of Lisbon added a third admissibility scenario enabling private applicants to directly challenge specific categories of general acts producing immediate legal effects (eg prohibiting a specific economic activity).[141]

According to the new scenario, private applicants may challenge 'regulatory acts' which are of 'direct concern' to them and do 'not entail implementing measures'. Scholars and practitioners used to express high hopes for the new scenario. However, the ECJ opted for its most restrictive interpretation.[142] It held that the concept of 'regulatory acts' encompasses acts of general application except for legislative ones,[143] maintained the condition of 'direct concern' and interpreted the criterion of no implementing measures strictly, to maintain the decentralised character of the EU judicial system.[144] The existing practice has revealed that relying on the third scenario is possible in highly specific circumstances: when a general regulatory act deprives the applicants of their acquired rights,[145] prohibits a given economic activity[146] or generates a new and fully specified duty.[147] In most instances, the applicants cannot benefit from the third scenario because of the requirement of 'no implementing measures'. It is a rare situation that a generally applicable act, even non-legislative, will not require some implementing measures at the national level.[148] 'A mountain laboured and brought forth a mouse',[149] concluded Barents, observing a small number of actions brought based on the new admissibility scenario.

It is often argued that access to justice should not depend on the formal features of contested legal acts, but preferably on their practical effects.[150] In this vein, AG Jacobs proposed a liberal principle according to which 'an individual

[141] The idea was to avoid a situation in which a party seeking judicial review would have to first breach the contested act to receive a challengeable decision imposing a sanction. According to the previous case law, such a requirement would breach the right to effective judicial protection. Case C-432/05, *Unibet*, ECLI:EU:C:2007:163, para 50.

[142] See different proposals, AG Kokott, Case C-583/11 P, *Inuit Tapiriit Kanatami et al v Parliament and Council*, ECLI:EU:C:2013:21, paras 30–62, 38 and 117 (ultimately endorsed by the ECJ). AG Wathelet, Case C-132/12 P, *Stichting Woonpunt et al v Commission*, ECLI:EU:C:2013:335, paras 69–76. AG Cruz Villalón, Case C-456/13 P, *T & L Sugars v Council*, ECLI:EU:C:2014:2283, paras 16–48.

[143] Case C-583/11 P, *Inuit Tapiriit Kanatami et al v Parliament and Council*, ECLI:EU:C:2013:625, para 61.

[144] Case C-244/16 P, *Industrias Químicas del Vallés v Commission*, ECLI:EU:C:2018:177. Case C-384/16 P, *European Union Copper Task Force v Commission*, ECLI:EU:C:2018:176.

[145] Case T-434/13, *Doux v Commission*, ECLI:EU:T:2016:7.

[146] Case T-296/12, *The Health Food Manufacturers' Association v Commission*, ECLI:EU:T:2015:375.

[147] Case T-135/13, *Hitachi Chemical Europe et al v ECHA*, ECLI:EU:T:2015:253.

[148] See, for instance, Case C-541/14 P, *Royal Scandinavian Casino Aarhus*, ECLI:EU:C:2016:302, paras 44–47.

[149] Barents (n 3), 284. See also Denis Waelbroeck and Thomas Bombois, 'Des requérants "privilégiés" et des autres … À propos de l'arrêt Inuit et de l'exigence de protection juridictionnelle effective des particuliers en droit européen' (2014) 50 *Cahiers de Droit Européen* 21.

[150] Jürgen Bast, 'Legal Instruments and Judicial Protection' in Armin von Bogdandy and Jürgen Bast (eds), *Principles of European Constitutional Law* (Hart Publishing 2010). Jürgen Bast, 'New Categories of Acts After the Lisbon Reform: Dynamics of Parliamentarization in EU Law' (2012) 49 *Common Market Law Review* 885, 907.

who considers himself wronged by a measure which deprives him of a right or advantage under Community law must have access to a remedy against that measure and be able to obtain complete judicial protection'.[151] Authors participating in the debate on access to justice at the EU level advance numerous arguments in support of liberalisation of the access rules. They most often invoke the concept of 'effective judicial protection',[152] currently enshrined in Article 47 of the EU Charter, the standards of the European Court of Human Rights (ECtHR),[153] and comparative analyses.[154] Another often-invoked concept is the 'rule of law', understood as the practical amenability of legal acts to judicial review to rule out arbitrariness in the exercise of public power.[155]

When it comes to the regulation of emerging risks to public health and the environment, it is argued, scientific questions are enmeshed with pure politics. The EU institutions and bodies may conceal their political agenda (or that of powerful industrial lobbies) behind seemingly neutral 'science', and even bend the applicable higher-order law, without any opposition from privileged applicants.[156] None of the privileged applicants – the Member States and EU institutions – in this or other areas, such as the highly controversial EU economic governance in times of financial crises, may have an interest in challenging politically controversial EU measures.[157] Without allowing private parties and social actors to trigger the EU judicial review, and thus act as effective watchdogs of EU institutions and bodies, certain public interests and EU legal norms may remain without protection and

[151] AG Jacobs, Case C-50/00 P, *Unión de Pequeños Agricultores*, ECLI:EU:C:2002:197, para 38.

[152] See generally Takis Tridimas and Sara Poli, '*Locus standi* of Individuals under Article 230(4): The Return of Euricide' in Philip Moser and Katrine Sawyer (eds), *Making Community Law: The Legacy of Advocate General Jacobs at the European Court of Justice* (Edward Elgar 2008). Maria Bergström, 'Judicial Protection for Private Parties in European Commission Rule-Making' in Carl Fredrik Bergström (ed), *Rulemaking by the European Commission* (Oxford University Press 2016).

[153] Laurent Pech and Angela Ward, 'Effective Judicial Remedies before the Court of Justice' in Steve Peers, Tamara Hervey, Jeff Kenner and Angela Ward (eds), *The EU Charter of Fundamental Rights: A Commmentary* (Hart Publishing, CH Beck, Nomos 2014), 1245. Angela Ward, 'National and EC Remedies under the EU Treaty: Limits and the Role of the ECHR' in Catherine Barnard and Okeoghene Odudu (eds), *The Outer Limits of European Union Law* (Hart Publishing 2009), 332–33 and 343–47. Louise Fromont and Arnaud van Waeyenberge, 'La protection juridictionnelle effective en Europe ou l'histoire d'une procession d'Echternach' (2015) 51 *Cahiers de Droit Européen* 113, 114–15.

[154] Eric Stein and Joseph Vining, 'Citizen Access to Judicial Review of Administrative Action in a Transnational and Federal Context' in Francis Jacobs (ed), *European Law and the Individual* (North-Holland 1976). Denis Waelbroeck and A-M Verheyden, 'Les conditions de recevabilité des recours en annulation des particuliers contre les actes normatifs communautaires' (1995) 31 *Cahiers de Droit Européen* 399. Anatole Abaquesne de Parfouru, '*Locus Standi* of Private Applicants under the Article 230 EC Action for Annulment: Any Lessons to Be Learnt from France?' (2007) 14 *Maastricht Journal of European and Competition Law* 361–402.

[155] Anthony Arnull, *The European Union and its Court of Justice* (Oxford University Press 2006), 91–93.

[156] Lucas Bergkamp, 'Private Party Standing and EU Risk Regulation: Expanded Standing Rights in the Public Interest' (2016) 8 *European Journal of Risk Regulation* 557, 564.

[157] Kilpatrick (nn 15 and 16).

enforcement.[158] Last but not least, it is argued that broadly accessible judicial review is necessary given the persistent non-transparency and insufficient inclusiveness of EU law-, rule- and decision-making.[159]

IV. The Risks of Judicial Overload and Overreach

The 'floodgate' argument is usually invoked to explain why the EU Courts are clinging to the restrictive access rules. Were it not for the restrictive rules, the EU Courts could be paralysed by the influx of empirically complex and politically controversial cases.[160] This is why, as it is explained, the ECJ opts for the decentralised system of access judicial system where legality challenges must first pass through a filter provided by national courts.[161]

The floodgate argument does not reveal the full picture. The restrictive access rules may also be interpreted as curbing the judicial power vis-à-vis the law-makers, administration or other authorities subject to judicial supervision. Admittedly, Arnull argued that

> the Court is not an institution plagued with doubts about its own legitimacy and has in the past been willing to interpret previous versions of Article 263 *contra legem* in the interests of the rule of law. Therefore, it is uncomfortable with the notion of judicial review *per se*, and there is no counter-majoritarian difficulty in the Union because of its persistent democracy deficit.[162]

Nonetheless, it should be pointed out that judges have a comparative disadvantage to make complex assessments and are less democratically legitimised; their decision-making is even less transparent than that of the EU co-legislators, and they remain detached from mechanisms of democratic accountability. That legislative or administrative bodies of the EU do not satisfactorily fulfil their tasks is not a reason to transfer these tasks to the judiciary.

Considering the 'transmutation thesis', judicial review must be limited by procedural means to avoid judicial errors and, importantly, normative overreach.

[158] Carol Harlow, 'Towards a Theory of Access for the European Court of Justice' (1992) 12 *Yearbook of European Law* 213. Hans-Wolfgang Micklitz and Norbert Reich, *Public Interest Litigation before European Courts* (Nomos 1996). Hans-Wolfgang Micklitz, 'The ECJ Between the Individual Citizen and the Member States – A Plea for a Judge-made European Law on Remedies' in Hans-Wolfgang Micklitz and Bruno de Witte (eds), *The European Court of Justice and the Autonomy of the Member States* (Intersentia 2012).

[159] Arnull (n 7). Elspeth Berry and Simon Boyes, 'Access to Justice in the Community Courts: A Limited Right?' (2005) 24 *Civil Justice Quarterly* 224.

[160] Anthony Arnull, 'Private Applicants and the Action for Annulment since *Codorniu*' (2001) 38 *Common Market Law Review* 7, 51–52.

[161] Hjalte Rasmussen, 'Why Is Article 173 Interpreted Against Private Plaintiffs?' (1980) *European Law Review* 112.

[162] Arnull (n 7), 400.

By dint of liberal access rules, the EU Courts could be continuously asked to second-guess the EU institutions and bodies' discretionary choices.[163] Although the above concerns about the rule of law, effective judicial protection, and the legal accountability of EU institutions and bodies are perfectly valid, a simple relaxation of direct access to the EU Courts may produce significant adverse effects in the long term.[164]

The easier it gets to trigger judicial review, especially the judicial review of general acts, the more likely it is that the judiciary will decide politically sensitive issues with concomitant risks for its legitimacy.[165] By allowing class actions, public interest litigation, popular constitutional complaints and the like, courts may effectively transform into quasi-legislative assemblies.[166] The restrictive admissibility criteria for annulment actions have allowed the ECJ to focus its resources and authority on the enforcement of EU law towards national authorities, within the preliminary reference procedure. Thus, the ECJ fostered European integration rather than permanently second-guessing EU authorities' legislative and regulatory choices.[167] Allowing all kinds of actors to challenge all kinds of EU legal acts could result in a significant shift of authority and responsibility within the EU governance structure towards the judicial branch, which is not adapted to exercise this amount of authority.

The very capacity of substantive EU law to steer the exercise of political discretion within law-, rule- and decision-making is also highly uncertain due to the indeterminacy of EU legal norms at the legislative and constitutional level.[168] The EU co-legislators, acting in a quasi-diplomatic fashion, struggle to set clear priorities between competing values and interests, which hampers subsequent judicial review of administrative action.[169] In interpreting EU constitutional or legislative norms, the ECJ cannot draw from a social consensus regarding basic value judgements that support constitutional review in more organic, national communities, or from the experience of parallel and lower-instance courts.[170] The many

[163] Paul Craig, 'Standing, Rights and the Structure of Legal Argument' (2003) 9 *European Public Law* 493, 525.

[164] See Carol Harlow, 'Accountability Through Law' in Carol Harlow (ed), *Accountability in the European Union* (Oxford University Press 2002), 166.

[165] Maartje de Visser, 'A Cautionary Tale: Some Insights Regarding Judicial Activism from the National Experience' in Elise Muir, Marc Dawson and Bruno de Witte (eds), *Judicial Activism at the European Court of Justice* (Edward Elgar 2013), 193 and 199.

[166] Harm Schepel and Ekhard Blankenburg, 'Mobilizing the European Court of Justice' in Joseph Weiler and Grainne de Búrca (eds), *The European Court of Justice* (Oxford University Press 2001), 41. Craig (n 163), 524.

[167] Anne-Marie Burley and Walter Mattili, 'Europe before the Court: A Political Theory of Legal Integration' (1993) 47 *International Organization* 41.

[168] Joana Mendes, 'Executive Discretion in the EU and the Outer Boundaries of Law' in Joana Mendes (ed), *EU Executive Discretion and the Limits of Law* (Oxford University Press 2019).

[169] Niamh Moloney, 'The European Supervisory Authorities and Discretion: Can the Functional and Constitutional Circles be Squared?' in Joana Mendes (ed), *EU Executive Discretion and the Limits of Law* (Oxford University Press 2019), 88–89.

[170] Gareth Davies, 'Does the Court of Justice Own the Treaties? Interpretative Pluralism as a Solution to Over-constitutionalisation' (2018) 24 *European Law Journal* 1, 6.

differences between Member States' legal, social and economic systems, and their varied interests, 'render an overarching concept of substantive justice for the EU unattainable',[171] while only such a common concept could support and inform broadly available judicial review. On top of that, the EU judicial review is 'an elitist and closed process deriving its legitimacy from contestable sources. The Treaties have never received the kind of popular endorsement that would have legitimised it as a political constitution'.[172] Therefore, it is unclear how highly indeterminate legal norms, such as fundamental rights, could legitimise the EU Courts to interfere in EU law- and rule-making regularly at the request of private parties.

Last but not least, the checks and balances at the EU level are skewed. Given the immensely arduous procedure for Treaty revision and political hurdles in carrying out any legislative change, it is complicated, often nigh on impossible, for the EU authorities and the Member States to overrule the decisions of the EU judicature.[173] While basing its judgments directly on the Treaty provisions regarding substantive EU policies, the ECJ 'constitutionalises' certain interpretive choices, withdrawing them from ordinary political debate.[174] Lawyers and political scientists have also observed that the EU judicature's interpretive choices, treated as objective and neutral, may have a considerable impact on subsequent law- or rule-making processes.[175]

V. Conclusion

The stream of litigation before the EU Courts involving complex and uncertain technical, scientific and political appraisals is likely to increase in the future. Within the current judicial structure, it seems risky to liberalise the access rules of EU judicial review to allow litigation by social actors and public interest organisations, including against legislative and regulatory acts. In case of a liberalisation, would the EU Courts have to reach back for a deferential standard of review? How to avoid swamping the EU Courts with cases exceeding their cognitive and

[171] Sionadh Douglass-Scott, 'Justic, Injustice and the Rule of Law in the EU' in Dimitry Kochenov, Gráinne de Búrca and Andrew Williams (eds), *Europe's Justice Deficit* (Hart Publishing 2015).

[172] Deirdre Curtin, *Executive Power of the European Union: Law, Practices, and the Living Constitution* (Oxford University Press 2009), 15.

[173] Marcus Horeth, 'The Least Dangerous Branch of European Governance? The European Court of Justice under the Checks and Balances Doctrine' in Bruno de Witte, Elise Muir and Marc Dawson (eds), *Judicial Activism at the European Court of Justice* (Edward Elgar 2013). Gareth Davies, 'Legislative Control of the European Court of Justice' (2014) 51 *Common Market Law Review* 1579.

[174] Dieter Grimm, 'The Democratic Costs of Constitutionalisation: The European Case' (2015) 21 *European Law Journal* 460.

[175] However political scientists' views differ regarding the precise scope of this impact: Susanne K Schmidt, *The European Court of Justice and the Policy Process: The Shadow of Case Law* (Oxford University Press 2015). Dorte Sindbjerg Martinsen, *An Ever More Powerful Court? The Political Constraints of Legal Integration in the European Union* (Oxford University Press 2015).

functional capacities and the very steering capacity of EU law remains an unresolved puzzle.

What is the role of auxiliary review mechanisms in this context? They have unfolded over the last 20 years: internal review, boards of appeals, the Ombudsman and the like. They have hitherto attracted comparatively little scholarly attention. Some have been specifically intended to address the shortcomings of judicial review, including its limited accessibility and thoroughness. Because of somewhat weaker safeguards of independence, the lack of binding powers and the perceived lack of the same kind of authority as that bestowed upon the EU Courts by the EU Treaties, these auxiliary mechanisms are usually considered to provide a second-rate form of legal protection, not tantamount to or interchangeable with judicial review. The following chapters will seek to verify this assumption. They will examine what kind of authority extra-judicial review mechanisms can bestow upon the EU legal acts, thereby supplementing the judicial review by the EU Courts.

3

The Bits and Pieces of Review Mechanisms

The EU legal scholarship has been working tirelessly, sleuthing out any remaining and newly emerging gaps in the EU judicial review. Underlying these efforts has been a never-ending struggle of public lawyers to minimise the risk of arbitrariness in the exercise of public authority by EU institutions and bodies. By the same token, public lawyers wish to maximise legal certainty and predictability, the accountability of EU institutions and bodies, and the legal protection of individuals. Simply put, they wish to implement the ideal of the rule of law.

As this chapter will argue, certain functions traditionally attributed to judicial review might be discharged by mechanisms formally labelled as extra-judicial. Such mechanisms have recently proliferated at the EU level. One of the main problems of the EU judicial review is that it is conceived as a one-size-fits-all solution. The EU judges are expected to hear all kinds of cases, specialisation being ruled out due to prioritising the objective of uniformity in the application of EU law across variegated regulatory sub-fields.[176] A uniform procedural framework is applied to the judicial review of all kinds of legal acts, not providing engaged fact-finding on the side of the EU Courts. How do extra-judicial mechanisms, more specialised or perhaps capable of utilising more far-reaching investigatory measures, supplement the EU judicial review?

This chapter fleshes out distinctive functions of judicial and extra-judicial review. It also pinpoints institutional and procedural devices for these functions' implementation. It is based on a survey of theoretical and comparative law literature regarding a deep normative rationale of judicial and extra-judicial review. Simultaneously, it advances the approach to the study of the EU governance structure based on the idea of 'relative authority'. According to this analytical framework, the allocation of any kind of authority, including the authority to review legal measures and decision-making processes on various grounds, should be guided by 'legitimacy assets' that particular mechanisms can instil into the legal order. In the context of EU judicial and extra-judicial review, the legitimacy assets are argumentative resources that can be invoked in support of the authority of EU

[176] Another reason is the specific system in which the EGC judges are recruited. The candidates are first recruited by the Member States. For political and practical reasons, it would be difficult to 'distribute' specialisation of the judges among the Member States.

measures subject to review.[177] These arguments are relative to distinctive institutional and procedural features of particular mechanisms: their decision-making independence, their power to thoroughly scrutinise the applied legal interpretation or factual appraisals, their accessibility to the affected parties, and their participation-oriented procedural framework.

Different review mechanisms may be attuned to the character of cases and regulatory fields with which they deal. However, they also display common characteristics. Four institutional and procedural features, proposed in this chapter, structure the analysis presented in this book. They do not imply any specific benchmarks. The point is not to evaluate extra-judicial review against the gold standard of judicial review but, rather, to examine whether legitimacy assets offered by the respective mechanisms are somehow complementary, thereby furthering the authority of EU law-, rule- and decision-making.

Section I argues that the discussion regarding contemporary challenges to the EU judicial and extra-judicial review must take account of the context in which these mechanisms operate. This context relates to the character of legal acts amenable to review, the precision of applicable substantive law, and the legitimacy assets generated by the mechanisms' specific institutional and procedural features. Section II identifies the distinctive functions of judicial and extra-judicial mechanisms in a governance structure. Section III discusses institutional and procedural features that are deemed adequate to discharge these different functions. Section IV presents conclusions.

I. A Change in the Methodological Approach

A. From a Syllogistic to Contextual Approach

Supporting the normative claims for more accessible and thorough judicial review are usually the concepts of effective judicial protection and the rule of law, currently enshrined in Article 47 of the EU Charter of Fundamental Rights, and Articles 2 and 19(1) TEU. The concept of effective judicial protection has played a paramount role in the ECJ case law regarding the protection of EU rights at the domestic level.[178] The concept of the rule of law has also enabled the EU Courts to subject a great variety of binding legal acts adopted by EU institutions and bodies to judicial review.[179] It comes as no surprise that EU legal scholars have

[177] Mendes and Venzke (n 30), 77–81.

[178] Marek Safjan and Dominik Düsterhaus, 'A Union of Effective Judicial Protection: Addressing a Multi-level Challenge through the Lens of Article 47 CFREU' (2014) 33 *Yearbook of European Law* 3.

[179] Case 294/83, *Les Verts v Parliament*, ECLI:EU:C:1986:166, para 23. Case C-72/15, *Rosneft*, ECLI:EU:C:2017:236, para 66. Graham Butler, 'Implementing a Complete System of Legal Remedies in EU Foreign Affairs Law' (2018) 24 *Columbia Journal of European Law* 637.

taken the EU Courts' lead in tracking down 'gaps' in effective judicial protection. Such a gap is understood as a practical impossibility to subject an aspect of EU law-, rule- or decision-making which affects rights or interests of individuals[180] to comprehensive judicial scrutiny, irrespective of the act's binding or non-binding form. Hindrances in this regard may stem from jurisdictional limitations, rigorous standing rules or an insufficiently thorough review technique.

The case for comprehensive and accessible judicial review at the EU level relies on syllogistic reasoning.[181] The implicit premise seems to be that in the ideal state of the realisation of the rule of law, any aspect of any measure affecting rights or interests of individuals should be amenable to exhaustive judicial scrutiny. Any exercise of public power, even one that the law considers discretionary, should be framed and constrained by courts to rule out arbitrariness.[182] Otherwise, a breach of the rule of law or the principle of effective judicial protection may occur. From this premise followed AG Jacobs' proposals to increase the accessibility[183] and improve the thoroughness of EU judicial review.[184] This is also why scholars emphasise the potential of vigilant NGOs and social actors who could foster the rule of law at the EU level through public interest litigation before the EU Courts.[185]

The case for comprehensive and accessible judicial review, noble as it is, should not underestimate the structural limitations of the EU judicial review mechanism. This mechanism is not an infallible safeguard. It was initially designed to protect the private interests of resourceful market actors. It may not be equally efficient as a check and balance upon the policy and regulatory choices of EU institutions and bodies put at civil society's disposal. The EU Courts rely on partisan evidence, whereas public interest organisations may not be capable of producing or commissioning by themselves technical or scientific evidence enabling meaningful judicial review of EU legal acts.

The principles of the rule of law and effective judicial protection at the EU level should be interpreted following the common constitutional traditions of the Member States. Domestic legal orders across the EU express very different ideas about the range of legal acts amenable to judicial review before administrative and constitutional courts, and the range of potential applicants. In particular,

[180] The addressee of non-binding acts may reasonably feel obliged to follow the act due to the authority of the author or in fear of negative repercussions.

[181] Renato Nazzini, 'Administrative Enforcement, Judicial Review and Fundamental Rights in EU Competition Law: A Comparative Contextual-Functionalist Perspective' (2012) 49 *Common Market Law Review* 971, 973. Nazzini made this observation with regard to the literature dealing with the EU competition law enforcement regime. In my view, this observation applies more widely to the large part of literature dealing with the EU-level system of judicial protection.

[182] Joana Mendes, 'Bounded Discretion in EU Law: A Limited Judicial Paradigm in a Changing EU' (2017) 80 *Modern Law Review* 443, 461.

[183] AG Jacobs, Case C-50/00 P, *Unión de Pequeños Agricultores v Council*, ECLI:EU:C:2002:197.

[184] AG Jacobs, Case C-269/90, *Technische Universität München*, ECLI:EU:C:1991:317, para 13.

[185] See, for instance, various contributions to Micklitz and Reich (n 158).

public interest litigation is not equally facilitated in all procedural systems.[186] Also, the ideas differ regarding when and under which circumstances judicial review cases should reach the courts.[187] Some systems allow direct legality challenges only against individual administrative decisions and only incidental and indirect challenges against basic acts of general application.[188] Opportunities for private constitutional challenges to parliamentary legislation may be constrained to a great extent or even ruled out.[189]

Very different ideas and practical solutions have also been employed regarding how public law courts may engage with empirical and normative discretion of primary decision-makers.[190] These ideas and solutions give expression to divergent conceptions of the allocation of authority to the law-makers, the executive rule-makers, the administration and the judiciary. Underlying these divergent conceptions is a complex set of normative and empirical assumptions, in particular as to how far public law can and should frame and constrain discretionary powers, or how capable the courts are of verifying complicated factual assessments.

The ECJ case law admittedly leads to fragmentary harmonisation of domestic procedural laws, including judicial review procedures.[191] Some of the judgments have proven quite controversial.[192] However, the ECJ still leaves significant leeway to the Member States to develop their procedural systems in terms of the accessibility of administrative courts and the thoroughness of judicial review.[193] Nor does the ECtHR case law provide a universal and exhaustive model of judicial protection. The standards elaborated under Article 6 European Convention on

[186] Mariolina Eliantonio, *Standing Up for your Right(s) in Europe: A Comparative Study on Legal Standing (Locus Standi) before the EU and Member States' Courts* (Intersentia 2013). See in particular chapter 4 regarding access to administrative courts.

[187] Athanase Popov, 'La complémentarité entre les recours en annulation formés par des particuliers et les renvois préjudiciels en appréciation de validité avant comme apprès l'entrée en vigueur du Traité de Lisbonne et l'accès au prétoire de l'Union européenne. Est-il (encore) légitime d'évoquer l'existence d'une "tache dans le paysage du droit communautaire que constitute la jurisprudence sur la recevabilité"?' (2012) *Cahiers de Droit Européen* 166.

[188] Chris Backes and Mariolina Eliantonio, *Cases, Materials and Text on Judicial Review of Administrative Action* (Hart Publishing 2019), 205ff. Note, in particular, restrictions on challenging directly general administrative measures in Germany and the Netherlands. Similar restrictions are not known in France. Regarding the standing of NGOs see, ibid, 270ff, especially restrictions in Germany and Austria.

[189] Maartje de Visser, *Constitutional Review in Europe: A Comparative Analysis* (Bloomsbury 2014). See in particular chapter 2 regarding access of individuals to constitutional courts.

[190] Mariolina Eliantonio, *Europeanisation of Administrative Justice? The Influence of the ECJ's Case Law in Italy, Germany and England* (Europa Law Publishing 2009), 181ff and 197ff.

[191] It has been observed that the ECJ tends to prescribe to domestic courts dealing with EU law cases its own solutions regarding the thoroughness of judicial review. Rob Widdershoven, 'The European Court of Justice and the Standard of Judicial Review' in Jurgen de Poorter, Ernst Hirsch Ballin and Saskia Lavrijssen (eds), *Judicial Review of Administrative Discretion in the Administrative State* (Springer 2019).

[192] See Warin (n 126) and Lohse (n 126).

[193] Regarding the ECJ case law on standing before domestic courts to enforce EU rights see Lenaerts and others (n 3), 119ff. Regarding the ECJ case law on the evidence regime, see Backes and Eliantonio (n 188), 417–25, 438.

Human Rights (ECHR) are inherently minimal and context-specific to accommodate many differences between European judicial systems. Be that as it may, the ECJ itself[194] and the ECtHR[195] have already recognised the system of EU judicial review as generally compliant with human rights standards.

B. The Relative Authority of Review Mechanisms

The discussion regarding the rule of law and effective judicial protection at the EU level have hitherto been focused on adjusting the one-size-fits-all judicial review to novel challenges. It might benefit from a more contextual approach.[196] The relevant context consists of, on the one hand, the nature of challenges posed by increasingly complex EU legal acts, and on the other hand, by the institutional resources available to the EU Courts, data that can be offered by the litigants, available procedural tools to clarify contentious legal and empirical issues, and the limits of judicial expertise. The emergence and proliferation of extra-judicial review also forms part of the relevant context. A shift towards examining the EU Courts in the context of other review mechanisms could expand our understanding of the legitimacy assets and weaknesses of judicial and extra-judicial review alike.

The proposed contextual approach is not entirely new. It has already been argued that the EU judicial review should be examined and improved according to a functionalist-comparative approach which takes account of a variety of factors: the legitimate interests of affected parties, additional or substitute procedural safeguards, the potential costs of judicial review and the prerogatives of primary law-, rule- or decision-makers to have the final word on some issues. In particular, procedural safeguards at the formally pre-judicial stage may justify the subsequently light-touch judicial review.[197] The same contextual way of thinking leads to questioning whether a one-size-fits-all judicial review model adequately responds to challenges posed by a wide range of measures requiring different kinds of expertise.

That judicial and extra-judicial review are associated with the rule of law and effective legal protection does not yet explain their specific contribution to the governance structure. In what way or by what means do they bring us closer to

[194] Case C-456/13 P, *T&L Sugars*, ECLI:EU:C:2015:284, paras 44–51. Case C-389/10 P, *KME v Commission*, ECLI:EU:C:2011:816, paras 118–37. Case C-501/11 P, *Schindler Holding and Others v Commission*, ECLI:EU:C:2013:522, paras 33–39.

[195] ECtHR, Case 17502/07, *Avotiņš v Latvia*, paras 101ff in which ECtHR upheld the presumption of the equivalence between the fundamental rights protection guaranteed by ECtHR and that guaranteed by the EU judicial system. See also Case 43509/08, *Menarini Diagnostics Srl v Italy*, ECLI:CE:ECHR:2011:0927JUD004350908, paras 57–67.

[196] On the contextual nature of due process, see Devika Hovell, *The Power of Process. The Value of Due Process in Security Council Sanctions Decision-Making* (Oxford University Press 2016).

[197] Nazzini (n 181). For instance, a compensatory safeguard might be reinforced independence and impartiality of the primary decision-maker.

the realisation of the said principles? The authority exercised by review mechanisms and other public institutions is *relative* to different 'legitimacy assets', which Mendes and Venzke define as 'argumentative resources that an institutional actor can invoke in support of its authority'.[198] An actor can seek to justify its authority on institutional and procedural grounds, with reference to its composition and organisation, expertise, decision-making techniques or the structure of proceedings. These institutional and procedural features should allow an actor to perform a certain important governance function. They should help individuals rationally comply with decisions coming from the governance structure.

It is necessary to examine and compare the institutional and procedural legitimacy assets of EU judicial and extra-judicial review.[199] Moreover, it is necessary to confront the legitimacy assets of the review bodies with those of the primary law-, rule- or decision-makers. What is the specific added value of judicial or extra-judicial review? Thinking in terms of 'relative authority' is a 'tool that furthers the critique of existing institutional arrangements, which may guide the assessment of institutional practices that enact current allocations of authority'.[200]

The idea of relative authority is associated with the idea of procedural or institutional justice. In contrast to the accounts focused on substantive justice, as put forward by Carolan, procedural or institutional justice is interested in a grounded estimation of whether specifically designed institutions and procedural arrangements are likely to generate just outcomes. In other words, it is more interested in the rational public perception of the institutions and procedures as 'fair' or 'just' rather than an assessment of individual outcomes.[201]

Carolan and Curtin have argued that this kind of approach is particularly suitable to analysing the distribution of authority within the EU governance structure due to its fragmentation, constant evolution and the ubiquity of informal arrangements supplementing or overcoming formal institutional and procedural rules. 'Institutional balance' has turned out to be an empty shell and the tripartite separation of powers too under-defined and not corresponding to the practice of EU governance.[202] The relative authority approach, on the contrary, encourages a

[198] Mendes and Venzke (n 30), 78. This analysis, needless to say, leaves out evaluation of the substantive justice or de facto authority of the outcomes of specific mechanisms among its audiences. Specific mechanisms may also be meaningfully assessed in relation to how they have dealt with specific substantive social problems or how they are perceived by their audiences, such as litigators, policy-makers, legal doctrine and other scholars, civil society and any other kinds of stakeholders.

[199] ibid, 79.

[200] ibid, 99.

[201] Eoin Carolan, *The New Separation of Powers: A Theory for the Modern State* (Oxford University Press 2009), 80.

[202] Suffice it to note that the EU has not managed to develop a consistent conception of legislative matters (reserved to the Parliament and the Council) and regulatory matters (reserved to the Commission). A myriad of special legislative acts or *sui generis* acts is adopted. The defining features of delegated and implementing acts are blurred. Certain regulatory acts are 'hybrids', resembling individual administrative decisions and vice versa, etc. Moreover, EU legislative frameworks, resulting from difficult intergovernmental and institutional negotiations, often lack the precision normally expected of parliamentary legislation in view of the protection of legal certainty. Executive and administrative power

realist enquiry aimed at developing an improved understanding of how EU mechanisms operate in practice, and what specific institutional or procedural values they do or should deliver.[203]

II. The Models of Review Mechanisms

A. The Functions of Review in a Legal Order and Governance Structure: The Instrumental and Deliberative Models

Theoretical and comparative literature frames the functions of judicial and extra-judicial review in different terms. It is possible to identify at least two types of justifications that correspond to the two main conceptions of procedural justice: the instrumental and the non-instrumental or deliberative model.[204] These models are not mutually exclusive. They express different visions of law and its ability to frame and constrain the exercise of public authority.[205] Each model must accommodate procedural economy: reasonable time and cost of proceedings for any actors involved.

In the instrumental model, review increases the chances of a *correct* outcome of law-, rule- or decision-making from the legal, technical or scientific perspective, depending on the applicable review criteria.[206] The review body verifies the interpretation of applicable law and the legal qualification of relevant factual circumstances. Correctness, broadly understood, is the overarching legitimacy asset or process value in this model.[207] Underlying this model is a vision of law as an objectively cognisable system of legal norms, with predetermined content, intended to bring about the best overall balance of substantive justice. The instrumental model fits the context of substantive law which is relatively precise or, at least, which is supposed to unfold through case law incrementally, and where binding and stable rulings are preferred to ensure a high level of legal certainty and uniformity.

The instrumental model may take two forms. In the more classical form, legal processes are seen as 'transmission belts' for implementing the will of a legitimate law-maker (in the case of the judicial review of administrative action) or

is often delegated to a myriad of expert committees or agencies, formally exercising only 'technical' discretion, but in fact regularly making political choices.

[203] Eoin Carolan and Deirdre Curtin, 'In Search of a New Model of Checks and Balances for the EU: Beyond Separation of Powers' in Joana Mendes and Ingo Venzke (eds), *Allocating Authority: Who Should Do What in European and International Law?* (Hart Publishing 2018).

[204] Solum (n 31) who relies on John Rawls, *A Theory of Justice* (Harvard University Press 1971), 85–86.

[205] Hovell (n 196), 58.

[206] Legal, technical or scientific criteria may overlap as contemporary public law tends to incorporate these other standards.

[207] This conception corresponds to the Rawlsian 'perfect procedural justice', Rawls (n 204), 85.

constitution-maker (in the case of the constitutional review of parliamentary legislation). In this understanding, the instrumental model is a principal-agent model in which the agents (judges or other adjudicators) are supposed to correctly enforce the true will of their principal (a parliament or a constitutional assembly).[208]

The transmission belt model does not correspond to the reality of contemporary constitutional review, due to the indeterminate substance of constitutional norms and ensuing normative discretion attributed to constitutional courts.[209] The EU constitutional norms, such as fundamental rights or the principle of proportionality, are evidently and deliberately open-ended. In cases of legality challenges to legislative acts, the EU judicature enjoys significant interpretive discretion.

Neither does the transmission belt model correspond to the reality of the contemporary judicial review of executive rule-making. Over the previous century, significant amounts of regulatory powers were shifted away to a complex, bureaucratic and technocratic administrative sphere.[210] Administration can no longer be regarded merely as a 'transmission belt' of legislative commands. It has its own vast discretionary powers and may adopt legal acts of general application, only loosely constrained by legislation or constitutional norms, which is particularly true in the EU context. The executive and administrative part of the governance structure is supposed to 'create the best solution rather than find it in a previously enacted statute'.[211]

According to a younger version of the instrumental model, legal processes – including review mechanisms – contribute to the aggregation and analysis of data regarding public and private interests affected by legislative or administrative action. This way, they contribute to hammering out possibly best laws, rules and decisions or those that express the best possible balance of substantive justice. In this understanding, the instrumental model is a 'trustee' model in which the judges, trustees of the political system, ensure by dint of their specific institutional and procedural assets that law-, rule- and decision-making produce the best possible outcomes.[212] The overarching legitimacy asset of correctness is consequently to be understood as the optimal balance of substantive justice.

[208] Hovell (n 196), 63–68.

[209] Arthur Dyevre, 'Technocracy and Distrust: Revisiting the Rationale for Constitutional Review' (2015) 13 *International Journal of Constitutional Law* 30.

[210] Bernardo Sordi, '*Revolution, Rechtstaat* and the Rule of Law: Historical Reflections on the Emergence and Development of Administrative Law' in Susan-Rose Ackerman, Peter Lindseth and Blake Emerson (eds), *Comparative Administrative Law* (Edward Elgar 2017).

[211] Javier Barnes, 'Towards a Third Generation of Administrative Procedure' in Susan-Rose Ackerman and Peter Lindseth (eds), *Comparative Administrative Law* (Edward Elgar 2010). Richard B Stewart, 'The Reformation of American Administrative Law' (1975) *Harvard Law Review* 1667–813. Peter Lindseth, 'Always Embedded Administration: The Historical Evolution of Administrative Justice as an Aspect of Modern Governance' in Christian Joerges, Bo Stråth and Peter Wagner (eds), *The Economy as a Polity: The Political Constitution of Contemporary Capitalism* (UCL Press 2010), 117.

[212] Dyevre (n 209).

An empirical assumption behind the instrumental model in both versions is that legislative, executive and administrative bodies pursue their own political agenda.[213] Members of Parliament and high-level executives focus on their re-election or reappointment, whereas middle-level administration is regularly approached by powerful lobbies and, at any rate, is continuously at risk due to the 'revolving door' phenomenon. Susceptible to public opinion and political pressure, politicians, executives or administrators are likely to breach higher-order laws and neglect some unpopular private or public interests. Moreover, law-, rule or decision-makers may not have perfect knowledge about the matter to be regulated or the case to be decided. Structural bias may also come into play. Administrators deciding individual cases have traditionally been seen as prioritising the social goals of enforced policies, or the interests of administration over the rights and interests of individuals.[214] Nowadays, there is also a fear that politicians and executives will prioritise the interests of powerful economic lobbies rather than important public interest goals.

Insulated from ordinary politics or political accountability, and equipped with legal expertise, judges or other independent adjudicators offer epistemic superiority in interpreting and applying higher-order laws 'objectively', fostering the overall balance of justice and, in particular, safeguarding the rights of minorities, general values and permanent interests.[215] They should ensure the voicing of all kinds of interests within the supervised law-, rule- and decision-making, especially when the channels of political participation are somehow impaired.[216] By responding to minority claims, courts or other adjudicators perform a portion of democratic or administrative tasks.[217]

Especially when it comes to legal acts producing general effects, granting the right to demand review to affected individuals is a useful way of bringing information on violations of their rights to light. The applicants for judicial or extra-judicial

[213] Samuel Freeman, 'Constitutional Democracy and the Legitimacy of Judicial Review' (1990–91) 9 *Law and Philosophy* 327.

[214] Jerry Mashaw, 'Conflict and Compromise among Models of Administrative Justice' (1981) *Duke Law Journal* 181.

[215] Alexander Bickel, *The Least Dangerous Branch: The Supreme Court at the Bar of Politics* (Yale University Press 1986), 25–26. Other theorists add the 'more deliberative, contemplative quality of the judicial process' – see Jesse Choper, *Judicial Review and the National Political Process* (University of Chicago Press 1980), 60 – or emphasise judicial competence, portraying judges as experts on rights – see Ronald Dworkin, *Law's Empire* (Harvard University Press 1986), 344–45. Ronald Dworkin, *Freedom's Law: The Moral Reading of the American Constitution* (Harvard University Press 1997), 344–45.

[216] John Hart Ely, *Democracy and Distrust: A Theory of Judicial Review* (Harvard University Press 1980), 102.

[217] Dimitrios Kyritsis, *Where Our Protection Lies: Separation of Powers and Judicial Review* (Oxford University Press 2017). Cristina Lafont, 'Philosophical Foundations of Judicial Review' in David Dyzenhaus and Malcolm Thornburn (eds), *Philosophical Foundations of Constitutional Law* (Oxford University Press 2016). Aileen Kavanagh, 'The Constitutional Separation of Powers' in David Dyzenhaus and Malcolm Thornburn (eds), *Philosophical Foundations of Constitutional Law* (Oxford University Press 2016).

review could be excellent sources of information about the actual effects of adopted policies. Moreover, for people and groups who have little political power or influence (mainly due to insufficient financial resources), and are disenfranchised in primary law-, rule- or decision-making, judicial or extra-judicial review may be a substitute channel of political participation.[218] Therefore, there has been a noticeable move, in particular in common law States, towards a more liberal standing regime and increased thoroughness of judicial review.[219] In particular, the point of concern has moved from correcting a wrong perpetrated by an executive or administrative body against an individual applicant towards ensuring the objective legality of administrative action and appraising whether it fosters the overall balance of justice.[220]

This aggregative model might explain the elevated expectations towards judicial review at the EU level. The transmission belt model might still offer some explanatory potential with regard to purely individual decisions, but such are increasingly rare before the EU Courts in the annulment procedure and before the other review bodies examined in this book.[221] Higher-order legislative and other *sui generis* acts concretising Treaty policies accommodate difficult inter-institutional and intergovernmental compromises. They are usually drafted in insufficiently explicit terms as to effectively reduce normative discretion to choose between competing substantive values and interests. This choice is delegated to the Commission and other administrative bodies, despite the ECJ's attempts to transplant from the domestic level a doctrine of 'essential' policy choices that should be decided in a legislative act.[222] Consequently, the adoption of EU regulatory acts of general application and even individual decisions involve technical and political discretion. Individual decisions in fields such as competition, State

[218] Aileen Kavanagh, 'Participation and Judicial Review: A Reply to Jeremy Waldron' (2003) 22 *Law and Philosophy* 456, 481. Nick O'Brien and Brian Thompson, 'Human Rights and Accountability in the UK: Deliberative Democracy and the Role of the Ombudsman' (2010) *European Human Rights Law Review* 504, 508. Peter Cane, *Administrative Tribunals and Adjudication* (Hart Publishing 2009), 229–33.

[219] Peter L Strauss, 'Politics and Agencies in the Administrative State: The U.S. Case' in Susan-Rose Ackerman, Peter L Lindseth and Blake Emerson (eds), *Comparative Administrative Law* (Edward Elgar 2017).

[220] Carolan (n 201), 67ff. Against this background, the powerful EU regulatory and administrative machinery protected from extensive judicial review by means of the restrictive *locus standi* criteria for private applicants appears to be an aberration to many authors, in particular to those with a common law background.

[221] Public procurement decisions concern a group of competitors for tenders and may involve complex technical appraisals. Access to documents decisions implement a significantly open-ended transparency regulation and have general impact on the transparency practices of the institutions. Competition, State aid and anti-dumping decisions and regulations are almost always based on highly contentious empirical and normative considerations and affect multiple market participants rather than only specifically indicated operators. EU legal acts regarding public health and environment naturally affect society in its entirety.

[222] Ton van den Brink, 'Danger! Glyphosate may Expose Weaknesses in Institutional Systems: EU Legislation and Comitology in the Face of a Controversial Reauthorisation' (2020) 11 *European Journal of Risk Regulation* 436.

aid, anti-dumping or the regulation of risks to public health and the environment, financial supervision and the like, affect not only the interests of their formal addressees, but also third parties and society in general.

This normative rationale of judicial review may generally apply to extra-judicial review. Some theorists argue that the instrumental function of constitutional review of law-making could be performed by institutions other than courts, enjoying some degree of independence from primary law-makers, and equipped with appropriate institutional and procedural features.[223] Some ombudsmen or specialised parliamentary panels, for instance, already play a part in ensuring the constitutionality of parliamentary legislation.[224] Moreover, the extra-judicial review of administrative action by officials and bodies other than courts *stricto sensu*—such as administrative tribunals and ombudsmen – is firmly established in many states. Terms such as 'accountability sector', 'network of accountability' or 'administrative justice system' have been proposed to denote internally diversified systems of review authorities.[225]

Different review bodies may formally apply different 'criteria' of review. Courts deal with 'constitutionality' or 'legality'. Administrative tribunals, and the like, must also consider the 'merits' or 'expediency' of administrative acts, including scientific and technical standards.[226] Ombudsmen enforce standards of 'good administration' which are to reach beyond mere legality but are at the same time more procedural in nature.[227] 'Merits' and 'good administration' are therefore supposed to be more than legality, but 'good administration' should at the same time be more procedural and uninterested in the substance of policy choices.

However, common to these criteria is that they all relate to the potential of law, and other normative standards to which the law refers, to guide and constrain the exercise of public authority and discretion, leading to optimal results. These criteria are not entirely distinct. The difference between the criteria may consist in the scope and intensity of review, depending on the legal mandates, the epistemic capacities of adjudicators and the applicable legal frameworks. Courts may intensify legality review to such an extent that it comes close to merits review. Process-oriented ombuds-review may become exceptionally thorough, capable of inducing substantive policy changes. Consequently, an examination of the formal criteria of review applied by different review mechanisms should consider the actual practice of review.

[223] Freeman (n 213). Kyritsis (217), 146–48.

[224] De Visser (n 189), chapter 1, regarding the role of non-judicial actors in upholding the Constitution (see 'Finland'). The Polish Commissioner for Human Rights can scrutinise the constitutionality of parliamentary legislation and petition the Constitutional Tribunal in this regard.

[225] Cane (n 218), 255. Trevor Buck, Richard Kirkham and Brian Thomson, *The Ombudsman Enterprise and Administrative Justice* (Routledge 2017), 19.

[226] Dacian C Dragos and David Marrani, 'Administrative Appeals in Comparative European Administrative Law: What Effectiveness?' in Dacian C Dragos and Bogdana Neamtu (eds), *Alternative Dispute Resolution in European Administrative Law* (Springer 2014), 544.

[227] Backes and Eliantonio (n 188), 894–903.

At the same time, review mechanisms of any kind perform a prospective or standard-setting function. They are instrumental to incrementally developing the meaning of general legal norms and shaping the standards of the accessibility, transparency or accountability of governance processes. Those review mechanisms with broad jurisdictional remits (like high courts or ombudsmen) may thus foster cross-fertilisation, mutual learning and uniformity in the application of law across the variegated regulatory areas.[228]

In turn, the deliberative model was proposed by theorists dissatisfied with instrumentalist accounts of the constitutional review of parliamentary legislation. It could also be employed to justify the judicial review of administrative acts of general application and general effects, which are only loosely bound by open-ended constitutional and legislative norms. In the deliberative model, the role of a review mechanism is to enhance the level of deliberation among the interested parties, so that the resulting decisions are rationally acceptable to everybody. Review mechanisms provide additional fora for public deliberation.

Underlying this conception is a vision of law as a deliberative undertaking. Rather than containing directives with predetermined content, substantive law provides arguments by means of which the participants in public deliberation may substantiate their normative propositions.[229] What bestows authority upon laws, rules and decisions is this democratic deliberative process itself rather than compliance with higher-level substantive standards.[230] The interpretation and application of law is an unavoidably creative rather than reconstructive process. Laws, rules and decisions should be responsive to the most convincing arguments articulated within a deliberative and participation-oriented process. In this way, citizens and other private parties have reasons to perceive themselves as co-authors of laws, rules and decisions to which they are simultaneously subjected.[231] The deliberative conception assumes, at the same time, not only an aggregation of subjective interests, but also mutual understanding, persuasion and transformation of preferences.[232]

[228] Joanne Scott and Susan Sturm, 'Courts as Catalysts: Rethinking the Judicial Role in New Governance' (2007) 13 *Columbia Journal of European Law* 565.

[229] This conception corresponds to the Rawlsian 'pure procedural justice'. Rawls (n 204), 85–86.

[230] As Habermas put it, 'under the conditions of cultural and societal pluralism, the constitution must also not be conceived as a concrete legal order that imposes a priori a total form of life on society as a whole. Rather, the constitution sets down political procedures according to which citizens can, in the exercise of their right to self-determination, successfully pursue the cooperative project of establishing just (i.e., relatively more just) conditions of life. Only the procedural conditions for the democratic genesis of legal statutes secures the legitimacy of enacted law'. Jürgen Habermas, *Between Facts and Norms: Contributions to a Discourse Theory of Law and Democracy* (MIT Press 1996), 209.

[231] Jerry L Mashaw, 'Administrative Due Process: The Quest for a Dignitary Theory' (1981) 61 *Boston University Law Review* 885. Richard B Saphire, 'Specifying Due Process Values: Towards a More Responsive Approach to Procedural Protection' (1978) 127 *University of Pennsylvania Law Review* 111. In this context, Hovell links the deliberative model – to which she refers as 'public interest model' – to the conception of responsive law. Hovell (n 196).

[232] Christopher Zurn, 'Judicial Review, Constitutional Juries and Civic Constitutional Fora: Rights, Democracy and Law' (2011) 58 *Theoria: A Journal of Social and Political Theory* 63, 67.

Judicial or extra-judicial review of law-, rule- and decision-making may be seen as forming part of the democratic process. Review mechanisms multiply the sites, means and opportunities for public deliberation. They enable private parties to voice their grievances against legal acts affecting them and engage in a reasoned exchange of arguments with public authorities, and induce genuine reconsideration of the contested laws, rules or decisions.[233] By offering participation in the process and individualised justifications of impugned laws, rules and decisions, review mechanisms give to individuals additional reasons to internalise these laws, rules or decisions.[234] In this context, individualistic rules of standing encapsulating reductionist definitions of direct interest, and the like, are at odds with deliberative ideals. They preclude civic-minded private parties from entering the democratic process and deprive the review authority of a large portion of its potential impact.[235]

The deliberative model fits a court or court-like adjudicatory framework, as well as any other mechanism enabling a contestation, deliberation and candid reconsideration of legal acts, including one equipped with only soft powers.[236] An ideal-type deliberative model supports broad access by citizens and their associations who wish to participate in the democratic process in the public interest. It also supports extensive participation rights, which enable unfettered deliberation, maximise the range of reasoned arguments, and mobilise law-, rule- or decision-makers in an open and collective deliberation in the aim of reaching the most persuasive and broadly acceptable outcomes.[237]

Table 3.1. summarises the main features of the instrumental and deliberative models. However, this book does not aim to categorise different judicial and extra-judicial mechanisms according to these models. They are not mutually exclusive. It is even difficult to identify a predominance of one of them in the functioning of a given mechanism. At first sight, courts may seem more instrumentalist and ombudsmen more deliberative. Upon a closer inspection, however, courts may be seen as enhancing deliberation just as ombudsmen are instrumental to optimal administrative action.[238] Whether courts, administrative tribunals and

[233] Alon Harel, *Why Law Matters* (Oxford University Press 2014). Alon Harel and Adam Shinar, 'Between Judicial and Legislative Supremacy: A Cautious Defense of Constrained Judicial Review' (2012) 10 *International Journal of Constitutional Law* 950.

[234] Matthias Kumm, 'Institutionalising Socratic Contestation: The Rationalists Human Rights Paradigm. Legitimate Authority and the Point of Judicial Review' (2007) 1 *European Journal of Legal Studies* 153. Matthias Kumm, 'Democracy is Not Enough: Rights, Proportionality and the Point of Judicial Review' in Matthias Klatt (ed), *The Legal Philosophy of Robert Alexy* (Oxford University Press 2009).

[235] Conrado Hübner Mendes, *Constitutional Courts and Deliberative Democracy* (Oxford University Press 2013), 162.

[236] Christopher Zurn, 'A Question of Institutionalization: Habermas on the Justification of Court-Based Constitutional Review' in Camil Ungureanu, Klaus Guenther and Christian Joerges (eds), *Habermas' Discourse Theory of Law and Democracy: From the Nation-State to Europe and the Postnational Constellation* (Ashgate 2011). Harel and Shinar (n 233), 974. Zurn (n 21).

[237] Hübner Mendes (n 235), 107.

[238] By the same token, specific procedural tools may be interpreted in instrumental or deliberative terms. For instance, a procedure for third-party intervention in pending proceedings may be seen as

ombudsmen should be interpreted in accordance with the instrumental or deliberative model largely depends on the vision of law to which one subscribes. This book's argument is rather that the primary instrumental and deliberative functions must be balanced, in the functioning of specific judicial or extra-judicial mechanisms, against limited resources and time available to review mechanisms and the litigants. Also, review mechanisms should bring some added value rather than replicating each other's assets in order not to waste limited resources. The following subsections will discuss how different comparative models conceive of the way in which the systems of justice should use their limited resources to foster their primary goals.

Table 3.1 The instrumental and deliberative models of judicial and extra-judicial review

Function of review mechanisms	Transmission belt	Interest aggregation	Deliberation
Conception of substantive law	Objectively ascertainable directives of law- or constitution-makers	Indication of private or public interests to be protected	Basis for reasoned normative propositions
Process value	Correct application of legal or extra-legal standards	Finding a correct balance between competing interests	Responsiveness to the most convincing arguments
Legitimacy asset	Independent verification of facts and legal interpretation	Independent verification of whether all affected interests have been properly balanced	Enhancing open, unbiased and reasoned deliberation on public matters

B. The Responsibility of the Parties to the Process: The Inquisitorial and Adversarial Model

The organisation of the judicial and extra-judicial review system requires significant public resources. Applicants, defendants and interested third parties also need resources to prepare litigation or intervention. Financial and non-financial costs may be generated by persisting legal uncertainty as to the final form and effects of contested legal acts. For this reason, the judicial or extra-judicial review should be considered a limited public good. Different legal systems make different choices as to which social groups should benefit from it, where its priorities lie, and how to balance the pursuit of the review's primary goals and the system's overall economy.

instrumental to increasing the availability of data pertinent to the subject matter of review, as well as enabling broader deliberation.

One way of setting this balance is to devise the review process as adversarial or inquisitorial. The main criterion of this distinction is the parties and adjudicators' responsibility for reaching the correct outcome. This distinction, popular in the comparative law literature, has traditionally been used to express the contrast between the Anglo-American and the continental administration of justice. Nowadays, however, legal processes and mechanisms rarely implement one of the models in their pure form.

The adversarial model generally charges the parties with litigation costs and occasionally tolerates substantively incorrect outcomes due to the parties' procedural mistakes. An adversarial process unfolds as an engagement of two adversaries before a relatively passive adjudicator.[239] The adversaries bear the responsibility to obtain and adduce relevant evidence and advance legal arguments to make their case before the impartial adjudicator. The adjudicator's task is limited to assessing the arguments and evidence adduced by the parties. Fuller argued that the adversarial adjudicatory framework is the most likely to yield correct outcomes. He saw the adversaries' active participation as lying at the heart of adjudication as a decision-making method, distinct from voting or negotiations. To him, adjudication is adversarial by definition. Active participation facilitates the collection and the analysis of relevant data by the adjudicators. The parties have the best knowledge of their own case and access to relevant evidence, which the adjudicators might not be able to identify or gather by themselves. By dint of partisan advocacy, the adjudicators become acquainted with both sides of the story and can make an impartial judgement.[240] However, the adversarial process may occasionally produce substantively wrong results if one of the parties proves unable to effectively plead her case (due, for instance, to lack of sufficient resources to be able to afford professional legal representation).[241]

Fuller warned that the adversarial adjudication is less attuned to solve strongly polycentric disputes. Where several different types of competing interests are at stake, the adjudicators might have difficulty in conceiving the consequences of their ruling for all the interests affected.[242] When it comes to public law disputes, the public institutions and bodies are expected to represent and consider all kinds of relevant public interest goals. In reality, however, public institutions and bodies are often criticised for a bias towards certain interests and judicial review is expected to be a form of their public accountability. This problem explains the proliferation of third-party interventions and *amici curiae* briefs by public interest organisations and social actors, as well as expectations of increased transparency of proceedings before high courts, which all reflect the growing instrumental and deliberative function of review mechanisms.

[239] Mirjan R Damaška, *The Faces of Justice and State Authority: A Comparative Approach to the Legal Process* (Yale University Press 1986), 3.
[240] Lon Fuller, 'The Forms and Limits of Adjudication' (1978) 92 *Harvard Law Review* 353.
[241] Damaška (n 239), 102.
[242] Fuller (n 240), 394.

The inquisitorial model charges the system of justice with the responsibility and potentially high costs of reaching the correct outcome. In Fuller's words, the task of an active inquisitor is more demanding than that of a passive adjudicator. An active inquisitor must develop the most effective statement of the case for each party and then proceed to 'view with distrust … the products of his best mental efforts'.[243] In other words, a passive arbiter plays only one role in the process, whereas an active inquisitor must somehow play all three: the representative of each of the parties and the objective decision-maker.[244] An active inquisitor may also need to bear the costs of additional fact-finding and legal analysis. The inquisitorial model is by no means opposed to active participation and deliberation among the parties, but the adjudicators themselves must supplement the cases presented by the parties if necessary with a view to reaching the correct outcome. The adjudicators may also be obliged to go beyond or against the parties' demands, raising specific legal issues or obtaining evidence on their own motion, in the public interest. The duty to seek the 'substantive truth' in each case demands an investment of more public resources in the administration of justice.[245]

Historically, the adversarial and inquisitorial models were underpinned by different visions of the government's role and the administration of justice. Damaška argued that the adversarial process was historically linked to the liberal government maintaining social peace and providing the citizens with the framework to solve their disputes. On the contrary, the inquisitorial process was historically linked to the more activist government enforcing social policies. In brief, the principal function of the adversarial process was peaceful dispute settlement, whereas that of the inquisitorial process was the enforcement of public policies.[246]

Damaška also observed that the adversarial process was originally linked to coordinate, single-instance, ad hoc adjudicatory structures (such as juries) and lay adjudicators. These adjudicators operated without the use of commonly established and written sources of law. They mostly relied on oral proceedings concentrated in a single procedural event (an oral hearing) during which they could directly assess the evidence and hear the arguments. Conversely, the inquisitorial process was more often associated with robust, bureaucratic and hierarchical structures, staffed by officials (professional judges) specialised in applying codified law and adjudication based on written case records collected over multi-instance proceedings.[247]

Notably, the inquisitorial model of judicial or extra-judicial review proceedings implies greater responsibility and power of the review adjudicators vis-à-vis primary decision-makers than in adversarial proceedings, in which the

[243] ibid, 382–83.
[244] ibid, 353.
[245] Solum (n 31) distinguishes in this respect a balancing model of procedural justice, in which the seeking of truth is balanced against the need to keep the cost and time of proceedings reasonable.
[246] Damaška (n 239), 3–12.
[247] ibid, 181ff.

applicants must convince the adjudicators that primary decision-makers have been wrong. Simultaneously, the inquisitorial model presupposes a relatively precise set of legal norms, stemming from a legitimate law-maker, and the practical possibility of getting to the bottom of 'objective truth', for which the adjudicator is responsible. Nowadays, a mixture of solutions pertaining to divergent or even opposing procedural logics is introduced to strike a balance between a few different goals: the enforcement of public policy, the protection of individual rights and interests, and the overall economy of the system.[248]

Within the EU Courts, the inquisitorial and adversarial logics are combined. On the one hand, the Article 267 TFEU preliminary reference procedure before the ECJ is inquisitorial inasmuch as the ECJ may reformulate the questions referred by the national court to provide it with a more 'useful' response, or seek clarifications from the national court if the order of reference is formulated in an unclear manner. This procedural setting presupposes a policy-enforcement function on the side of the ECJ, according to Damaška's classification. The 'policy' is the entirety of EU law as following from the Treaties and secondary law, laid down by EU institutions and bodies. The ECJ's task consists in making it operational before the national courts, regardless of conflicting national laws and practices. Crucially, the ECJ is not restrained by procedural acts and potential mistakes committed by an individual acting before the referring court or by the referring court itself.

On the other hand, the procedural approach of the ECJ somewhat changes in Article 267 TFEU references concerning the *validity* of EU legal acts. The ECJ confines itself to examining whether anything in the order of reference affects the validity of the act in question instead of authoritatively identifying and examining any potentially problematic aspects of the act. The adversarial dispute-settlement function is also clearly visibly in the Article 263(4) TFEU action for annulment in which it is the applicant's task to set out all relevant pleas in law and offer evidence to refute the presumption of legality attributed to the impugned legal acts. A different procedural setting, in which the EU Courts would play a more inquisitorial role in the annulment proceedings, autonomously examining the legality of impugned acts regardless of the applicant's initiative and activity, is perfectly conceivable. However, the more inquisitorial role in the Article 263(4) annulment proceedings would imply accretion of judicial responsibility and power for concretising the 'policy' to be enforced, ie higher-order (and essentially open-ended) legal norms such as fundamental rights and general principles. Overall, the combination of the policy-enforcement function in the preliminary reference procedure and the dispute-settlement function in the annulment procedure results in a limitation of the EU Courts' power vis-à-vis the EU institutions and bodies, but not vis-à-vis the Member States.

[248] Backes and Eliantonio (n 188), 417 ff. Compare in particular the inquisitorial approach of the German administrative courts with the approach of the Dutch courts, which has arguably evolved from a more inquisitorial towards an adversarial approach, and the approach of the French courts, which is generally adversarial except for complex cases.

Table 3.2. summarises the main features of the inquisitorial and adversarial review proceedings. However, rather than classifying discrete procedural solutions into the two opposing theoretical models, it may be more fruitful to examine how 'active' the adjudicator is in a particular type of proceedings. What matters is not only procedural arrangements 'in the books', but also the adjudicators' actual conduct, their everyday practices and informal arrangements. Following research into some novel forms of administrative adjudication in traditionally adversarial legal systems, it has been observed that most proceedings may be located somewhere between the adversarial and inquisitorial models and that these 'hybrids' merit more attention. Hence, a model of more or less 'active adjudication' is proposed as a non-dichotomous alternative occupying a broad interstice between the adversarial and inquisitorial models.[249] An active adjudicator may foster the reaching of a correct decision or facilitate and steer a fruitful deliberation between the parties through informal practices, irrespective of the formal characteristics of the procedural setting.

Table 3.2 The inquisitorial/adversarial spectrum in judicial or extra-judicial review

Procedural model	**Adversarial**	**Inquisitorial**
Responsibility for the outcome	Applicant	Adjudicator
Costs for the justice system	Low	High
Balance of power	Protection of primary decision-makers from excessive interference by the courts or other review bodies	Possible shifts of power and responsibility towards the courts or other review bodies

C. Broadly Available or Thorough Review? The Objective and Subjective Model

Yet another influential classification, generally based on the comparative analysis of the French and German administrative courts, divides the review mechanisms into those that emphasise the enforcement of 'objective law' and those that emphasise the protection of 'subjective rights'.[250] This distinction is mostly concerned with the accessibility of administrative courts to interested parties and their powers vis-à-vis the supervised administration. Likewise, the two models may be

[249] Samantha Green and Lorne Sossin, 'Administrative Justice and Innovation: Beyond the Adversarial/Inquisitorial Dichotomy' in Laverne Jacobs and Sasha Baglay (eds), *The Nature of Inquisitorial Processes in Administrative Regimes: Global Perspectives* (Ashgate 2013).

[250] Jean-Marie Woehrling, 'Le contrôle juridictionnel de l'administration eu Europe et la distinction entre droit objectif et droits subjectifs' in Jürgen Schwarze (ed), *L'état actuel et les perspectives du droit administratif européen Analyses de droit comparé* (Bruylant 2010).

seen as embodying different choices regarding the allocation of limited resources to the system of administrative justice. Should the review of administrative action be broadly accessible but focused on a rather thin notion of legality or, instead, restricted in terms of accessibility but more thorough on the merits of the case?

Clearly, the contemporary administrative court systems have been evolving to the extent that neither of these models is currently implemented in its pure form.[251] Arguably, a general tendency is to increase both the accessibility of judicial review and the responsibility of courts for the cases' final outcomes, in the name of both the individual rights of litigants and the legal accountability of public institutions. Therefore, specific administrative court systems traditionally assigned to one or another category may nowadays operate similarly.

In the French model of 'objective legality review' (*recours objectif*) the administrative courts were focused on ensuring the prevalence of the rule of law on the administration or, in other words, the objective legality of administrative action. Any notification of potential irregularities in administrative action, either of individual or general nature, was a good reason to inquire into the matter, which explained the broad accessibility of administrative courts to private parties having some sort of legal interest. In return, court actions had no automatic suspensory effects. At the same time, the administrative courts were traditionally concerned only with the relatively thin notion of legality rather than the merits or political and technical expediency of administrative action. If the contested action was unlawful, the court was empowered to annul it and remit the case to the administration.

In the German model of 'subjective legality review' (French: *recours subjectif*) the administrative courts were focused on protecting the subjective rights of private parties in individual cases. In other words, the administrative courts were to make sure that the administration had delivered to private parties what was guaranteed to them by law. This is why to trigger the judicial review of administrative action, the applicants must indicate a specific subjective right conferred upon them by legislation or the Constitution. A 'protection of rights doctrine' has been developed to establish whether a legal provision grants an actionable individual right or solely protects a 'general public interest'.[252] At the same time, the administrative courts dealt mostly with individual administrative acts inflicting personalised harm to the applicants rather than administrative acts of general application. In return, court actions had a suspensory effect. In the course of the process, the court raised all relevant legal issues and made appropriate factual determinations. If the contested act was unlawful, the court was also empowered to issue injunctions against the administration to make sure that the subjective rights of the applicants would be realised.

The French model served as a blueprint for the annulment proceedings before the EU Courts regarding the lack of the action's automatic suspensory effect, the

[251] Backes and Eliantonio (n 188), 113ff.
[252] ibid, 114–15.

criterion of 'legality', and the judicial power to, in principle, only annul the unlawful act.[253] The German conception, however, inspired the restrictive access rules for private parties. The point was to shield the fledgling supranational institutions from constant legality challenges by private parties.[254] Nowadays, the restrictive access rules may be seen as being at odds with the judicial review's instrumental function pertaining to the aggregation of interests and even more so with the deliberative function. Likewise, light-touch judicial review, merely focused on an outer layer of formal legality, has been abandoned in some jurisdictions and areas of administrative law for underestimating the potential of judicial review to improve administrative action.[255]

III. Independence, Powers, Accessibility, Activity

It follows from the foregoing analysis that different jurisdictions embrace different choices as to the distribution of limited resources within the system of justice. These choices may result from past and present political decisions, as well as traditional and incrementally developed juridical conceptions of priorities assigned to the system of justice. Such conceptions tend to change slowly due to a typical juristic attachment to existing intellectual constructs and lawyerly practices. However, even if well established, they must be subject to criticism and revised considering the changing social and political context.

At least until recently, the general trend has been the growing expectation towards both the instrumental and deliberative functions of the constitutional review of parliamentary legislation and the judicial review of administrative action. Nowadays, with concerns about over-empowered constitutional courts[256] and the cognitive limitations of generalist administrative courts,[257] the time is ripe for exploring mechanisms that could support, supplement, relieve or even fill gaps in the EU judicial review, by discharging some of their instrumental and deliberative functions. Even though the EU law-makers have been willing to experiment with extra-judicial review, relatively little is still known about the practical advantages and disadvantages of the specific mechanisms they designed.

To perform the instrumental and deliberative functions, a judicial or extra-judicial review mechanism must comprise several institutional and procedural

[253] René Barents, 'EU Procedural Law and Effective Legal Protection' (2014) 51 *Common Market Law Review* 1437–62. Barents interprets the narrow access to the EU Courts as forming part of the objective conception. However, this interpretation is at odds with the comparative law literature. See Woehrling (n 250).

[254] Fromont (n 99).

[255] Marc Clément, 'La jurisprudence administrative en droit de l'environnement: Entre technique et acteurs' (2020) *Revue juridique de l'environnement* 51–61.

[256] Davies (n 170).

[257] Vos (n 89).

features. These features are distinguished below for analytical purposes but, as will become apparent, are strongly interrelated and the boundaries between them may become blurred.

First, a logical prerequisite for genuine review is *independence* from primary law-, rule- or decision-makers. Objectivity and neutrality towards competing interests and reasoned arguments is seen as resulting from insusceptibility to external pressure by political bodies, concentrated societal powers or concerns about the popularity of decisions.[258] Hence, independence is usually considered a compulsory element of due process.[259] A form of independence that is usually idealised by lawyers is 'judicial independence' with fixed terms of office, safeguards against arbitrary dismissals, immunities and the like, as well as safeguards of impartiality within specific proceedings, such as the right to demand recusal of adjudicators involved in a conflict of interests. Since no one can penetrate the mind of an adjudicator and verify her decisions' real motives, what is often emphasised in fundamental rights case law on judicial independence is the external 'appearance of independence', assessed from the perspective of a reasonable observer. This concept has recently gained importance in the ECJ case law.[260]

Considering the growing technicality and scientification of legislative and administrative action at the EU level, functional independence should also be seen as a corollary of possessing relevant technical or scientific knowledge. Without specialist knowledge, an adjudicator is unable to reach an independent judgment. She may have no choice but to defer, for instance, to whichever evidence presented by one of the parties appears prima facie more convincing. Institutional safeguards of independence may therefore include safeguards of access to specialist knowledge and support by specialised staff.

At the same time, independence from external pressure does not necessarily imply complete objectivity and political neutrality. Due to limited resources, review bodies such as superior courts or ombudsmen may be vested with discretion to filter out, select or even initiate the cases with which they choose to deal, or set their priority goals. Without being bound by explicit criteria, other than 'legal uniformity' or 'systemic problems', such a selection or prioritisation is, to some extent, political. The result is that the review body may be subject to criticism for its choice of cases on political grounds, just like any other political body,

[258] A so-called 'regulatory capture' occurs especially in situations of 'revolving doors' between, for instance, specialised administrative tribunals and law firms operating in the relevant sector. As a result, the administrative tribunal may acquire bias in favour of the sector it is supposed to supervise. Zurn (n 21), 254 and 269–70.

[259] Martin H Redish and Lawrence C Marshall, 'Adjudicatory Independence and the Values of Procedural Due Process' (1986) 95 *Yale Law Journal* 455, 77.

[260] Michał Krajewski and Michał Ziółkowski, 'EU Judicial Independence Dencentralized' (2020) 57 *Common Market Law Review* 1107.

with concomitant risk for the perception of its objectivity and neutrality towards different societal interests.

Second, a review body must be vested with *powers* to intercede in the impugned law-, rule- and decision-making to correct their outcomes or offer a candid reconsideration of these outcomes. The powers of review bodies depend on the practical scope of their jurisdiction, the remedies they may grant, and the review technique (including specific criteria of review) they employ. Instrumentalist accounts traditionally emphasise the advantages of bestowing courts and court-like bodies with powers to grant peremptory remedies. Deliberative accounts, highlighting the need for a 'genuine reconsideration' of the impugned acts, should accept review bodies without binding powers.[261]

An important and challenging question is what degree of interference into the law-, rule- and decision-making – expressed as the criteria, grounds, standard, intensity or, more generally, the technique of review – can be justified by the independence and expertise of the review authority. Expertise in a specific field, which an ordinary judge lacks but a member of a specialised tribunal possesses, may be perceived as a factor justifying more substantial interferences within the complex empirical basis of legislation or administrative action.[262]

Third, the *accessibility* of review mechanisms strongly determines their capacity to ensure the systemic correctness or enhance the deliberative credentials of law-, rule- or decision-making. In the instrumentalist perspective, liberal access rules enable private parties to seek protection against potentially detrimental legal acts, thereby providing the review bodies with useful data informing the review process. The wider the access to review, the greater the chances of unlawful acts being detected and eliminated. In the deliberative perspective, liberal access rules enable individuals to enter the democratic process of law-, rule- or decision-making, voice their concerns and submit reasoned arguments. Third-party interventions and *amici curiae* briefs can perform the same function.[263]

Fourth, review mechanisms fulfil their goals by dint of the parties' and the adjudicators' *activity* in the course of proceedings. In the instrumentalist model, the activity of the parties enables and facilitates data collection and analysis. The scope of the adjudicators' task of proactive truth-seeking may vary according to the specific procedural model. In the deliberative model, an open, reasoned and comprehensive deliberation on contentious issues provides the affected parties with reasons to perceive themselves as morally obliged to comply with the final decision, irrespective of its substance.[264] An active adjudicator may facilitate constructive

[261] For instance, Harel (n 233), Harel and Shinar (n 233).
[262] Kyritsis (n 217), 154ff. Cane (n 218), 251.
[263] Zurn (n 21), 271.
[264] Solum (n 31), 259–60.

deliberation among the parties. However, extensive procedural opportunities for participation and deliberation may slow down proceedings, require additional resources and consequently affect the overall efficiency of the system of justice.

Table 3.3 The instrumentalist and deliberative interpretation of review mechanisms' procedural features

Feature/interpretation	Instrumentalist	Deliberative
Independence (from the primary decision-makers and the parties, from political accountability)	Cognitive superiority in objective legal interpretation and fact-finding	Precondition of a candid reconsideration of the disputed matter
Powers (to quash or modify the act, or to issue non-binding proposals)	Authoritative declaration of the correct outcome	Performing or inducing a candid reconsideration of the matter
Accessibility (to the main applicants, third-party interveners or *amici curiae*)	Provision of relevant or useful data	Voicing of grievances and arguments
Procedural activity (of the parties and the adjudicators within the review proceedings)	Verification of factual data and applicable laws	Reasoned deliberation

IV. Conclusion

This chapter has proposed how to dissect the deeper normative meaning of 'the rule of law' and 'effective judicial protection' in the context of judicial and extra-judicial review. This move has been necessary as the legal systems of EU Member States profess very different conceptions as to how far constitutional or administrative law and courts can strive to frame and constrain public authority exercise. These divergent conceptions are manifested in different *locus standi* criteria, judicial review techniques and adjudicators' activity during review proceedings.

Based on a literature survey, the chapter has distinguished the instrumental and deliberative functions of judicial review. Judicial or extra-judicial review mechanisms may be instrumental to improving the legal and empirical correctness of law-, rule- and decision-making. They may also enhance the deliberative quality of these processes. However, the specific design and performance of judicial or extra-judicial mechanisms depend on the distribution of limited resources and the traditional priorities of the system of justice.

To understand the changing functions of EU judicial review and the added value of extra-judicial review, the chapter has advanced an analytical framework based on four institutional and procedural features: the *independence*, *powers*, *accessibility* and procedural *activity* of judicial or extra-judicial review bodies. The design and operation of these four features determine how review mechanisms discharge their instrumental and deliberative functions and what specific legitimacy assets they generate. Such legitimacy assets are argumentative resources that can be invoked to support the authority of law-, rule- or decision-making subject to judicial or extra-judicial review.

4

Judicial Review: Justice and Efficiency

The EU judicature is an extensive bureaucratic structure operating under pressure to achieve efficiency, primarily to expedite the time and increase the number of closed proceedings. Various public documents and extra-judicial statements of members of the EU Courts suggest that they have embraced efficiency as the primary yardstick of their judicial activity.[265] Moreover, other EU institutions and the Member States have called upon the EU judicature to improve efficiency.[266] Seeing its docket rocketing, the EU judicature has introduced several procedural and organisational reforms, such as recasting its rules of procedure,[267] introducing internal deadlines[268] and digitalising case processing.[269] On the one hand, internal statistics of the EGC demonstrate a consistent decrease in the time necessary to draft a preliminary report based on the parties' written pleadings. On the other hand, the time of proceedings is steadily determined by the time necessary to complete the written procedure and the translation of written pleadings.[270] The EU Courts are currently seeking more procedural discretion to measure out the parties' activity in the proceedings on a case-by-case basis in the name of efficiency.

[265] ECJ, 'Annual Report 2018: Judicial Activity', 8 and 159–60. Eleanor Sharpston, 'Making the Court of Justice of the European Union More Productive' (2014) 21 *Maastricht Journal of Comparative and European Law* 763. Marc Jaeger, '25 Years of the General Court: Looking Back and Forward' in Vesna Tomljenović (ed), *EU Competition and State Aid Rules: Public and Private Enforcement* (Springer 2017), 24 ('all my mandates as the President of this court have been directed at improving efficiency in dealing with cases … This is the priority I have set').

[266] Christoph Krenn, 'The European Court of Justice's Financial Accountability: How the European Parliament Incites and Monitors Judicial Reform through the Budgetary Process' (2017) 13 *European Constitutional Law Review* 453.

[267] See, below n 414.

[268] EGC, *Manuel des procédures internes* (internal procedural guidelines received on 16.4.2018, request 7/2018D), para 9.

[269] European Court of Auditors, 'Special Report: Performance Review of Case Management at the Court of Justice of the European Union' (14/2017), paras 53ff.

[270] EGC, 'Durée de l'instance par stade de procédure (en mois) – Affaires réglées par arrêt (…)' (internal document disclosed by email of 4.9.2020, request 17/2020D).

The main challenge for the EGC, which deals with annulment actions in the first and often the only instance, is the number and the great variety and complexity of cases. In its 2018 annual report, the EGC highlighted

> the great variety of areas of law in which the Court is involved. The extension of the spheres of the activity of the European Union is gradually being reflected in the case-law. Thus, the Court has had the opportunity to develop its case-law in new matters such as supervision of the financial sector …, or again in matters of great social importance, such as environmental and health protection.[271]

During a recent audit of case management at the EU Courts by the European Court of Auditors, the EU judges generally confirmed that the complexity and volume of case documentation most frequently affect the duration of the case after the written procedure has been closed.[272] Is the time ripe for specialisation of judicial review by the EGC, or would it rather endanger the uniformity of case law across the variegated fields of EU law?

Notwithstanding its shortcomings, the EU judicial review is assumed to be the gold standard of legal protection. This chapter explores the relative authority of EU judicial review, that is the practice of the Article 263(4) TFEU annulment procedure as triggered by private parties.[273] It specifically looks into the operation of the institutional and procedural features affecting the judicial review's *independence*, *powers*, *accessibility* and the *activity* of the parties to proceedings. This way, it complements and verifies the findings of the scholarship summarised in Chapter 2.

Section I discusses the independence of the EU Courts, highlighting some of its weak points. Section II examines how the EU Courts have been exercising their powers, including what kind of acts fall within their jurisdictional remit, the review technique and its limits in empirically uncertain cases, and the rate of successful actions. Section III seeks to grasp how accessible the EU judicial review is in reality. It analyses the applicants (such as economic operators, trade unions, public interest organisations) and legal acts falling into different categories (individual decisions, general regulations) in the annulment cases closed in 2014–18. It also explores the number and categories of third-party interveners. Section IV examines the parties and the EU judges' activity in the course of annulment proceedings, drawing from procedural statistics and different procedural documents. Section V presents this chapter's conclusions.

[271] ECJ (n 265), 161.
[272] European Court of Auditors (n 269), 33.
[273] It also considers the Article 267 TFEU validity reference procedure.

I. Judicial Independence: Safeguards, Resources and Expertise

The authority of judicial review is relative, first and foremost, to the institutional safeguards of the judges' independence from political actors and concentrated societal powers and their impartiality in the course of proceedings.[274] These attributes are associated with objectivity and neutrality in the application of law. Strong legal safeguards protect the EU judges from external pressure.[275] In particular, EU judges can be dismissed early for no longer meeting the conditions or fulfilling the obligations arising from the judicial office only by a *unanimous* decision of ECJ members; an option which has never been used.

However, scholars have pointed out problems in the appointment procedure, related mainly to its non-transparency and the lack of objective criteria for the scrutiny and selection of candidates. The EU judges are elected by a common accord of the Member States.[276] The candidates have been scrutinised since 2010 by an independent panel, the members of which are appointed by the Council at the ECJ President's initiative.[277] The Member States have always respected the panel's non-binding opinions,[278] but the criteria it applies have been established internally, and individual opinions are not made public. It has also been pointed out that the ECJ President has a decisive influence on the composition of the panel, which is seen as a form of emerging judicial self-governance at the EU level, with concomitant advantages and risks.[279]

The main problem regarding the independence of EU judges is the possibility of their reappointment every six years. Reappointment of a sitting judge for the next term of office creates the risk of political influence on the candidate, or at least reasonable suspicions in this regard.[280] A compensatory safeguard is

[274] Dominique Ritleng, 'The Independence and Legitimacy of the European Court of Justice' in Dominique Ritleng (ed), *Independence and Legitimacy in the Institutional System of the European Union* (Oxford University Press 2016).

[275] These safeguards have the status of EU primary law. They are contained in Title I of the Statute of the Court of Justice which *cannot* be subject to an ordinary legislative amendment, under Article 281 TFEU.

[276] Judges of specialised courts, which currently do not exist, are to be elected by the Council.

[277] Article 255 TFEU. The members of the panel are appointed by the Council upon a recommendation by the ECJ President, mainly from among the highest national judges and former judges of EU Courts.

[278] 'Fifth Activity Report of the Panel Provided for by Article 255 TFEU', 14.

[279] Judicial self-governance may secure the objectivity of the appointment process but, as the experience of some countries shows, may also generate the risk of arbitrary appointments and the over-empowering of court leadership or senior judges. Michal Bobek and David Kosař, 'Global Solutions, Local Damages: A Critical Study in Judicial Councils in Central and Eastern Europe' (2014) 15 *German Law Journal* 1257.

[280] The terms of office of the ECtHR judges have been prolonged, and no reappointments are currently allowed.

the collegiality of the EU judicature's decision-making and the lack of dissenting opinions. As a result, national governments cannot know their judge's vote in individual cases.[281]

The EU judges lack specialised resources which they could use in empirically complex cases.[282] They are appointed from among legal generalists. They rely on highly qualified legal assistants (*référendaires*). They can also get support in the form of the preliminary analysis of new cases and comparative research notes drafted by the internal Documentation and Research Directorate. The ECJ manages the distribution of these internal resources, which has given rise to tensions with the EGC. At one point, the EGC required more resources to manage its skyrocketing workload.[283] Recently, another conflict between the ECJ and the EGC concerned the vision of the EU judicial architecture in light of what might seem like an increasing backlog.[284] While the ECJ opted for the enlargement of the EGC, the option which finally prevailed, the EGC called for more support staff. Since the enlarged EGC now has spare workforce capacity, the ECJ intends to transfer to the EGC some of its jurisdiction in infringement proceedings,[285] and perhaps also in preliminary references. Another confirmation of the EGC's spare capacity is that more cases are currently assigned to the chambers of five rather than three judges.

The ECJ itself cannot be enlarged without a Treaty change and, arguably, without risking the uniformity of case law. In the future, the ECJ may need to extend the use of its case filtering device, which is currently applied to some appeals from the EGC rulings.[286] In this context, the EGC is likely to retain its character of a generalist administrative court responsible primarily for the uniformity of case law across the variegated subfields of EU administrative law. The ECJ will not be able to take greater responsibility for maintaining the uniformity of case law of specialised EGC chambers.

[281] Naturally, this safeguard does not apply to advocates general, who publish their opinions individually.

[282] An economic advisor was employed for six years at the EU Courts in 1990s. Castillo de la Torre and Gippini Fournier (n 71), 257 (fn 144).

[283] Marc van der Woude, 'Towards a European Council of the Judiciary: Some Reflections on the Administration of the EU Courts' in Flora ANJ Goudappel and Ernst MH Hirsch Ballin (eds), *Democracy and Rule of Law in the European Union: Essays in Honour of Jaap W de Zwaan* (Springer 2016).

[284] Alberto Alemanno and Laurent Pech, 'Thinking Justice Outside the Docket: A Critical Assessment of the Reform of the EU's Court System' (2017) 54 *Common Market Law Review* 129.

[285] This initiative was halted by the Commission, which suggested waiting for the analysis of the results of the enlargement of the EGC. Commission, 'Opinion on the draft amendments to Protocol No 3 on the Statute of the Court of Justice of the European Union, presented by the Court of Justice on 26 March 2018' (COM(2018) 534 final).

[286] See further, Section IV.D.

II. The Reach of Judicial Power

A. Acts with Strong and Weak Legal Effects

How much authority judicial review can bestow upon law-, rule- or decision-making is relative to how much power the judges can exercise. Judicial powers depend, first and foremost, on the jurisdictional remit. Law-, rule- and decision-making through which EU institutions and bodies may affect the rights and interests of individuals have no clear boundaries. Therefore, the jurisdiction of EU Courts in the Article 263(1) TFEU action for annulment is framed by a malleable concept of acts adopted by EU institutions and bodies producing legal effects vis-à-vis third parties.[287] Occasionally, controversy may arise about whether an entity that adopted an act is or is not an EU institution or body. For instance, the ECJ held that the Commission and the ECB's participation in the Eurogroup meetings did not make them the Eurogroup statement's co-authors. This ruling raised controversies as the statement exerted a considerable impact on domestic policies.[288]

Doubts arise more frequently as to whether a contested act produces 'legal' effects. An 'act' is usually a written document, but it may also be an act of oral communication.[289] An act produces legal effects, the EU Courts assume, when it brings about 'a distinct change in the rights and obligations of a third party'.[290] To identify legal effects, the EU Courts look at the act's substance and context rather than only its formal characteristics. They ascertain whether a conscientious, prudent and well-informed person could reasonably perceive herself as obligated by the contested act to undertake specific conduct, even if only out of reasonable fear of sanctions.[291] Apart from the wording of contested provisions,[292] the EU Courts consider the powers of the act's author to adopt binding legal norms in the same field,[293] potential enforcement and sanctioning mechanisms, the character of procedure for the act's adoption and publication,[294] the relationship to binding

[287] Case 22/70, *ERTA*, ECLI:EU:C:1971:32. In the EU Courts' understanding, it is the second sentence of Article 263(1) TFEU that effectively contains a general principle setting out their jurisdiction (ie a challengeable act is one producing legal effects vis-à-vis third parties).

[288] Joined Cases C-105/15 P to C-109/15 P, *Mallis et al v Commission and ECB*, ECLI:EU:C:2016:702, para 57.

[289] Case T-3/93, *Air France v Commission*, ECLI:EU:T:1994:36, paras 57–59. Case T-85/03, *Cayman Islands v Commission*, ECLI:EU:T:2003:83, para 60.

[290] Joined Cases C-463/10 P and C-475/10 P, *Deutsche Post and Germany v Commission*, ECLI:EU:C:2011:656, paras 36–37 and the case law cited therein.

[291] AG Jacobs, Case C-301/03, *Italy v Commission*, ECLI:EU:C:2005:550, paras 70–71 (fn 26). Case T-496/11, *UK v ECB*, ECLI:EU:T:2015:133, para 32.

[292] Case T-713/14, *IPSO v ECB*, ECLI:EU:T:2016:727, paras 22–24.

[293] Case T-678/14, *Slovakia v Commission*, ECLI:EU:T:2015:66. Joined Cases C-105/15 P to C-109/15 P, *Mallis et al v Commission and ECB*, ECLI:EU:C:2016:702, paras 52–56.

[294] Case T-713/14, *IPSO v ECB*, ECLI:EU:T:2016:727, paras 34–35.

legal norms[295] and eventually the author's actual intent.[296] In practice, the EU Courts have accepted reviewing the legality of letters written by the Commission staff,[297] policy frameworks[298] and even oral statements.[299] By dint of this flexible approach, the EU institutions and bodies should not escape judicial review by manipulating the form of a legal act.

It is still possible that even such a broad and flexible jurisdiction may leave out certain acts indirectly affecting the rights and obligations of third parties. The EU institutions and bodies adopt various acts, generally labelled as 'soft law', by which they may, for instance, creatively concretise the interpretation of open-ended EU law provisions.[300] AG Bobek recently posited that such acts might be effectively directing the interpretation of binding EU acts or domestic law by domestic judges due to their authors' de facto authority.[301] However, the ECJ has not taken advantage of this to expand its jurisdiction to encompass soft law acts,[302] which contrasts with its recent approach to the acts falling within the Common Foreign and Security Policy (CFSP).[303] As will be demonstrated in Chapter 6, the Ombudsman's remit has proved to be more flexible than that of the EU Courts. She accepts review of instances of soft law-making in which the EU Courts do not currently intercede.

Due to the hierarchical structure of the EU legal order, applicants for judicial review may raise pleas relating to the unlawfulness of any parent act of general application that has influenced the substance of the act directly contested.[304] According to the conception of the decentralised judicial architecture, the EU acts of general application, the majority of which are subject to implementation by domestic authorities, should be subject to judicial review on private parties' initiative using Article 267 TFEU validity references from domestic courts. The ECJ jurisdiction can turn out broader in the indirect validity avenue than in the direct

[295] AG Jacobs, Case C-301/03, *Italy v Commission*, ECLI:EU:C:2005:550, paras 68–69. Case T-258/06, *Germany v Commission*, ECLI:EU:T:2010:214, paras 26–28 and 128. See also as regards informational and scientific acts, Case T-334/12, *Plantavis and NEM v Commission & EFSA*, ECLI:EU:T:2015:376.

[296] Case T-713/14, *IPSO v ECB*, ECLI:EU:T:2016:727, para 27.

[297] Case C-322/09 P, *NDSHT v Commission*, ECLI:EU:C:2010:701.

[298] Case T-496/11, *UK v ECB*, ECLI:EU:T:2015:133.

[299] Case T-3/93, *Air France v Commission*, ECLI:EU:T:1994:36, paras 57–59. Case T-85/03, *Cayman Islands v Commission*, ECLI:EU:T:2003:83, para 60.

[300] Eliantonio and Stefan (n 40).

[301] AG Bobek, Case C-16/16, *Belgium v Commission*, ECLI:EU:C:2017:959.

[302] Case C-16/16, *Belgium v Commission*, ECLI:EU:C:2018:79. In Case C-72/15, *Rosneft*, ECLI:EU:C:2017:236, the ECJ did not shy away from reinterpreting a Treaty clause ruling out the judicial review of CFSP measures so as to broaden its jurisdiction.

[303] Butler (n 179).

[304] For instance, Case T-526/10, *Inuit Tapiriit Kanatami et al v Commission*, ECLI:EU:T:2013:215. The EU Courts allow such indirect challenges against a wide range of acts of general application, not only binding regulations, but also internal administrative guidelines, on condition that their application has genuinely influenced the content of contested decisions. Case C-171/00, *Liberos v Commission*, ECLI:EU:C:2002:17. Case C-189/02, *Dansk Roindustri v Commission*, ECLI:EU:C:2005:408, paras 214 and 237. Case T-176/01, *Ferriere Nord v Commission*, ECLI:EU:T:2004:336, para 136.

annulment avenue. In the former, the ECJ may arguably review any 'act', rather than only a *legal* act, which has a bearing upon the result of proceedings before the referring domestic courts.[305] Underlying such a far-reaching liberal meaning of an 'act' in the validity proceedings might be the willingness of the ECJ to keep its monopoly on the judicial review of the full range of EU acts that may find application in cases before domestic courts.[306]

B. Science on Trial

The EU judicature's review technique revolves around the concept of 'legality'.[307] This concept is further specified by the types of pleas which the applicants can raise in the annulment proceedings: 'lack of competence, infringement of an essential procedural requirement, infringement of the Treaties or of any rule of law relating to their application, or misuse of powers'.[308] The concept of 'legality', known in some domestic administrative justice systems, curbs the powers of judicial review courts vis-à-vis those of the administration or political bodies. The courts do not repeat the challenged decision-making process – or, in other words, they do not review the 'merits' or 'expediency' of the case – but only focus on its crucial procedural and substantive aspects which can be linked to specific legal norms.

In practice, the concept of 'legality' review has become increasingly capacious, as discussed in Chapter 2, conforming with the expectations of national courts, scholars and legal practitioners. By recognising a justiciable 'duty of care' on the side of the EU institutions and bodies, the EU judicature simultaneously asserted a power to delve into the empirical basis of impugned legal acts, including to verify which empirical factors are relevant and how they should be assessed under the applicable law. Nowadays, many consider the EU judicial review, especially in competition law cases, to be comprehensive.[309] The procedural setting of the annulment proceedings, which imposes on applicants the burden of advancing convincing legal arguments and adducing relevant evidence,[310] may still constrain the EU judicature's scope of autonomous engagement with purely empirical matters. Another limitation to detecting 'manifest errors' stems from limitations of

[305] AG Bobek, Joined Cases C-83/19, C-127/19 and C-195/19, *Asociația 'Forumul Judecătorilor din România' v Inspecția Judiciară*, ECLI:EU:C:2020:746, paras 123–27.

[306] It has been posited that acts such as ECB guidelines or purchase programmes produce weak legal effects by giving rise to certain legitimate expectations as to future moves of the ECB. Alexander H Türk and Napoleon Xanthoulis, 'Legal Accountability of European Central Bank in Bank Supervision: A Case Study in Conceptualizing the Legal Effects of Union Acts' (2019) 26 *Maastricht Journal of Comparative and European Law* 151.

[307] Article 263(1) TFEU.

[308] Article 263(2) TFEU. The fourth ground, of little practical significance, is a transplant of a French concept (*détournement de pouvoir*).

[309] Castillo de la Torre and Gippini Fournier (n 71), 285–86.

[310] Section IV in this chapter.

judicial expertise and ability to process, comprehend and critically assess abstruse empirical data.

The EU Courts seek to compensate for the lack of specialised advisory bodies or expert witnesses with meticulous scrutiny of the partisan evidence (usually delivered in the form of voluminous annexes to the applications and written submissions) and accompanying legal arguments. The technique of review applied by the EU Courts naturally relates to its largely adversarial procedural setting.[311] However, no matter how scrupulous, the EU judicial review of uncertain empirical appraisals is inherently restricted by the applicant's ability to obtain sufficient evidence to substantiate the doubts regarding the impugned acts' empirical foundation.

Cases concerning the authorisation or restriction on the marketing of chemical substances, food additives or pharmaceuticals are arguably among the most difficult which the EU Courts, especially the EGC, have to examine. Non-governmental environmental organisations recently sought to bring litigation against (in their view) a dubious empirical basis of such EU measures. It seems they did not possess enough resources to produce scientific studies providing definitive conclusions as to the Commission's empirical mistakes. Instead, they expected the EU Courts to autonomously assess whether the data relied on by the Commission had been sufficient to state that the public interest was not in danger.[312] However, annulment proceedings' adversarial logic attributed a relatively strong presumption of correctness to the EU administration's acts. The judicial review applicants were required to discharge the burden of proof, something they were ill-equipped to do in a case involving uncertain and controversial scientific appraisals.[313] In its current institutional and procedural setting, the EU judicature does not seem able to more thoroughly engage with the uncertain empirical basis of EU measures, acting as a fully autonomous 'check and balance' upon the EU administration.[314] Epistemic uncertainty surrounding contemporary scientific findings and administrative measures makes the criterion of legal and empirical 'correctness' elusive. The EU judges were recently called to assess, for instance, whether new scientific

[311] The procedural setting of EU Courts will be further discussed in Section IV of this chapter.

[312] As illustrated by a dispute regarding the internal review by the Commission of its measure authorising modified soya beans, Case T-177/13, *TestBioTech et al v Commission*, ECLI:EU:T:2016:736, para 224: 'the first applicant does not dispute … that … it had not provided any evidence in support of the arguments put forward and that it had simply stated that there were no data on the effects of other technical treatments used to process soybeans and that, therefore, no conclusions could be drawn as to the effects on consumers and animals … a third party challenging a marketing authorisation for products must adduce substantial evidence liable to raise serious doubts as to the lawfulness of the grant of that authorisation. Since the first applicant has not demonstrated that there were serious doubts surrounding the lawfulness of the grant of the marketing authorisation for products containing the modified soybean, the fourth complaint must be rejected as unfounded'.

[313] AG Szpunar, Case C-82/17 P, *TestBioTech et al v Commission*, ECLI:EU:C:2018:837, para 68, as followed by the ECJ.

[314] Another issue is the scope of its legal mandate to engage with the EU administration's empirical findings.

findings had revealed risks to public health that would justify a restriction upon the use of a specific chemical or pharmaceutical substance, or whether the EU administrative response in this regard had been proportionate.

A study of the cases closed by the EU Courts with a definitive ruling issued in 2014–18 and involving problems of epistemic uncertainty relating to public health and the environment[315] demonstrated that the thoroughness of judicial review hinged upon the applicant's activity. During the examined period, the EGC was called to assess the weight of scientific arguments and counter-arguments,[316] their relevance to the case at hand,[317] the methodology and quality of data,[318] or the causal links between the data and public health or environmental risks.[319] In such cases, the applicant's ability to expose scientific flaws and convince the judges of legitimate and meaningful doubts about the empirical foundation of impugned measures appeared crucial.[320] In the absence of convincing evidence and arguments from the applicant, the EU judges had no choice but to recapitulate the challenged administration's reasoning, even if it appeared prima facie uncertain to a non-specialist reader.

The EU judges' ability to assess the contested measure's proportionality and adequacy is limited in a similar way. They may have difficulty assessing whether available alternatives to the restricted chemical substance might pose a higher risk to public health.[321] A simple verification of whether the EU administration has provided some prima facie reasonable explanation of its choice for the measure in

[315] Twenty-five annulment cases were identified, in which the EGC scrutinised the accuracy of uncertain empirical and normative appraisals under the heading of 'error of assessment', 'proportionality' or similar. In this period, the ECJ did not second-guess the EGC assessments in this regard. The appeals to the ECJ are formally limited to points of law, but a point of law may also encompass an error of empirical assessment by the EGC, which gives to the ECJ leeway in moderating the intensity of its appellate review. Giulia Gentile, 'The ECJ as the EU Court of Appeal: Some Evidence from the Appeal Case-law on the Non-contractual Liability of the EU' (2020) 13 *Review of European Administrative Law* 73.

[316] For instance, in Case T-368/11, *Polyelectrolyte Producers Group et al v Commission*, ECLI:EU:T:2013:53, the applicant alleged that the Commission had not considered a report containing data regarding a range of risk-reduction measures relating to acrylamide based on their likely effectiveness, practicality, economic impact and monitorability. In para 34, the EGC assumed that if this report was mentioned in the impact assessment report, it must have been considered.

[317] For instance, to what extent a difference in the application method of a substance in different countries is relevant for the reliability of data, ibid, para 48; to what extent a production method resulting with carcinogenic impurities of a substance not applied in the EU is nonetheless relevant in light of the precautionary principle, Case T-400/17, *Deza v Commission*, ECLI:EU:T:2018:712, paras 27–39.

[318] For instance, to what extent the EGC can assess the 'realistic and foreseeable' conditions of the 'correct usage' of the product in question, Case T-368/11, *Polyelectrolyte Producers Group et al v Commission*, ECLI:EU:T:2013:53, paras 55–62.

[319] For instance, in Case T-400/17, *Deza v Commission*, ECLI:EU:T:2018:712, paras 46–49, the EGC approved the explicitly uncertain *assumption* by a scientific committee that a carcinogenicity was due to the substance in question itself rather than its impurity, given a low presence of this impurity in the tested sample.

[320] For instance, Case T-135/13, *Hitachi et al v ECHA*, ECLI:EU:T:2015:253, paras 59–60 and 76 regarding whether the substance in question led to respiratory sensitisation.

[321] Case T-368/11, *Polyelectrolyte Producers Group et al v Commission*, ECLI:EU:T:2013:53, para 81.

the statement of reasons, a prior impact assessment, or in the course of the administrative process may be the only way out.[322]

Crucially, the EU Courts visibly avoided scrabbling around in the scientific opinions of independent committees, forming the basis and shaping the substance of the Commission's measures.[323] Invoking such committees' independence and scientific expertise, the EU Courts confined themselves to making sure that the scientific opinions appeared intelligible and logical. This technique undoubtedly warranted some degree of meaningful review. When conflicting evidence was available, a committee was expected to justify why specific evidence was preferred.[324] Notably, in a recent case, among several pleas in law, some related to potential substantive errors by a scientific committee, the ECJ concentrated on one that related to the procedural requirement of impartiality of the committee's rapporteur.[325]

In practice, the scientific opinions enjoyed a strong presumption of correctness, and it was up to the applicants to persuade the judges, with clear evidence, that such opinions were tainted with errors.[326] Otherwise, the EU Courts confined themselves to underscoring the characteristics of contested opinions that could reasonably warrant their scientific validity: compliance with established methodological standards (control groups, randomising), a variety of data and sources, an agreement between the experts, or a brief response or acknowledgement of the applicant's counter-arguments or doubts voiced during the administrative proceedings.[327] The fact that the Commission had followed the expert opinion – although it was authorised to depart from it on specific grounds – was invoked as an indicator of the contested measure's scientific validity.[328]

[322] ibid, paras 85–97. Evidently, the EU judicature may be able to declare the contested measure unlawful in an extreme scenario in which the Commission has not carried out or is unable to prove any prior impact assessment. Case T-584/13, *BASF Agro et al v Commission*, ECLI:EU:T:2018:279, paras 157–73.

[323] Case T-189/13, *PP Nature-Balance Lizenz v Commission*, ECLI:EU:T:2014:1056, paras 33–34 and the previous case law cited therein.

[324] ibid, paras 52 and 59–62.

[325] In the first instance (Case T-672/14, *August Wolff and Remedia v Commission*, ECLI:EU:T:2016:623), the EGC engaged with complex substantive pleas regarding the lawfulness of a pharmaceutical authorisation. On appeal (Case C-680/16 P, *August Wolff and Remedia v Commission*, ECLI:EU:C:2019:257), the ECJ focused on the procedural problem of impartiality.

[326] For instance, Case T-400/17, *Deza v Commission*, ECLI:EU:T:2018:712, paras 46–54 and 57.

[327] For instance, Case T-539/10, *Acino v Commission*, ECLI:EU:T:2013:110, paras 95–98, 101–03.

[328] Case T-189/13, *PP Nature-Balance Lizenz v Commission*, ECLI:EU:T:2014:1056, paras 45–49. Case T-96/10, *Rütgers Germany et al v ECHA*, ECLI:EU:T:2013:109, para 129. Case T-539/10, *Acino v Commission*, ECLI:EU:T:2013:110, paras 80–81; Case T-368/11, *Polyelectrolyte Producers Group et al v Commission*, ECLI:EU:T:2013:53, para 48. The EU Courts might, moreover, try to quash a party's arguments by pointing out their inconsistency. For instance, in Case T-135/13, *Hitachi Chemical Europe et al v ECHA*, ECLI:EU:T:2015:253, paras 67, 77 and 115–16. In Joined Cases T-339/16, T-352/16 and T-391/16, *Ville de Paris v Commission*, ECLI:EU:T:2018:927, paras 129, 136 and 142–43, the EGC noted that the Commission defended 'coefficients' to account for the 'overestimation' of car pollution while measured in practical use rather than in a laboratory, having at the same time argued that the methods for measuring car pollution in the actual use have been significantly improved.

In the examined period, this review technique only allowed the EGC to quash an impugned act for lack of any proof of appropriate scientific assessment.[329] In general, the EU judges seemed able to solve by themselves relatively evident problems regarding the evidential value of scientific studies,[330] but their epistemic ability to scrutinise more intricate methodological problems might give rise to doubts.[331] The outcome of another case in which the EU Courts found that a relevant scientific factor had not been appropriately considered proved controversial.[332] It was argued that the inclusion of this factor would change the whole methodological approach of the disputed scientific analysis and imply more tolerance for potential risks to public health and the environment. Arguably, the applicable legislation could have been deemed as leaving normative discretion to the Commission to define the acceptable risk level and, consequently, to choose the corresponding methodological approach.[333]

When the EU administration takes measures to prevent or moderate a newly discovered risk of a chemical or pharmaceutical substance, it makes a normative choice as to the acceptable level of risk and the ensuing level of required evidence as to the existence or seriousness of this risk. This underlying normative choice is based on subjective axiological choices and preferences of the decision-makers. The applicable legal frameworks only loosely bind these normative choices.

The entanglement of normative and empirical uncertainty leads to two simultaneous but opposing questions. On the one hand, do the institutional and procedural assets of the EU Courts justify them second-guessing normative choices as to the acceptable level and required evidence of risk made by the primary decision-makers? The latter are politically accountable at the EU or domestic level, besides enjoying specialist expertise and institutional back-up. On the other hand, how can affected economic operators effectively defend themselves in the procedural setting that makes them responsible for persuading the judges that the empirically uncertain evidence against their products is too weak or that the level of acceptable risk should be higher? The applicants may be required to prove their products' perfect safety or the absence of any risk whatsoever, which may be nigh on impossible for practical reasons.[334] By the same token, how could the non-governmental

[329] In Case T-584/13, *BASF Agro et al v Commission*, ECLI:EU:T:2018:279, the Commission was unable to prove that any impact assessment had taken place.

[330] For instance, in Case T-135/13, *Hitachi Chemical Europe et al v ECHA*, ECLI:EU:T:2015:253, para 74, the weakness of the evidence submitted by the applicant seemed rather clear.

[331] For instance, Case T-400/17, *Deza v Commission*, ECLI:EU:T:2018:712, paras 70–88 concerned whether a specific method of feeding the studied animals affected the test results, indicating a higher risk of the carcinogenicity of the substance in question.

[332] Case C-691/15 P, *European Commission v Bilbaína*, ECLI:EU:C:2017:882, discussed in Chapter 2, Section II.

[333] Leonelli (n 68).

[334] For instance, Case T-584/13, *BASF Agro et al v Commission*, ECLI:EU:T:2018:279, paras 137–44. In Case T-201/13, *Rubinum v Commission*, ECLI:EU:T:2015:311, paras 73–75, the applicant claimed that a potential detection of a gene usually associated with chloramphenicol in a species of bacteria used by the applicant and in other related species is not sufficient proof that the product may provoke a resistance to antibiotics, especially that even the European Food and Safety Authority used

environmental organisations benefit from access to the EU Courts, which they continuously demand?[335] Without a change of procedural setting, they would be required to offer strong empirical evidence to refute the presumption of correctness attributed to the EU measures. Would they have sufficient resources and practical possibilities to produce such evidence?

C. Measuring the Impact of Judicial Power

In the annulment procedure, the EU Courts are, in principle, empowered only to *annul* the unlawful measures.[336] Unlike certain BoAs, they cannot modify these measures' substance or impose injunctions.[337] Only specific provisions confer upon the EU Courts the 'unlimited jurisdiction' to modify the amounts of fines imposed on private undertakings[338] or modify the substance of decisions in intellectual property cases.[339] In order not to assume the responsibility and power of primary decision-makers,[340] the EU Courts are supposed only to review the legality of impugned acts based on the facts and the law as they stood at the time when the act was adopted.[341] The EU institutions and bodies to which the case has been remitted for re-examination must follow the reasoning of the EU Courts,[342] which extends the practical effects of the judgments and the underlying motives beyond a formal annulment of the impugned act.[343]

The rate of successful annulment actions (which resulted in at least a partial annulment of the contested measure) provides a picture of the judicial review's

a phrase 'strongly suggests' rather than 'proves'. See also Case T-96/10, *Rütgers Germany et al v ECHA*, ECLI:EU:T:2013:109, paras 128–29.

335 At present, they may get access to the EU Courts to litigate against EU measures having environmental impact only indirectly, through initiating first the internal review procedure. See the illustration provided by Case T-177/13, *TestBioTech et al v Commission*, ECLI:EU:T:2016:736.

336 As regards the incidental objection of illegality against a parent act of general application, the EU Courts declare its 'inapplicability' in the case at hand. As regards the Article 267 TFEU validity references, the EU Courts may declare the 'invalidity' of the contested act. An annulment and declaration of invalidity produce *ex tunc* and *erga omnes* effect (the act is eliminated from the legal order as if it has never existed, although the EU judicature may indicate the effects of the act which remain final under Article 264(2) TFEU). Formally, a declaration of inapplicability produces only *inter partes* effects in the case at hand, but the institution concerned is obliged to draw all the consequences from such a declaration under Article 266 TFEU. Barents (n 3), 303.

337 Case T-120/10, *Client Earth v Birdlife International*, ECLI:EU:T:2011:646, paras 28–29. Case T-436/09, *Dafour v ECB*, ECLI:EU:T:2011:634, paras 39–40.

338 Article 261 TFEU.

339 Article 262 TFEU.

340 Case C-510/11 P, *Kone et al v Commission*, ECLI:EU:C:2013:696, para 26.

341 Joined Cases 15/76 and 16/76, *France v Commission*, ECLI:EU:C:1979:29, para 7. Regarding the ECJ's latitude in validity references, see Lenaerts (n 3), 471.

342 Article 266 TFEU.

343 Competition law scholars used to argue for a revision of the EU judicial review to allow the EU Courts to make substantive decisions rather than only 'review' the decisions of the Commission, which leads back to the discussion of how much resources the EU Member States and law-makers are ready to invest to enable the EU Courts to further develop the technique of judicial review. See above nn 51–52.

impact on EU law-, rule- and decision-making. There is no universal indicator of the 'appropriate' or desired rate of successful actions. Interpreted in light of the 'transmission belt' model (which considers courts as ensuring the objectively correct application of law), the rate of successful actions provides a measure for the rule of law. It shows the extent to which public authorities comply with higher-order law in their decision-making.[344] Interpreted in the light of the 'aggregative' model (which considers courts as enabling aggregation and balancing of affected interests), the rate of successful actions may reveal judicial deference or, quite the contrary, the readiness of courts to constrain the discretion of primary decision-makers. Interpreted in the light of the deliberative model (which sees courts as enhancing reasoned deliberation on public matters), the rate of successful actions for judicial review may reveal the size of the gap between the values professed by the courts and primary decision-makers.[345] On the contrary, a very high rate of successful court actions might encourage even more litigation, raising concerns about the risk of courts' normative overreach. It will also be interesting to see whether the rate of successful actions evolves or remains relatively stable.

A unique dataset was compiled including 798 annulment cases initiated by private parties[346] and closed by a judgment or reasoned order issued in 2014–18.[347] The dataset did not include the cases rejected as *manifestly* bound to fail at the level of the EGC[348] (and the like[349]), those withdrawn by the applicants themselves,

[344] There would still be a possibility that a certain number of unlawful acts had not been challenged.

[345] Takis Tridimas and Gabriel Gari, 'Winners and Losers in Luxembourg: A Statistical Analysis of Judicial Review before the European Court of Justice and the Court of First Instance (2001–2005)' (2005) 35 *European Law Review* 131, at 134–35.

[346] The cases initiated exclusively by Members States, public agencies, local governments or third countries were not included.

[347] The dataset included the Article 263(4) TFEU annulment cases completed either at the level of the EGC (in the first instance or after a referral by the ECJ) or the ECJ (on appeal) with a definitive ruling issued between 1.1.2014 and 31.12.2018. In other words, the case was included in the database if a *definitive* ruling closing the case was announced either by the EGC or the ECJ in the said period (even if the first-instance ruling was issued before 2014). Orders announcing the appeal withdrawal or orders relating to costs or a subsequent interpretation of the ruling were not considered. An appellate annulment ruling by the ECJ was considered definitive if the case was not referred back to the EGC. The annulment actions are often combined with actions for damages; if the appeal concerned only the damages, it was not included in the dataset. If the EGC reduced the amount of the penalty imposed on the applicant within the 'unlimited jurisdiction' under Article 261 TFEU, the action would be considered at least partially successful.

[348] In practice, such cases – dismissed under Article 126 RPGC (the Rules of Procedure of the General Court, below n 414) – are often directed against non-EU acts or non-EU institutions (for instance, against domestic authorities or even other international courts; in such cases, the EU Courts declare lack of jurisdiction), against non-challengeable EU acts, or where the applicants do not fulfil the admissibility or formal criteria (for instance, the duty to have legal representation or the deadline for lodging the action). The EGC may deal with the substance of the case, under Article 126 RPGC, by declaring the action as 'manifestly deprived of any foundation in law' but it uses this option only rarely. See further Section IV.C. Conversely, the dataset included the appeals dismissed by the ECJ under Article 181 RPCJ (the Rules of Procedure of the Court of Justice, below n 414) as manifestly inadmissible (for instance, due to lack of clear arguments or arguments relating to points of law only) or manifestly unfounded, because the ECJ uses this simplified procedure very often, as an ordinary means to deal with appeals. See further, Section IV.D.

[349] In a handful of cases, the EGC rejected the case due to an absolute bar to proceedings under Article 129 RPGC.

as well as intellectual property (trademark) cases.[350] Considering the definitive outcomes, 665 of 798 cases (83.3%) were declared admissible,[351] so the EU Courts dealt with their substance. The remaining cases were dismissed as inadmissible by a reasoned order adopted upon a formal objection raised by the defendant and following an exchange of written pleadings on the issue of admissibility.[352]

Figure 4.1 Rate of successful actions for annulment brought by private applicants and settled by the EU Courts with a definitive ruling in 2014–18 (% of admissible actions)

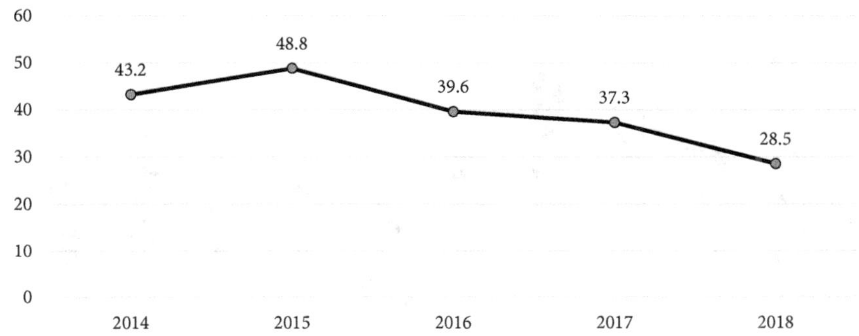

Overall, from among 665 admissible cases, as many as 262 (39.4%) were at least partially successful, ie at least one plea in law was upheld leading to an at least partial annulment of the contested act.[353] Figure 4.1 demonstrates the rate of at least partially successful admissible cases per year (the yearly number of admissible cases varied between 125 and 149 cases). The rate of success was slightly dropping in the examined period.[354] It is unknown if this drop is a new trend, which might raise concerns about judicial deference, or a temporary and random result,[355] or if it might be linked to the EGC enlargement between 2016 and 2020 and related organisational disruptions. This drop occurs in all policy fields. At the same time, the rate of all successful *appeals* recorded in the database

[350] Due to their highly specific nature, distinct procedural framework, review technique and remedies. Moreover, technically they have a separate legal basis (Article 262 TFEU). The same approach was applied by Tridimas and Gari (n 345).

[351] The dataset does not consider individual pleas in law that might have been declared inadmissible (for instance, due to lack of clarity) in these cases.

[352] Under Article 130 RPGC. As already mentioned above, the cases declared as *manifestly* bound to fail and dismissed in the Article 126 or 129 RPGC simplified procedure by the EGC were not considered. Also, no successful appeal against such an order was identified.

[353] More specifically, 135 actions were fully successful and 127 were partially successful.

[354] A similar drop can also be observed in the aggregate data regarding all direct actions before the EGC (excluding intellectual property cases and staff cases) closed by a judgment: from about 40% in 2014 to about 22.8% in 2018. EGC, 'Affaires clôturées – Sens de la décision' (versions 2014–2018, internal documents received by emails of 15.2.2018 and 21.4.2020, requests 4/2018D, 2-5/2020D).

[355] As concerns the aggregate data relating to all direct actions before the EGC, in 2019 the rate of success rose again to 38.3%. Ibid.

amounted to 23 per cent,[356] which means that the appeal proceedings have a considerable impact on the overall annulment proceedings' outcomes.[357]

Figure 4.2 Rate of successful actions for annulment brought by private applicants and settled by the EU Courts with a definitive ruling between 2014 and 2018 (% of admissible actions) in different policy fields

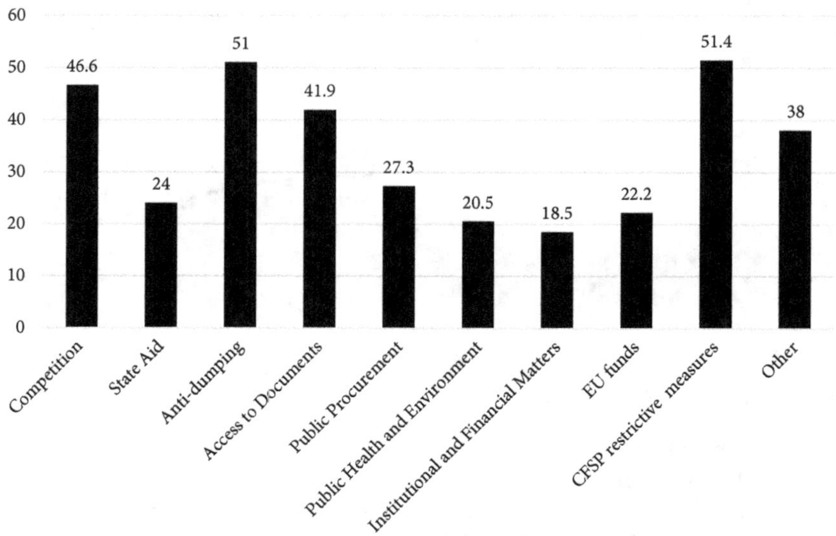

Figure 4.2 demonstrates the rate of successful cases per policy field. One of the highest rates of successful cases characterised the area of CFSP restrictive measures (individual asset freezing).[358] The general concern in this area is that restrictive measures may be imposed upon the individuals by the Council and the Commission, in the implementation of UN Security Council decisions, despite

[356] This rate relates to all appeals recorded in the dataset, including subsequent appeals in cases referred back to the EGC. As mentioned above, the unsuccessful appeals from EGC orders declaring the action as *manifestly* bound to fail were *not* considered. Cross-appeals and parallel appeals against the same EGC ruling were not recorded separately.

[357] Not only by changing the overall outcome, but also, for instance, by requesting the EGC to examine or re-examine some additional aspects of the case. The aggregate rate of at least partially successful appeals for all types of appeals closed in 2014–18 (a broader and, temporally, somewhat different dataset) is slightly lower: 17.3%. Calculated based on ECJ (n 265), 133 (excluding 'appeals removed from the register/no need to give a decision'). It could be added that, on average, 20–27% of all challengeable EGC rulings issued in 2014–18 were appealed each year before the ECJ. This rate was visibly higher in State aid (19–41%) and competition cases (29–60%), and lower in intellectual property cases (16–23%). EGC, 'Décisions du Tribunal ayant fait l'objet d'un pourvoi devant la Cour de justice' (31.12.2019, internal document received on 21.4.2020, request 2-5/2020D).

[358] An even higher rate of success was recorded with regard to the Economic and Monetary Union (EMU) (mostly, the supervisory decisions of the ECB). However, the number of cases was low, and the successful cases formed a series relating to the same subject matter.

weak evidence.[359] As regards the cases concerning EU internal policies, the highest rate of successful actions was observed in anti-dumping and competition law cases; the fields in which scholars and litigators have been most vocal about their expectations of thorough judicial review, in which large corporations can afford costly litigation, and in which the EGC judges and their supporting staff have, arguably, gained extensive expertise. A lower rate characterised State aid cases. This lower rate may testify to a somewhat more deferential attitude of the EU Courts to the Commission's assessments regarding the fairness of domestic tax arrangements.

A distinctly lower rate of successful actions was also observed in cases which often raise empirically complex and uncertain questions – those relating to public health (the regulation of pharmaceuticals, pesticides or chemical substances) and the environment (for instance, the CO_2 emissions trading scheme). In contrast, in access-to-documents cases, which do not raise complex empirical issues, the success rate was higher. In public procurement cases, which are usually not considered empirically problematic, the success rate was moderate. There are some factors pertaining to the latter field's specificity, which might explain a somewhat lower than average rate of successful cases, such as high litigiousness of companies regularly applying to provide services to the EU institutions and bodies. As repeat players, these companies are prepared to litigate even in cases in which they have low chances of success.

No significant difference was observed concerning the rate of successful actions against individual decisions, decisions formally addressed to Member States (but challenged by private parties) and regulations of general application, mostly implementing ones, many of which were 'hybrid' acts (ie of individual application to specific applicants).

The ECJ reviewed in the examined period a considerable number of legal acts of general application in response to validity references from domestic courts. Through a search of characteristic expressions in the operative part and motives of the ECJ rulings,[360] 82 validity rulings under Article 267 TFEU were identified in the examined period.[361] As many as 91.4 per cent related to legal acts of general applications. 36.6 per cent related to legislative acts (instances of the 'constitutional' review of legislation), and 54.9 per cent to implementing and other regulatory acts

[359] Christina Eckes, 'EU Restrictive Measures Against Natural and Legal Persons: From Counterterrorist to Third Country Sanctions' (2014) 51 *Common Market Law Review* 869.

[360] These expressions included a word 'validity', 'invalid' and the like, or 'consideration of the question referred has disclosed nothing to affect the validity …'. I am grateful to Stein Arne Brekke for his help in this regard.

[361] Some preliminary references which formally concern interpretation of legal acts may in fact relate to their validity. The identification of such 'hidden' validity references requires subjective assessment and may prove controversial. Hence, the 'hidden' validity references were not considered. A perfect example is the ruling in Case C-62/14, *Gauweiler*, which was framed as *the interpretation of the ECB Statute* but in fact related to *the validity of the ECB press release* announcing its Outright Monetary Transactions programme.

(instances of the judicial review of executive rule-making). The overall rate of at least partially successful validity challenges was 22 per cent; and more specifically, 37.8 per cent regarding regulatory (non-legislative) acts and only 6.6 per cent regarding legislative acts (two cases).[362] It may therefore seem that legislative acts enjoy a strong presumption of 'constitutionality'.[363]

III. Restrictive Access and the Court's Administrative-Economic Profile

A. Litigants and Cases

The extent to which judicial review fulfils its instrumental and deliberative goals depends on its accessibility. The applicants offer reasoned arguments and useful data which inform the review process. The accessibility of judicial review hinges upon a myriad of formal and technical issues. Unlike at the domestic level, the EU judicial review is not limited by court fees. On the contrary, an important hindrance has turned out to be the duty to be represented by an 'independent lawyer'.[364] A duty to deliver written pleadings to the EU Courts' headquarter in Luxembourg also caused practical problems.[365]

The main cause of concern for many lawyers and scholars has always been the restrictive admissibility criteria of annulment actions for private parties. As discussed in Chapter 2, the EU Courts' gates are open to the intended addressees of individual administrative decisions or 'hybrid' regulations, who tend to be

[362] However, the distinction between validity and interpretation references being blurred, the ECJ may address doubts as to the 'Euro-constitutionality' of EU legislative acts by indirectly providing their 'pro-constitutional' interpretation, not necessarily by declaring them invalid. The ECJ enjoys procedural freedom to reformulate the questions obtained from the domestic courts and may decide if its ruling should be framed as providing interpretation or assessing validity. See Case C-516/16, *Erzeugerorganisation Tiefkühlgemüse*, ECLI:EU:C:2017:1011.

[363] Objections of illegality against basic acts under Article 277 TFEU did not play a significant role in the examined period.

[364] This concept rules out representation by an in-house lawyer or a lawyer in a permanent employment relationship with the applicant. Well established in France but unknown in many Member States, this concept causes confusion. See below n 450. Not explicitly provided for in the Statute of EU Courts or their Rules of Procedure, it leads to a number of actions being rejected on this formal ground.

[365] In some States, court pleadings are considered to be delivered when submitted at a public post office. The EU Courts applied double standards: they considered their own documents delivered to their addressees when submitted at a post office, but the applicants' pleadings were considered submitted only when *physically* delivered to the EU Courts' headquarters. See Case C-138/14 P, *Faktor i Gęsina v Commission*, ECLI:EU:C:2014:2256, paras 17–27.

individual economic operators. The gates remain closed to trade unions, consumer associations and other social actors, or public interest organisations, wishing to challenge EU institutions and bodies' substantive policy choices.

Figure 4.3 Types of private applicants in admissible annulment actions closed by the EU Courts with a definitive judgment in 2014–18 (% of admissible actions)

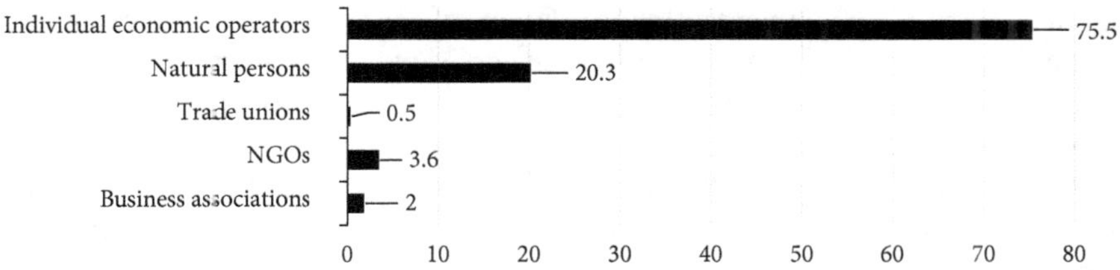

Figure 4.3 demonstrates how many cases were brought by different categories of applicants. In the examined period, as expected, the EU Courts dealt mostly with individual administrative decisions and 'hybrid' regulations challenged by individual economic operators. Almost 90 per cent of the applicants in the cases declared admissible[366] were the intended addressees of the challenged acts, ie persons formally indicated as the addressees, or whose individual situation was explicitly considered in the adoption process. In 66.5 per cent of admissible cases the applicants were individual economic operators intended as the addressees of contested acts, and only in 9 per cent of cases were the economic operators not the intended addressees of contested acts but, rather, the latter's market competitors, who nonetheless managed to satisfy the strict criteria of direct and individual concern. Admissible cases brought by individual economic operators concerned mostly competition law decisions (31.5% of this cluster), State aid decisions (13.9%), anti-dumping acts (9.8%), public procurement decisions (10%) and CFSP restrictive measures (12%).[367] Conversely, the actions by public interest organisations were mainly confined to cases regarding access to documents and grants awarded by EU institutions and bodies.[368] Actions by natural

[366] As to the design of the dataset see above (n 347ff).

[367] Only a few admissible actions were lodged by business associations representing small and medium-size operators, Cases T-140/13, *Netherlands Maritime Technology Association v Commission*, ECLI:EU:T:2014:1029. T-49/14, *Zentralverband des Deutschen Bäckerhandwerks v Commission*, ECLI EU:T:2015:755. T-623/13, *Unión de Almacenistas de Hierros de España v Commission*, ECLI:EU:T:2015:268. T-342/11, *CEEES and Asociación de Gestores de Estaciones de Servicio v Commission*, ECLI:EU:T:2014:60.

[368] A few cases were also brought by universities or research institutes relating to the award of grants.

persons mainly concerned CFSP restrictive measures. Likewise, the number of 'class actions' by associations of smaller and medium-size economic operators[369] and trade unions[370] was marginal.

Only 16 cases were identified in which the applicants successfully invoked the new Lisbon admissibility scenario. In practice, this new scenario turned out to be serving mostly individual economic operators, or industry associations,[371] contesting the Commission's implementing regulations of general application (including non-hybrid acts), which imposed upon the applicants directly applicable obligations or restrictions (for instance, the manufacturing or marketing of chemical substances[372]), or immediately modified their rights (in cases regarding State aid general schemes[373] or agricultural policy[374]). Therefore, the third admissibility scenario did not improve the possibility of bringing class actions or carrying out public interest litigation.[375]

Two-thirds of actions declared as inadmissible, following a written procedure,[376] were lodged by persons other than the intended addressees of impugned acts; most often, by individual economic operators.[377] In most cases, the unsuccessful applicants failed to meet the criterion of direct and individual concern to contest a decision conferring benefits upon their competitors, or they directed their actions against legal acts that needed national implementing measures. Therefore, the admissibility criteria still constitute a significant obstacle to private parties seeking legal protection against EU institutions and bodies. Occasionally, the unsuccessful applicants directed their actions against bodies not considered EU bodies or they designated a wrong defendant or missed the deadline. Interestingly, almost one-third of inadmissible cases were directed against acts not considered by the EU Courts as challengeable (letters, communications, preparatory measures), which suggests that the concept of 'acts producing legal effects' does not in practice encompass all the categories of EU measures by which private parties may subjectively consider themselves to be adversely affected.

[369] For instance, Case T-134/10, *FESI v Council*, ECLI:EU:T:2014:143.

[370] The actions brought by trade unions were rather specific as the trade unions in question represented the civil servants of EU authorities and challenged, on procedural grounds only, new EU civil service legislation. Cases T-456/14, *TAO-AFI and SFIE-PE v Parliament & Council*, ECLI:EU:T:2016:493. T-17/14, *U4U et al v Parliament & Council*, ECLI:EU:T:2016:489. T-713/14, *IPSO v ECB*, ECLI:EU:T:2016:727.

[371] Joined Cases T-454/10 and T-482/11, *ANICAV and AGRUCON v Commission*, ECLI:EU:T:2013:282.

[372] For instance, Case T-134/13, *Polynt and Sitre v ECHA*, ECLI:EU:T:2015:254.

[373] For instance, Case T-219/13, *Ferraci v Commission*, ECLI:EU:T:2016:485.

[374] For instance, Case T-397/13, *Tilly-Sabco v Commission*, ECLI:EU:T:2016:8.

[375] A few public interest organisations in the examined period tried to break through the admissibility criteria, without any success.

[376] As mentioned above, actions immediately rejected prior to a written procedure as manifestly bound to fail under Articles 126 and 129 RPGC were not considered.

[377] This number does not include cases rejected as manifestly bound to fail.

Figure 4.4 The types of challenged acts in admissible action for annulment closed by the EU Courts with a definitive ruling in 2014–18 (% of admissible actions)

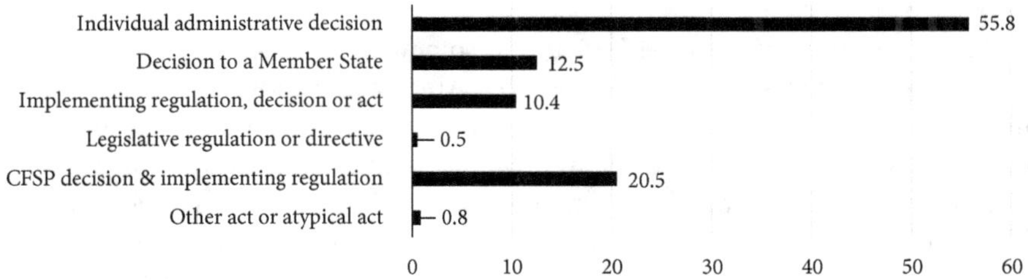

Figure 4.4 demonstrates the categories of contested acts in admissible cases. The admissible annulment actions by private parties were mostly brought against individual administrative decisions, and much less often against decisions formally addressed to Member States (in State aid and some environmental cases), as well as implementing regulations, directives or general decisions, some of which nonetheless constituted so-called 'hybrid' acts (akin to individual administrative decisions). Many actions were brought against acts imposing restrictive measures governed by the specific CFSP legal regime. Only two cases were successfully brought against legislative acts, but in rather specific circumstances.[378] Rarely did the EU Courts engage with legislative acts at the request of private parties in response to incidental Article 277 TFEU objections of illegality.[379]

In the examined period, a few economic operators unsuccessfully tried to break through the well-established restrictive interpretation of access rules and challenge legislative acts regarding the new rules on the safety of plant breeding,[380] conservation of fish stocks[381] and mutual recognition of professional qualifications.[382] One should also note a high number of rejected actions concerning regulatory acts of general application, especially implementing regulations (23.3% of

[378] These cases were particular because the actions were brought by unions of EU civil servants in order to enforce their right to be consulted on amendments to legislative regulations pertaining to the EU civil service. On top of that, another case was declared admissible against the Council regulation regarding the Common Customs Tariff, based directly on the Treaties, and thus occupying a rank equivalent to a legislative act.

[379] Case T-296/12, *The Health Food Manufacturers' Association et al v Commission*, ECLI:EU:T:2015:375, 175–98.

[380] Case T-560/14 (order of 18.05.2015), *ABZ et al v Parliament & Council*, ECLI:EU:T:2015:314. Case T-559/14 (order of 18.05.015), *Ackermann Saatzucht et al v Parliament & Council*, ECLI:EU:T:2015:315 (on appeal, Joined Cases C-408/15 P and C-409/15 P, *Ackermann Saatzucht et al v Parliament and Council*, ECLI:EU:C:2016:893).

[381] Case T-121/10 (order of 26.03.2015), *Conte et al v Council*, ECLI:EU:T:2015:196.

[382] Case T-185/14 (order of 7.01.2015), *Freitas v Parliament & Council*, ECLI:EU:T:2015:14.

inadmissible actions), as well as atypical acts (33.8% of inadmissible actions), such as, for instance, interpretive competition law guidelines[383] or a declaration of the Eurogroup.[384]

Access to justice before the EU Courts is somewhat widened by the procedure for validity references from national courts. Among 82 validity references identified in the examined period,[385] the vast majority were made in the context of disputes opposing individual economic operators and administrative authorities regarding adopted or planned decisions or general rule-making acts implementing EU acts of general application. Some were also made in the context of domestic constitutional review, or civil or labour disputes. In only 7.3 per cent of these cases did the preliminary reference procedure allow an NGO or a civil society member to challenge before the ECJ an EU act of general application.[386] In more than 70 per cent of cases the beneficiaries of this procedure were individual economic operators. However, as many as 37.8 per cent of references were directed against legislative acts, and 54.9 per cent against regulatory acts, which confirms that the validity reference procedure is mainly open to challenges against EU acts of general application, unlike the annulment proceedings by private parties.

Can rejected direct actions against acts of general application come back via the validity reference procedure? The available data do not provide a clear answer. The number of rejected direct actions and admissible references contesting legislative acts is similar. However, there may still be a large number of general acts, raising constitutional and legal controversies, that do not come before the ECJ due to a lack of domestic legal avenues or national judges' unwillingness to make references.

Through the restrictive admissibility criteria, overall, the EU Courts limited their role – as regards the direct engagement with private parties – to that of a two-instance administrative court, dealing with the legality of individual administrative

[383] Case T-694/14 (order of 23.11.2015), *EREF v Commission*, ECLI:EU:T:2015:915.

[384] Case T-330/13 (order of 16.10.2014), *Chatziioannou v Commission & ECB*, ECLI:EU:T:2014:904. Many actions were rejected as directed against acts of a contractual nature. In such cases, in other words, the applicants chose the wrong procedure (the action for annulment instead of arbitration clause). See, for instance, Cases T-134/12, *Investigación y Desarrollo v Commission*, ECLI:EU:T:2014:31 (Case C-102/14 P, *Investigación y Desarrollo v Commission*, ECLI:EU:C:2016:737) and T-314/14, *Borde and Carbonium v Commission*, ECLI:EU:T:2015:197 (Case C-279/15 P, *Borde and Carbonium v Commission*, ECLI:EU:C:2016:297).

[385] These references were identified through characteristic expressions used in the operative parts of the rulings by means of the search engine at curia.europa.eu. Inadmissible references were not considered.

[386] Case C-362/14, *Schrems*, ECLI:EU:C:2015:650. Joined Cases C-293/12 and C-594/12, *Digital Rights Ireland and Seitlinger et al*, ECLI:EU:C:2014:238. Case C-444/15, *Associazione Italia Nostra Onlus*, ECLI:EU:C:2016:978. In one case, the national proceedings that led to a validity reference had been brought by a professional association of lawyers (Case C-543/14, *Ordre des barreaux francophones and germanophone et al*, ECLI:EU:C:2016:605). In another case, the national proceedings were brought by a group of citizens adversely affected by EU austerity measures (Case C-526/14, *Kotnik et al*, ECLI:EU:C:2016:570).

decisions. A popular narrative tends to portray the ECJ as the constitutional court of the EU. However, the EU Courts infrequently perform the 'constitutional' review of EU legislative acts at the request of private parties.

Another characteristic feature of the EU judicial review is the economic profile of applicants in annulment proceedings, at least as far as legal acts embodying and implementing EU internal policies are concerned. The applicants' profile determines the types of legal claims and arguments that the EU Courts are confronted with. In their actions, economic operators usually allege breaches of those legal norms that protect their private interests. They are less likely to allege that an EU authority has been insufficiently protective of a public interest, such as public health, animal welfare or the environment. A certain number of legal acts that could otherwise be deemed in breach of some legally protected public interests may never reach the EU Courts due to the lack of an interested and authorised applicant representing the public interest.[387]

B. Third-Party Intervention

A separate set of admissibility criteria applies to the right of third parties to intervene in pending annulment proceedings. The intervention allows third parties affected by the prospective ruling to seek protection of their interests. From the instrumentalist perspective, interveners may offer to the judges potentially useful empirical data or legal arguments. From the deliberative perspective, the intervention may play a crucial role in broadening the access to the judicial forum on which essential matters of public policy and discretionary choices are discussed. It is important to note, in this respect, that the EU Courts do not accept *amici curiae* briefs – less formalised forms of public participation in judicial proceedings by civil society members. Therefore, access to intervention is all the more important due to the character of many EU legal acts subject to judicial review. Even if such acts are formally of individual application to specific operators, they tend to affect third parties and society.

The intervention does not grant the same procedural rights as the applicant's status; it is limited to supporting or opposing the remedy sought and pleas in law formulated by one of the parties. Interveners cannot widen the subject matter of the dispute but only advance new arguments which amplify the pleas already raised by the parties.[388] The intervention still offers ample opportunities to influence the

[387] Take, for instance, Case T-673/13, *European Coalition to End Animal Experiments v ECHA*, ECLI:EU:T:2015:167 in which an NGO for animal welfare had no standing before the EU Courts to claim that the ECHA, in its decision-making practice concerning the testing of chemicals on animals, was insufficiently protective of animal welfare, even though it was one of the public interests explicitly protected by the applicable legislation.

[388] For instance, Joined Cases T-394/08, T-408/08, T-453/08 and T-454/08, *Regione autonoma della Sardegna et al v Commission*, ECLI:EU:T:2011:493, paras 42–43. Joined Cases C-471-473/09 P, *Diputación Foral de Vizcaya et al v Commission*, ECLI:EU:C:2011:521, paras 109–11, 117–19.

outcome of annulment proceedings. Interveners receive the non-confidential versions of written submissions of the main parties, they can submit their own submissions and participate in the oral hearing.[389] Simultaneously, however, intervention may significantly increase the time and cost of proceedings as it requires preparation of non-confidential versions of the main parties' submissions.[390]

In interpreting the scope of the right to intervene, the EU Courts balance the instrumental and deliberative gains and drawbacks for procedural economy. Pursuant to the Statute of the EU Courts, any person establishing an *interest* in the result of a case may intervene in that case.[391] What constitutes sufficient 'interest' is indeterminate, leading to 'casuistic case law, which is not free of contradictions'.[392] The criteria for intervention are nonetheless more lenient than those for lodging the action for annulment. A person may be admitted as an intervener if she establishes that her *legal position* or *economic situation* may be *directly* affected by the ruling's operative part. Notably, an intervener cannot merely rely on being in a similar position to the main applicant[393] or having an interest in pleading before the EU judicature in favour of expounding case law principles from which it could hypothetically benefit in the future.[394]

In principle, the scope of potential interveners extends to those who fulfil admissibility criteria to lodge an independent action,[395] as well as their market competitors[396] but not necessarily business partners.[397] Industry associations may be admitted as interveners, given instrumental and procedural economy gains

[389] Interventions by private parties are allowed only in proceedings initiated by private applicants. Case C-40/10, *Commission v Council*, ECLI:EU:C:2010:713.

[390] Par G Muguet-Pullennec and Daniele P Domenicucci, 'L'intervention devant le Tribunal après l'entrée en vigueur du nouveau règlement de procédure: entre droit d'ingérence et urgence judiciaire' (2015) *Revue Lamy de La Concurrence* 61, at 62.

[391] Article 40 of the Statute. Intervention in preliminary reference procedures is governed by national procedural laws. See Case C-61/14, *Orizzonte Salute*, ECLI:EU:C:2015:655, paras 32–39.

[392] Barents (n 3), 498. The incoherence in the case law may stem from the fact that applications for intervention are not examined collegially but by a single judge – the Presidents or Vice-presidents of the EGC and the ECJ.

[393] Case T-370/08 (order of 24.03.2011), *Csepeli Áramtermelő v Commission*, ECLI:EU:T:2011:116, para 12.

[394] For instance, Case T-310/18, *EPSU and Goudriaan v Commission*, ECLI:EU:T:2019:757.

[395] For instance, Case T-587/08 (order of 17.02.2010), *Fresh Del Monte Produce v Commission*, ECLI:EU:T:2010:42. These may be also non-economic operators, Case 410/15 P(I) (order of 6.10.2015), *Comité d'entreprise de la SNCM v Commission*, ECLI:EU:C:2015:669, paras 4–6, 10–11.

[396] Case T-210/01, *General Electric v Commission*, ECLI:EU:T:2005:456, paras 28–29. Case T-201/04 R (order of 22.12.2004), *Microsoft v Commission*, ECLI:EU:T:2004:372, para 91. Case T-119/09 (order of 12.1.2010), *Protégé International v Commission*, ECLI:EU:T:2010:9, para 8. Case C-385/07 P (order of 21.2.2008), *Duales System Deutschland v Commission*, ECLI:EU:C:2008:114. Case T-54/07 (order of 21.1.2011), *Vitesse Networks v Commission*, ECLI:EU:T:2011:15. Joined Cases T-415/05, T-416/05 and T-423/05, *Greece et al v Commission*, ECLI:EU:T:2010:386.

[397] Case C-362/15 P(I) (order of 06.10.2015), *Etairia Larymnis Larko Larko v Commission*, ECLI:EU:C:2015:682, paras 19–20. See also Case C-589/11 P(I) (order of 8.6.2012), *Schenker v Air France and Commission*, ECLI:EU:C:2012:332, paras 14–15. Case C-33/14 P (order of 27.2.2015), *Mory et al v Commission*, ECLI:EU:C:2015:135, paras 4 and 11.

(avoiding multiple individual interventions).[398] The condition is that they represent an appreciable number of undertakings active in the sector concerned and that the case raises questions of principle affecting the functioning of the sector concerned. Conversely, trade unions are unlikely to be admitted in a case concerning related employer companies. Their interest in such cases has been deemed 'only indirect and hypothetical' as there is no certainty what effect a decision addressed to an employer will have on its employees' welfare.[399] The EGC held that a trade union willing to intervene should prove the causal link between the challenged act and deterioration of workers' situations, which seems in practice nigh on impossible.[400]

Surprisingly, the EU Courts admitted interventions from public interest organisations, when the subject matter and the territory of their activity corresponded to the subject matter of the case, especially when they had been involved in protection programmes or studies relating to the region and sector concerned. For instance, in joined cases concerning restrictive measures against members of the Iranian regime, the EGC examined several reports and publications on human rights violations in Iran issued by the organisation applying to intervene.[401] The EGC adopted a similarly lenient approach to applications of environmental organisations. Prior submission of a scientific study concerning a risky chemical substance or prior involvement in relevant administrative proceedings were enough to establish an interest in cases pertaining to these substances.[402]

Most recently, the ECJ approach to intervention evolved. On the one hand, not long ago the ECJ succinctly rejected an application to intervene made by an animal welfare organisation in proceedings concerning a decision by the ECHA in which the latter requested a chemical operator to conduct chemical

[398] Case T-37/04 R (order of 7.7.2004), *Autonomous Region of the Azores v Council*, ECLI:EU:T:2004:215, paras 57–71. Case T-245/11 (order of 18.10.2012), *Client Earth and International Chemical Secretariat v ECHA*, ECLI:EU:T:2012:557, para 12. Some economic associations may also promote environmental goals. Case T-694/18 (order of 7.5.2020), *DEI v Commission*, ECLI:EU:T:2020:211, paras 25–35.

[399] Case T-360/13 (order of 4.3.2014), *VECCO v Commission*, ECLI:EU:T:2014:130, paras 24–26 and the case law cited. Case C-418/15 P(I) (order of 6.10.2015 concerning *CAP Actions SNCM*), *SNCM v Commission*, ECLI:EU:C:2015:671, paras 17–22. A trade union may, however, intervene in proceedings concerning a decision which affects the trade union's procedural rights. Such a situation occurs, for instance, in the case of a Commission decision not to open a formal State aid investigation in which trade unions may participate as interested parties, Case C-410/15 P(I) (order of 6.10.2015 concerning *Comité d'entreprise de la SNCM*), *SNCM v Commission*, ECLI:EU:C:2015:669.

[400] The latter condition has not been fulfilled in the case at hand, Case T-385/12 (order of 16.9.13), *Orange v Commission*, ECLI:EU:T:2013:504, paras 28–38.

[401] Case T-273/13 (order of 25.3.2015), *Sarafraz v Council*, ECLI:EU:T:2015:243. Case T-274/13 (order of 25.3.2015), *Emadi v Council*, ECLI:EU:T:2015:202.

[402] Case T-636/17 (order of 5.3.2018), *PlasticsEurope v ECHA*, ECLI:EU:T:2018:154. Case T-429/13 (order of 21.10.2014), *Bayer CropScience v Commission*, ECLI:EU:T:2014:920, paras 73–99. See also Case T-57/11 (order of 6.11.12), *Castelnou v Commission*, ECLI:EU:T:2012:580, para 83. Case C-175/19 P (order of 22.10.2019), *Stena Line Scandinavia v Commission*, ECLI:EU:C:2019:1095, paras 57–58. It is, however, up to the applicant to intervene to prove its prior involvement in a given sector. See Case T-125/17 (order of 12.12.2017), *BASF v ECHA*, ECLI:EU:T:2017:931, para 24.

tests on animals. The ECJ stated that 'the fact that [the organisation] protects the interests of animals is not sufficient alone to show how its legal situation, or that of its members, would be affected by the Court's decision'.[403] On the other hand, in more recent cases concerning a regulation limiting the use of some specific pesticides harmful to bees and the tests on animals of a potentially dangerous chemical substance, the ECJ applied its test for interventions in a distinctively lenient way. It contented itself with finding that one of the applicants to intervene was campaigning against *all* pesticides harmful to bees, and the other one was generally active in campaigning against animal testing in the context of EU chemical regulation. Unlike its usual practice, it did not request proof that these organisations had been involved in protection programmes or studies relating to the *specific pesticides* concerned by the impugned regulation.[404] The EGC later adopted a similar approach.[405]

However, in the examined period the intervention procedure does not in practice have the effect of broadening access to justice before the EU Courts, at least from the perspective of independent public interest representation before the EU Courts. Interventions in annulment proceedings brought by private applicants were relatively rare. Interveners were allowed to support the applicant or the defendant at some point of proceedings in 120 cases (including some that were ultimately declared inadmissible), ie 15 per cent of all cases. As many as 70 per cent of all admissible interventions were made by economic operators (such as market competitors of the applicants) and 24 per cent by business associations. Only seven admissible applications for intervention came from social actors, such as a consumer association in a case regarding health claims on food products, or an environmental organisation in a case regarding State aid to energy infrastructure.[406]

IV. The Value and Cost of Procedural Activity

A. The Guiding Values of EU Procedural Law

The instrumental and deliberative performance of judicial review is relative, last but not least, to the activity of the adjudicators and the parties in the course of

[403] Case C-565/17 P(R) (order of 28.5.2018), *BASF v ECHA*, ECLI:EU:C:2018:340, para 37.

[404] Case C-499/18 P (order of 7.2.2019), *Bayer CropScience v Commission*, ECLI:EU:C:2019:107. Case C-471/18 P (order of 12.3.2019), *Esso Raffinage v ECHA*, ECLI:EU:C:2019:198, para 27.

[405] Case T-636/19 (order of 15.6.2020), *Chemours Netherlands v ECHA*, ECLI:EU:T:2020:276, paras 34–40.

[406] Case T-274/13 (order of 25.3.2015), *Emadi v Council*, ECLI:EU:T:2015:202. Case T-273/13 (order of 25.3.2015), *Sarafraz v Council*, ECLI:EU:T:2015:243. Case T-296/12 (order of 4.9.2014), *Health Food Manufacturers' Association et al v Commission*, ECLI:EU:T:2014:783. Case T-57/11 (order of 6.11.2012), *Castelnou Energía v Commission*, ECLI:EU:T:2012:582.

review proceedings. By advancing legal arguments and adducing evidence, the adjudicators and the parties influence the final rulings, whereas opportunities for open and reasoned deliberation provide the affected parties with moral reasons to perceive the rulings as binding sources of legitimate authority.[407] Moreover, the parties' activity during the proceedings has a significant impact on the technique and thoroughness of review.

Procedural law frames the activity of the adjudicators and the parties in the process of judicial review. It is much more than a set of discrete, technical and value-neutral arrangements. Quite the contrary, its role is to secure crucial legitimacy assets of courts and judicial review processes. It expresses a fundamental and essentially political choice regarding the right balance between judicial review's opposing goals: accuracy, deliberation and procedural economy. Hence, in continental Europe, procedural law is usually enacted as parliamentary legislation,[408] even though different actors claiming specialist expertise such as judges, litigators or legal scholars may be involved in the drafting process.

EU procedural law[409] is scattered among sundry primary and secondary sources. However, the EU judicature retains control over its creation and application. First of all, the EU judicature dictates the interpretation of Treaty provisions relating to its own powers.[410] Moreover, the ECJ has the right to propose amendments to the Statute of EU Courts, a protocol attached to the Treaties[411] that can be modified via the ordinary legislative procedure.[412] In practice, the ECJ has a considerable impact on the amendment process.[413] Furthermore, the ECJ and the EGC adopt their own rules of procedure, which concretise the parties' procedural rights and obligations (RPCJ and RPGC, respectively).[414] While the rules of procedure require approval by the Council,[415] the Council mostly seems

[407] Solum (n 31), 181.

[408] Jean-Paul Keppenne, 'Les procédures de révision du cadre réglementaire des juridictions de l'Union' (2017) *Cahiers de Droit Européen* 343.

[409] Lenaerts and others (n 3), vii. These authors define EU procedural law as that which sets out the remedies and mechanisms available to enforce EU law in the EU Courts to obtain judicial protection against unlawful action on the part of EU institutions and bodies.

[410] Article 47 of the EU Charter of Fundamental Rights, Article 19 TEU and Articles 251–84 TFEU.

[411] Protocol no 3 to the Treaties on the Statute of the Court of Justice of the European Union.

[412] Article 281 TFEU.

[413] Laurent Coutron, 'The Changes to the General Court' in Emmanuel Guinchard and Marie-Pierre Granger (eds), *The New EU Judiciary: An Analysis of Current Judicial Reforms* (Wolters Kluwer 2018). However, the Commission and the Council opposed the ECJ's proposal for an amendment of the Statute that would transfer jurisdiction in infringement proceedings to the EGC. They highlighted the need to await assessment of the EGC enlargement in late 2020. Commission, 'Opinion on the draft amendments to Protocol No 3 on the Statute of the Court of Justice of the European Union, presented by the Court of Justice on 26 March 2018' (COM(2018) 534 final). ECJ, 'Draft Amendment to Protocol No 3 on the Statute of the Court of Justice of the European Union – Letter of the President of the Court of Justice' (Council doc. 11180/18).

[414] Rules of Procedure of the General Court [2015] OJ L105/1 (as amended). Rules of Procedure of the Court of Justice [2012] OJ L265 (as amended).

[415] Article 253(6) TFEU and Article 254(5) TFEU. The draft of the RPGC must be approved by the ECJ, Article 254(5) TFEU.

to follow the EU Courts' proposals.[416] Notably, there are no rules delimiting the scope of matters to be regulated by the Statute and the rules of procedure, respectively. The EU Courts can choose freely in which of the said acts a given matter should be regulated.[417] Finally, there is no external review of fair trial standards applied by the EU Courts.[418] It is the EU Courts that must occasionally rule on the compliance of procedural rules – enacted by the courts themselves – with fundamental rights.[419] The accumulation by the EU judicature of different kinds of power over EU procedural law, predominantly composed of provisions drafted and approved behind closed doors, has given rise to doubts as to its democratic legitimacy.[420]

Various sources suggest that the EU Courts have embraced 'efficiency' as the primary yardstick of their activity. For instance, the reasoning given to back up a major procedural reform of the EGC completed in 2015, which has affected the procedural rights of the parties,[421] was replete with efficiency-related rhetoric: 'maximum effectiveness with minimum resources', 'a significant increase in the number of cases disposed', 'a need for increased judicial productivity', 'heavy budgetary constraints faced by the institution', while not mentioning fair trial equally often.[422] There is also external pressure coming from EU institutions and the Member States.[423] The internal and external pressure to achieve efficiency, coupled with the lack of judicial accountability for EU procedural law and practice, should raise scholarly interest in the critical evaluation of EU procedural law.

The procedural framework of annulment proceedings generally imposes on applicants the burden of adducing persuasive evidence and raising pertinent pleas in law together with supporting argumentation. This is why the parties benefit from several procedural tools for active participation and deliberation: exchanges of written pleadings,[424] an oral hearing,[425] measures of organisation of procedure

[416] Available sources indicate that in the process of approving recent procedural reforms the Council has focussed on selected issues relating to the procedural rights and interests of the Member States. Compare successive versions of the Draft RPCJ, Council doc. 11147/11, 5140/11, 6422/12, 8020/12, and Draft RPGC, Council doc. 7795/14, 15628/14, 16522/14. A Court insider gives assurances, however, about intense scrutiny by the Council, Marc-André Gaudissart, 'La refonte du règlement de procédure de la Cour de Justice' (2012) 48 *Cahiers de Droit Européen* 603.

[417] Keppenne (n 408), 356.

[418] Such a review could be provided by the ECtHR under Article 6 ECHR, following EU accession to the ECHR.

[419] For instance, regarding the prohibition against being represented by an in-house lawyer, Case C-464/16 P, *PITEE v Commission*, ECLI:EU:C:2017:291, paras 10–14 and 23–36. Regarding the obligation to lodge submissions in the EU Courts' headquarters, Case C-478/11 P, *Laurent Gbagbo et al v Council*, ECLI:EU:C:2013:258, para 63. On the possibility to dispense with the oral hearing and optional procedural steps, see Case C-666/16 P, *Lysoform v ECHA*, ECLI:EU:C:2017:569, paras 35–46.

[420] Christina Eckes and Vigjilenca Abazi, 'Closed Evidence in EU Courts: Security, Secrets and Access to Justice' (2018) 55 *Common Market Law Review* 753.

[421] The second round of written pleadings has become optional and certain procedural time limits have been shortened. EGC, 'Draft RPGC' (Council doc. 7795/14), 6. ECJ, 'Draft RPCJ' (Council doc. 11147/11), 2–3.

[422] EGC (n 421), 5–6.

[423] Krenn (n 266).

[424] Articles 76–83 RPGC. Articles 167–75 RPCJ.

[425] Articles 106–15 RPGC. Articles 76–85 RPCJ.

(eg written questions)[426] or comments on the evidence.[427] However, many of these tools depend on the judges' discretionary appraisal in individual cases, the rules of procedure providing only very general criteria in this respect.[428] In particular, most participation opportunities are curtailed if the case is promptly dismissed as manifestly bound to fail.[429]

The EGC judges may adopt a more active approach to, for instance, steering the deliberation among the parties on crucial points. Conversely, they do not raise new substantive pleas in law if the applicant has failed to raise relevant pleas, and do not collect new evidence on their own motion, which gives the annulment proceedings a distinctly adversarial character. However, the EU Courts are increasingly expected by litigants to scrutinise and autonomously reassess the uncertain empirical and normative assessments in scientifically and technically complex matters. This development may lead to doubts about whether the one-size-fits-all annulment procedural framework, adopted in the early days of European integration, is adequate for the contemporary challenges that the EU judicial review must face.

B. The System of Pleas and Partisan Evidence

An essential characteristic of the annulment procedure – in contrast to, for instance, the preliminary reference procedure – is that it is governed by what Barents has called a 'system of pleas'.[430] The system of pleas seeks to strike a fair balance between the process values related to the parties' participation and procedural economy.[431] According to Article 21 of the Statute of the EU Courts, an initial application for annulment must contain a brief statement of the pleas in law against the impugned act and the relevant evidence.[432] In its early days, the EU judicature derived the conclusion from this provision that – in principle – it is not competent to raise new pleas in law on its own motion in the course of proceedings (*ne ultra petita*).[433] The subject matter and limits of the dispute should be set from the outset by the initial application, in the interests of obtaining legal certainty for the litigants and any affected third parties.[434] The applicant cannot raise new pleas,

[426] Articles 89–90 RPGC. Articles 61–62 RPCJ.

[427] Articles 91ff RPGC. Articles 63ff RPCJ.

[428] The data do not cover intellectual property cases (mostly regarding trademarks), which are governed by a distinct procedural regime. Articles 171ff RPGC.

[429] Article 126 RPGC. Article 180 RPCJ.

[430] Barents (n 253).

[431] Case C-122/16 P, *British Airways v Commission*, ECLI:EU:C:2017:861, paras 86–87 and 89. Case C-272/09 P, *KME et al v Commission*, ECLI:EU:C:2011:810, para 102.

[432] A plea in law is an allegation that a contested act or conduct on the part of the institution constitutes an infringement of a legal norm. Barents (n 3), 618.

[433] Joined Cases 46 and 47/59, *Meroni v High Authority*, ECLI:EU:C:1962:44.

[434] Case C-272/12 P, *Commission v Ireland et al*, ECLI:EU:C:2013:812, paras 27–29. Case C-122/16 P, *British Airways v Commission*, ECLI:EU:C:2017:861, para 84.

or offer or demand new evidence at a later stage of the procedure, save in exceptional circumstances.[435]

The system of pleas does not reduce the role of EU Courts to passive observers of proceedings. The EU Courts are not bound by *specific argumentation* advanced by the parties in support of their pleas.[436] The EU judicature can, exceptionally, raise a 'plea relating to public policy' on its own motion. As has been explained by AG Jacobs, this judge-made concept assumes that certain pleas relate to fundamental values of the EU legal order, the interests of third parties and the general public rather those of only the persons directly concerned.[437] This concept encompasses pleas relating to the competence to adopt the impugned act[438] and essential procedural requirements,[439] eg motivation[440] and adoption rules.[441] Legal norms setting out competences and essential procedural requirements are believed to warrant legal certainty and observance of the principle of conferral. In contrast, pleas relating to breaches of ordinary procedural requirements, the misuse of powers and especially breaches of any substantive norms are not considered to relate to public policy. The EU judicature would seem to be cautious about broadening the catalogue of pleas relating to public policy, hesitating especially about the status of the right to be heard within administrative proceedings and the rights of defence.[442]

The system of pleas is complemented by the 'adversarial principle', according to which the EU judicature may consider only those procedural items made available to the parties' representatives and on which they have been allowed to express their views.[443] This principle is enforced strictly and must be applied even if the EU judicature raises a plea relating to public policy on its own motion.[444]

The system of pleas and the adversarial principle are often seen as a 'tandem' securing fair and efficient proceedings. The former obliges the parties to put 'all

[435] Pursuant to Article 84 RPGC, a new plea may be raised if it is based on facts that have come to light in the course of the proceedings. Pursuant to Article 85(2) and (3) RPGC, parties may produce or offer further evidence in the course of the proceedings provided that the delay in the submission of new evidence is justified.

[436] Case T-586/14, *Xinyi v Commission*, ECLI:EU:T:2016:154, paras 29–35 and the case law cited.

[437] Opinion of AG Jacobs, Case C-210/98 P, *Salzgitter v Commission*, ECLI:EU:C:2000:172, paras 141–42.

[438] For instance, Case T-676/13, *Italian International Film v EACEA*, ECLI:EU:T:2016:62, para 40.

[439] Case C-325/91, *France v Commission*, ECLI:EU:C:1993:245, para 26.

[440] Case C-415/14 P, *Quimitecnica.com and de Mello v Commission*, ECLI:EU:C:2016:58, para 57.

[441] Case T-284/08, *PMOI v Council*, ECLI:EU:T:2008:550, paras 25–27.

[442] The ECJ held that the breach of procedural rights did not relate to public policy, Case C-421/11 P (order of 7.2.2012), *Total and Elf Aquitaine v Commission*, ECLI:EU:C:2012:60, para 35. See, however, Opinion of AG Bot, Case C-43/15 P, *BSH v EUIPO*, ECLI:EU:C:2016:129. Case T-17/14, *U4U et al v Parliament and Council*, ECLI:EU:T:2016:489, paras 95–96. Case T-456/14, *TAO-AFI et al v Parliament and Council*, ECLI:EU:T:2016:493, paras 151–52. Case T-263/15, *Gdynia and Kossakowo v Commission*, ECLI:EU:T:2017:820, paras 70 and 89. Freya Clausen, *Les moyens d'ordre public devant la Cour de justice de l'Union européenne* (Bruylant 2018).

[443] Articles 65 RPGC and 62 RPCJ. For exceptions, see, Articles 104–05 and, among others, Joined Cases C-584/10 P, C-593/10 P and C-595/10 P, *Commission et al v Kadi*, ECLI:EU:C:2013:518, para 129.

[444] C-89/08 P, *Commission v Ireland*, ECLI:EU:C:2009:742, paras 38–40, 50–57 and 59–61. Arguably, this requirement stems from the case law of the ECtHR, Case 19075/91, *Vermeulen v Belgium*, para 33.

cards on the table' in their initial written submissions, and the latter obliges the judges to give to the parties equal opportunities to express their views. Thus, the risk of protracted proceedings due to a sudden broadening of their subject matter is minimised.[445] In the system of pleas, the judge's role is not in principle to redefine the subject matter of review proceedings – by modifying the remedy sought, by indicating additional legal acts or aspects thereof that should have been challenged or by supplementing the applicant's allegations against the impugned acts.

The system of pleas tends to be portrayed as a value-neutral and 'natural' characteristic of the annulment proceedings, in which the applicant bears the responsibility for its own interests. However, it is not common to the systems of judicial review across the EU. In certain domestic jurisdictions, administrative courts indeed play a more active role, raising on their own motion all relevant pleas in law and actively engaging in fact-finding. The system of pleas adopted in the EU annulment proceedings is just one of several existing models of judicial review proceedings.[446] It had been adopted in the early days of European integration and never fundamentally revised.[447] In those early days, the Court functioned in an emerging legal order without fully fledged public law standards at its disposal. Courts cannot be active in a legal vacuum, ie without specific pre-existing normative standards for their decisions.[448] Moreover, in those early days, the EU judicial review was to serve only powerful transnational corporations.

EU public law standards have been laboriously worked out over the years. The expectations regarding the instrumental and deliberative function of EU judicial review significantly increased. The EU judicial review is now expected to act as a check and balance upon the EU institutions and bodies, especially in the context of contemporary law-, rule- and decision-making, underpinned by epistemically uncertain scientific, technical and political appraisals. Some litigants, especially public interest organisations (if they could trigger judicial review), might not have sufficient resources to produce by themselves enough evidence to refute the presumption of correctness attributed to the empirical basis of EU measures. Finally, the system of pleas is not explicitly laid down in the EU Treaties or other EU procedural law sources. This lack of an unambiguous legal basis has allowed the EU Courts to transplant and creatively develop the concept of pleas relating to public policy.

[445] Koen Lenaerts, 'De quelques principes généraux du droit de la procédure devant le juge communautaire', *Mélanges en hommage à Jean-Victor Louis* (Editions de l'Université de Bruxelles 2003), 245–46. If the applicants were allowed to broaden the subject matter during the course of proceedings, they would also circumvent the time limit for bringing annulment proceedings set in Article 263(6) TFEU.

[446] The ECHR standards under Article 6 exclude neither the adversarial nor the inquisitorial system of administrative justice. AG Colomer, Case C-480/99 P, *Gerry Plant et al v Commission*, ECLI:EU:C:2001:359, paras 34–37.

[447] Barents (n 3), 877–81.

[448] Fuller (n 240), 372–73.

The system of pleas puts a great deal of responsibility for the case's outcome on the lawyer representing the applicant. Hence, the EU Courts cling to a strict interpretation of the duty to be represented by an independent lawyer (as opposed to in-house counsel),[449] although an equivalent concept of 'lawyer as an independent officer of the court' is not common to all EU Member States.[450] The reality, however, does not always align with the theory. As there is no distinct body of lawyers specialising in litigation before the EU Courts, the applicant's lawyer may not always succeed in setting out all relevant pleas correctly. Any mistake a lawyer makes may have broader repercussions; it could result in an unlawful act being upheld with concomitant risks for third parties. Much depends on the judge's appraisal in individual cases. The EU judicature has striven to minimise the drawbacks of the system of pleas. It has held that it is not bound by any specific argumentation in support of pleas.[451] It also admits new pleas provided they can merely be qualified as 'amplifying' those already raised by the initial application.[452] Still, it has been observed that appellants increasingly allege before the ECJ that the GC has failed to raise a public policy plea to remedy a lawyer's mistake.[453]

The applicant's lawyer also bears the responsibility for adducing or indicating the relevant evidence. The EGC enjoys discretion concerning the need to supplement information about the case.[454] It does not generally engage in independent fact-finding by summoning expert witnesses or ordering independent expert opinions, even though relevant procedural tools have been laid down in its rules of procedure. In the examined period, the EGC used its investigatory powers mostly to obtain confidential documents from the institutions regarding, for instance, evidence of competition law infringements,[455] a full State aid dossier,[456] or documents sought within the access-to-documents regime.[457] In some cases, the private

[449] For instance, Case T-702/15 (order of 20.11.2017), *BikeWorld v Commission*, ECLI:EU:T:2017:834.

[450] Joined Cases C-422/11 P and C-423/11 P, *PUKE & Poland v Commission*, ECLI:EU:C:2012:553, para 23. See also Case T-137/16 (order of 13.6.2017), *Uniwersytet Wrocławski v Research Executive Agency*, ECLI:EU:T:2017:407, in which the EGC rejected an action because the lawyer was also a professor at a university he represented. On appeal the ECJ endorsed a more searching and case-by-case assessment of the independence of a lawyer, Joined Cases C-515/17 P and C-561/17 P, *Uniwersytet Wrocławski & Poland v REA*, ECLI:EU:C:2020:73.

[451] Case T-586/14, *Xinyi v Commission*, ECLI:EU:T:2016:154.

[452] For instance, Case T-76/14, *Morningstar v Commission*, ECLI:EU:T:2016:481, para 54.

[453] Caroline Naômé, *Le pourvoi devant la Cour de justice de l'Union européenne* (Larcier 2016), 41.

[454] Joined Cases C-490/15 P and C-505/15 P, *Ori Martin v Commission*, ECLI:EU:C:2016:678, para 108.

[455] For instance, Case T-450/14, *Sumitomo Electronic Industries et al v Commission*, ECLI:EU:T:2018:455, para 23.

[456] For instance, Case T-162/13, *Magic Mountain Kletterhallen et al v Commission*, ECLI:EU:T:2016:341, para 25.

[457] For instance, Case T-476/12, *Saint-Gobain Glass Deutschland v Commission*, ECLI:EU:T:2014:1059, para 28.

parties applied for more elaborate inquiry measures such as commissioning an expert opinion,[458] hearing a partisan expert,[459] or hearing witnesses.[460] The EGC rejected such requests finding no added value in taking the requested evidence. It also highlighted that it is not under a duty to justify such rejections in precise terms.[461] In one case, it rejected a motion for obtaining a report assessing the application for a grant as it was of a highly scientific nature, whereas the applicant was unable to explain what this report could reveal specifically.[462] Some inquiry measures pertaining to written evidence in the administrative case file were adopted upon the EGC's own motion.[463] Even though oral testimony or expert witnesses are not commissioned, the EGC recently highlighted a general increase in the use of measures of inquiry.[464]

Nonetheless, the lack of independent fact-finding does not mean the lack of any judicial activity in proceedings. The judges actively steered the proceedings using measures of organisation of procedure in almost every case, such as written questions to the parties regarding clarifications of specific contentious issues.[465] The EGC recently reported a significant increase in the use of the measures of organisation of procedure. In 2020 the parties' written questions tended to replace oral hearings due to the public health crisis.[466]

Naturally, any relaxation of the system of pleas, implying more judicial activity and responsibility, would affect the procedural economy by slowing down proceedings and increasing costs. It is not unknown for case files, eg in competition law cases, to be several volumes thick.[467] It is furthermore open to debate whether any liberalisation of the system of pleas would result in a systemic increase in the correctness of acts adopted by EU authorities or would rather overburden the EU Courts with responsibility for primary law-, rule- and decision-making, and for empirically complex matters for the examination of which they were ill-equipped. A more active role for the EU judicature in annulment proceedings

[458] For instance, Case T-689/13, *Bilbaína de Alquitranes et al v Commission*, ECLI:EU:T:2015:767, para 21. Case T-700/14, *TV1 v Commission*, ECLI:EU:T:2017:35, para 67.

[459] For instance, Case T-463/14, *Österreichische Post v Commission*, ECLI:EU:T:2016:243, para 207.

[460] For instance, Case T-162/10, *Niki Luftfahrt v Commission*, ECLI:EU:T:2015:283, paras 253–69. Case T-468/16, *Verein Deutsche Sprache v Commission*, ECLI:EU:T:2018:207, paras 17–23.

[461] It referred to the standards of the ECtHR. It also held that it must be clear *ex ante* that hearing a witness would bring new elements that are not available in the written file. Case T-216/13, *Telefónica v Commission*, ECLI:EU:T:2016:369, paras 346 and 349.

[462] Case T-208/16, *Graziano Ranocchia v ERCEA*, ECLI:EU:T:2018:68, paras 142–51.

[463] Sometimes a formal measure of inquiry is necessary because the institution refuses a less formal measure of organisation of procedure to signal the importance of confidentiality issues. For instance, Case T-296/11, *Cementos Portland Valderrivas v Commission*, ECLI:EU:T:2014:121, paras 23–25.

[464] ECJ, 'Report provided for under Article 3(1) of Regulation 2015/2422' (available at the Court's website), 42.

[465] Under Article 89 RPGC, any such measure should serve to clarify contentious issues and promote the efficiency of the proceedings.

[466] ECJ (n 464), 42.

[467] Clausen (n 442), 287–88.

would also reinforce concerns about the fine line between judicial review and the actual replacement of challenged authorities in primary law-, rule- and decision-making.

C. Procedural Activity Before the General Court

In the proceedings, the applicants seek to prove the unlawfulness of impugned acts through written and oral submissions. For the sake of procedural economy, the EGC has been granted the option of dismissing actions on admissibility or substantive grounds without undergoing the full course of the procedure, if actions are considered manifestly bound to fail. Namely, if it is clear that the EGC has no jurisdiction to rule on the action, the action is 'manifestly inadmissible' or 'manifestly lacking any foundation in law', the EGC may dismiss the action by means of a reasoned order (providing a written justification as in a judgment) without taking any further procedural steps.[468] The ECJ has held that the application of this procedural option does not amount to a breach of the right to a fair trial, provided that the criteria for application of that provision are fulfilled.[469] While this practical device allows the EGC to moderate its workload, it curtails the parties' right to participate in the proceedings actively. The EGC can dispose of a case in this way at any stage of the proceedings,[470] even shortly after an action has been lodged.[471]

The aggregate yearly data pertaining to all direct actions (for annulment, for failure to act, for damages, and regarding arbitration disputes; but excluding intellectual property cases, staff cases and any auxiliary proceedings such as those regarding the taxation of costs or legal aid) brought by all (private and, rarely, privileged) applicants and closed in 2014–18 (of which actions for annulment represented approximately 82–93%[472]) demonstrate a moderate use of this simplified procedure. Each year, approximately 11–16 per cent of the direct actions[473] were closed this way.[474] Closer analysis has shown that these actions often suffer

[468] Article 126 RPGC.

[469] Case C-308/07 P, *Atxalandabaso v Parliament*, ECLI:EU:C:2009:103, paras 36–38.

[470] Irrespective of any other steps already undertaken, eg measures of organisation of procedure. Case C-547/03 P, *AIT v Commission*, ECLI:EU:C:2006:46, para 30.

[471] Case C-580/08 P, *Srinivasan v Ombudsman*, ECLI:EU:C:2009:402, paras 33–36.

[472] The direct actions discussed in this and the following sections include the most numerous actions for annulment (accounting for 92% of all direct actions in 2014, 90% in 2015, 87% in 2016, 82% in 2017 and 92% in 2018), actions for failure to act, actions for damages and arbitration disputes introduced by private parties and (much less often) by Member States. EGC, 'Affaires clôturées – Objet du recours' (internal document received by email of 21.4.2020, request 2-5/2020D).

[473] For intellectual property cases, which are more routinely brought against the decisions of the EUIPO BoAs, this rate is even lower: between 3.6 and 8.6% in the examined period. Ibid.

[474] The general rate calculated based on EGC (n 354).

from formal deficiencies, such as a lack of required legal representation or failure to meet a deadline. During the same period, 7–15 per cent of direct actions were closed by an order following a written exchange of pleadings regarding the issue of admissibility (mostly the admissibility criteria),[475] whereas 49–67 per cent of direct actions were closed with a judgment.[476] Moreover, the EGC rarely takes advantage of the option to promptly dismiss an action as 'manifestly lacking any foundation in law', ie 'manifestly' unfounded on substantive grounds. Each year, only 1.5–1.7 per cent of direct actions were dismissed in this way.[477] The use of this option has been narrowed down to cases in which the applicant's argumentation contradicts a consistent line of case law[478] or where the applicant's pleas are the same as those already dismissed in another case.[479] These data do not seem to suggest that the EGC must actively moderate its workload using simplified procedures, restraining the parties' activity.

Written and oral submissions by the parties support the correctness of decision-making and enable reasoned deliberation, but they also slow down the proceedings and generate costs for both parties (lawyers' fees) and for the court (time needed to process submissions, translations). This is why the judges enjoy leeway to tailor the activity of the parties. One exchange of written pleadings – the application and the defence – always takes place. The 2015 RPGC have maintained the provision enabling judges to dispense with the second exchange of written pleadings[480] – reply and rejoinder – and eased the requirement to hold the subsequent oral hearing.[481] In practice, the parties still enjoy ample opportunities for active participation,[482] although the EGC aims to reduce the length of proceedings by increasingly dispensing with second exchanges of written pleadings and oral hearings.

Limitations of these procedural stages in the name of efficiency mainly relate to more routine and technical intellectual property cases and to staff cases, the effects of which are limited to the persons directly involved. As reported by the EGC,

[475] Under Article 130 RPGC, an oral hearing may also be held to discuss the issue of admissibility.

[476] Between 2014 and 2017, this rate was 49–53.5% and in 2018 it amounted to 66.8%. The remaining direct actions were withdrawn or have become devoid of purpose. The general rates calculated based on EGC (n 354).

[477] ibid.

[478] For instance, Case T-206/17, *Argus Security Projects v Commission and EUBAM Libya*, ECLI:EU:T:2018:288, paras 60–72.

[479] For instance, Case T-506/17, *Makhlouf v Council*, ECLI:EU:T:2018:655, paras 38–59.

[480] Pursuant to Article 83 RPGC, a second exchange of written pleadings – a reply and rejoinder – takes place by default, unless the EGC decides that a second exchange of pleadings is unnecessary because the contents of the file in the case are 'sufficiently comprehensive'. The chamber president can also specify the matters to which the additional pleadings should relate.

[481] An oral hearing does not take place by default, pursuant to Article 106 RPGC. A party may file a request for an oral hearing, stating the reasons why it wishes to be heard. The EGC may dispense with an oral hearing if no request has been filed for one to be held and if it deems that 'it has sufficient information available to it from the material in the file'. Under the 1991 RPGC an oral hearing was always mandatory in annulment proceedings (but not in intellectual property cases).

[482] For instance, despite being authorised to lay down a formal decision limiting the size of written pleadings, the EU Courts have only adopted soft guidelines in this respect.

in 2017 as many as 90 per cent and in 2018, 87 per cent of proceedings concerning direct actions settled by judgment still involved a second exchange of written pleadings.[483] However, as regards 2019, the EGC reported a drop to 78 per cent.[484] The interviewees from the EGC reported that in the years of increased workload, most judges and legal secretaries could only find time to look at the case file after the second exchange had transpired and the written pleadings subsequently been translated. After the EGC embarked upon its expansion course, the judges may have increasingly more time to manage the proceedings actively.

As follows from its yearly reports, the EGC also aims at demonstrating efficiency by reducing the number of oral hearings. The previous President of the EGC, writing extra-judicially, has opined that accuracy and timely decisions are primary process values for the EGC. Providing the parties with an opportunity for a genuine hearing was relegated to a secondary value status.[485] In 2014–18 the aggregate number of direct actions settled by a judgment *without* an oral hearing was significant and varied each year between approximately 26 per cent in 2014 and 47 per cent in 2017.[486] It dropped to 29 per cent in 2018 and again rose to 39 per cent in 2019.[487] However, an examination of, more specifically, the annulment proceedings brought by private applicants demonstrated that the oral hearing was still relatively important, as indeed held in approximately 90 per cent of cases of this type closed in 2014–18 with a judgment. However, this number dropped to approximately 78 per cent in 2018.[488] In State aid and competition law cases, which are arguably among the most complex ones, the oral hearing took place in nearly every case.[489] Conversely, the yearly number of oral hearings was lower in the intellectual property field, where 42–57 per cent of cases were settled *without* an oral hearing.[490]

On the one hand, oral hearings increase the time of proceedings, mainly due to the need to draft and translate a report for the hearing, summarising the

[483] ECJ (n 265), 229–30. However, this data includes also staff cases. These rates are likely to be even higher (95%) when staff cases and some specific proceedings which by default do not provide for the second exchange of written pleadings are excluded. The additional data have been provided by the Registries of the EU Courts in response to the author's request 16/2020C on 21.9.2020.

[484] ECJ, 'Annual Report 2019: Judicial Activity', 274. More detailed data have not been disclosed. This drop might be due to the inclusion of staff cases (the intellectual property cases are not included).

[485] Marc Jaeger, 'The Court of First Instance and the Management of Competition Law Litigation' in Heikki Kanninen, Nina Korjus and Allan Rosas (eds), *EU Competition Law in Context* (Hart Publishing 2009), 7.

[486] In the previous period 2010–13, this number was lower: 21–28%.

[487] The rate calculated based on EGC, 'Affaires clôturées – Mode de clôture' (internal document disclosed by email of 21.4.2020, request 3-5/2020D).

[488] The rate calculated based on the procedural data provided by the EGC in its rulings (retrieved from the search engine at curia.europa.eu).

[489] EGC, 'Affaires clôturées – Mode de clôture – Affaire Aide d'Etat' et 'Affaire Concurrence' (internal documents disclosed by email of 21.4.2020, request 3-5/2020D).

[490] EGC, 'Affaires clôturées – Mode de clôture – Propriété intellectuelle' (internal documents disclosed by email of 21.4.2020, request 3-5/2020D).

facts, pleas and arguments of the parties.[491] On the other hand, oral hearings have paramount importance for the ideal of reasoned deliberation and a genuine reconsideration of the impugned acts. Applicants may see an opportunity to be heard face to face as essential to a fair trial.[492] The hearings are also likely to be particularly useful in factually complex cases. Although inquiry measures are rarely ordered, it is the court's well-established practice to take evidence informally at the oral hearing.[493] Despite not engaging in independent fact-finding, the judges generally do take an active and hands-on approach during the hearings. Apart from the opening and closing statements, the hearings are usually directed by judges' questions, although the parties may have an opportunity to comment on each other's responses. The judges may also invite the parties to focus on specific written questions or speak to the parties informally before the oral hearing about its envisaged course.[494]

With somewhat vague legal status, the oral hearing is still very close to being considered an applicant's right. Under RPGC, the party applying for the oral hearing must 'state the reasons for which that party wishes to be heard'.[495] Also, the Practice Rules stipulate that the application for an oral hearing

> must be based on a real assessment of the benefit of a hearing to the party in question and must indicate the elements of the case file or arguments which that party considers it necessary to develop or refute more fully at a hearing.[496]

However, the RPGC also states that the EGC may dispense with an oral hearing 'if there is no request' from the party. The latter provision would seem to imply that the application for an oral hearing is binding upon the judges. The motives of the draft RPGC,[497] the extra-judicial writings of the EGC's President,[498] and information from the interviewees corroborate the latter interpretation. Moreover, if the oral hearing does not take place, the EGC usually emphasises in the ruling's text that none of the parties applied for it.

In the examined period, the yearly average time of proceedings in all direct actions settled by a judgment at the EGC varied between 19.5 to 28.4 months, but in the most complex competition law cases, it could even amount to 51.5 months.[499] Internal statistics demonstrate that the EGC has managed to consistently decrease the average time necessary to draft the preliminary reports by the reporting judges

[491] ECJ (n 484), 274.
[492] For instance, Case C-682/13 P, *Andechser Molkerei Scheitz v Commission*, ECLI:EU:C:2015:356, paras 43–47.
[493] Case C-578/11 P, *Deltafina v Commission*, ECLI:EU:C:2014:1742, paras 57–68. Castillo de la Torre and Gippini Fournier (n 71), 247–48.
[494] See Article 98(4) RPGC.
[495] Under Article 106 RPGC, within three weeks of being notified of the close of the written procedure, each of the parties may apply for an oral hearing.
[496] EGC, 'Practice rules for the implementation of the Rules of Procedure of the General Court', para 180.
[497] EGC 'Draft RPGC' (Council doc. 7795/14), 107.
[498] Jaeger (n 265), 26.
[499] ECJ (n 265), 244.

based on parties' written submissions: from 12.1 months in 2014 to 5.8 months in 2018 in cases settled by a judgment and involving an oral hearing, and from 7.6 to 4.6 months in the same period in cases settled by a judgment but not involving an oral hearing.[500] According to available statistics, this tendency also relates to State aid and competition law cases, among the more complex ones. However, the time of proceedings is largely and steadily determined by time accorded to written submissions by the main parties and the interveners (7.9 to 7.7 months in cases with the oral hearing and 6.3 to 5.1 months in cases without the hearing), by the time needed to hold the oral hearing (2.1 to 2.4 months), as well as the time needed for the translation of written pleadings (1.5 months on average). In State aid and competition law cases, the time of written proceedings was constant or even somewhat increased. Therefore, the EGC may be inclined to seek further procedural flexibility and discretion to tailor the parties' activity in proceedings on a case-by-case basis.

In its report regarding the evaluation of the EGC enlargement, the ECJ urged the EGC to foster its 'prompt, active and smooth' case management process by, among other things, a prompt identification of actions manifestly bound to fail before notification to the defendant, adopting more measures of organisation of procedure, and limiting the use of the automatic second exchange of written pleadings. On top of that, the ECJ recommended

> requiring a more detailed statement of reasons in the main parties' requests for a hearing in order to enable the court to assess the merits of those requests and to ensure that only the elements justifying a hearing are actually included in the hearing, and developing the practice of replacing a hearing with written questions to the parties ....

The ECJ pointed out that, according to interviewed 'users' of the EGC, some oral hearings bring limited added value.[501] In response, the EGC declared that 'the central role of the hearing cannot be underestimated' and that the EGC

> must always remain at the service of the parties and be attentive to them. It is they who, within the parameters laid down by the rules of procedure, decide to bring their disputes before the General Court and who, ultimately, determine the content of those disputes.[502]

This passage seems to imply the EGC's scepticism regarding the limiting of the right to the oral hearing or, perhaps, a broader efficiency-oriented procedural approach promoted by the ECJ at the expense of the parties' active involvement in the proceedings. Given that the two EU Courts may have different visions

[500] This difference may be due to the general complexity of cases settled with and without an oral hearing. The time of deliberation after the oral hearing was also somewhat reduced: from 4 months in 2011 to 3.2 months in 2019. EGC, 'Durée de l'instance par stade de procédure (en mois) – Affaires réglées par arrêt (…)' (internal document disclosed by email of 4.9.2020, request 17/2020D).

[501] ECJ (n 464), 52.

[502] ibid, Annex 2.

of the legitimacy assets that should stem from judicial review proceedings, the procedural reforms at the EU Courts in the following years should be closely monitored.

D. Procedural Activity at the Court of Justice

Decisions given by the EGC may be subject to a right of appeal to the ECJ, on points of law only however.[503] In the examined period, the yearly rate of EGC rulings in direct actions (excluding intellectual property and staff cases) open to appeal that were indeed challenged before the ECJ varied between 21 and 32.9 per cent.[504] The yearly rate of successful appeals also varied between 14.8 and 25.3 per cent,[505] but it generally confirms the importance of appellate proceedings before the ECJ. The appellate procedure structure resembles the first-instance procedure; both consist of two exchanges of written pleadings (one mandatory and one optional) and an optional oral hearing.[506] However, the ECJ's procedural practice differs from that of the EGC since it increasingly leaves little space for the parties' active participation.

On the one hand, this tendency could be due to the ECJ's jurisdiction in appellate proceedings, which is limited, in principle, to questions of law. The ECJ seems to adopt rulings in a fashion more akin to adopting a piece of legislation, ie focussing on abstract questions of principle. It does not need to take advantage of the parties' activity and information because its role is usually not to settle fact-intensive cases.[507] On the other hand, however, the scant importance attached to parties' activity might mean that the ECJ applies a deferential standard of review to the EGC's rulings, perhaps wishing to discourage the frequent submission of appeals.[508] As has been reported elsewhere, the judges of the ECJ are said to have an aversion to appeals, which are considered to carry less weight in enhancing the Court's authority than do preliminary references.[509] The procedural practices of the ECJ are attuned to deliberation on matters of abstract question of legal

[503] Article 256(1), para 2, TFEU. Appellants may not raise new pleas before the ECJ. See Article 170 RPCJ and Case C-176/13, *Council v Bank Mellat*, ECLI:EU:C:2016:96, para 116.

[504] ECJ (n 265), 251.

[505] Based on the ECJ annual reports (excluding intellectual property cases and those removed from the register). For instance, ECJ (n 265), 252.

[506] Articles 167ff RPCJ.

[507] Jan Komarek, 'Reasoning with Previous Decisions: Beyond the Doctrine of Precedent' (2013) 61 *The American Journal of Comparative Law* 149–72, 158. The ECJ is, in this respect, similar to continental supreme courts that were established to make authoritative pronouncements on what the law is rather than settle concrete legal disputes. Ibid, 170–71.

[508] An observation by one of the interviewees.

[509] Angela Huyue Zhang, 'The Faceless Court' (2016) 38 *University of Pennsylvania Journal of International Law* 71, 121ff.

interpretation. It is considered that the EGC is better equipped to handle empirically complex issues.[510]

Crucially, the ECJ frequently dismisses appeals as 'manifestly unfounded' or 'manifestly inadmissible'[511] in a simplified procedure curtailing the right to active participation.[512] Internal procedural guidelines issued by the ECJ's President explicitly instruct ECJ judges that 'regarding the appeals, the application of Article 181 of the rules of procedure should be fully exploited'.[513] The difference in the wording of Article 181 RPCJ – which mentions appeals that are 'manifestly unfounded' – and Article 126 RPGC – which mentions actions 'manifestly lacking any foundation in law' – suggests that the ECJ enjoys greater (albeit self-granted) leeway to dismiss appeals on substantive grounds in the simplified procedure. In the examined period, the ECJ dismissed 47.6 per cent of all appeals (all categories of direct actions combined) by a reasoned order as manifestly inadmissible or manifestly unfounded.[514] For the appeals in the annulment proceedings brought by private parties, this number was, however, 31.6 per cent.[515]

This ECJ approach to appeals manifests itself through the frequency with which the ECJ uses optional procedural tools. At the EGC there are two exchanges of written pleadings by default, whereas the ECJ President[516] must actively authorise a second exchange, upon a duly reasoned application submitted by the appellant.[517] The President may also prescribe the length of the pleadings and indicate the points on which the parties should focus.[518] Requests for a second exchange are subject to scrutiny by the reporting judge and the advocate general. In practice, such requests are not accepted unless there is a need to respond to new issues raised in defence.[519] According to the available data, in 2017–18 the second exchange of written pleadings took place in about 47 per cent of appeal cases brought by private parties and settled with a judgment (excluding intellectual property cases).[520] This figure contrasts with the figures relating to the EGC where

[510] AG Bobek, Case C-352/19 P, *Région de Bruxelles-Capitale v Commission*, ECLI:EU:C:2020:588, paras 142–45.

[511] An appeal may also be dismissed as 'manifestly inadmissible' if it is unclear or merely repeats the argumentation already raised before the EGC.

[512] Article 181 RPCJ.

[513] ECJ President, 'Guide Pratique relative au traitement des affaires portées devant la Cour de Justice: Novembre 2019' (internal document received on 10.3.2020, request 6/2020D), para 42.

[514] Calculated based on ECJ (n 265), 134.

[515] The rate calculated based on the search engine at www.curia.europa.eu.

[516] In the appellate procedure, procedural decisions in the written procedure are taken by the ECJ President. Cases are allocated to chambers only after the written procedure and a discussion of the general meeting of judges.

[517] Article 175 RPCJ.

[518] Article 177(1) RPCJ.

[519] ECJ (n 421), 123.

[520] The data provided by the Registries of the EU Courts in response to the author's request 16/2020C on 21.9.2020.

the second exchanges of written pleadings are still commonplace. The ECJ may request the parties to provide additional arguments and information by addressing them with specific written questions (measures of organisation of procedure). The use of these measures lies entirely with the ECJ. Specific data relating to the frequency with which these measures were used were not available.

The ECJ assumes a similar approach to oral hearings is less generous than the approach of the EGC.[521] Pursuant to Article 76 RPCJ, the ECJ may decide not to hold an oral hearing if 'on reading the written pleadings or observations lodged during the written part of the procedure' it decides that 'it has sufficient information to give a ruling'. Parties may submit a reasoned request for an oral hearing, but as opposed to the practice adopted by the EGC, the discretionary decision rests with the ECJ entirely.[522] The general assumption is that before the ECJ oral hearings should always bring some instrumental added value.[523] If a hearing is organised, the ECJ will invite the parties to concentrate on one or more specified issues in their oral pleadings.[524] The ECJ judges also actively steer the course of oral hearings by addressing specific questions to specific parties. In principle, the parties may comment on each other's responses only in brief closing remarks.[525] In the examined period, oral hearings were held in 56.1 per cent of the appellate annulment proceedings brought by private parties and settled with a judgment, or in 38.4 per cent of all appellate annulment proceedings brought by private parties, closed with either a judgment or a reasoned order.

Thanks to procedural flexibility and jurisdiction limited to the points of law, appeal proceedings before the ECJ were shorter than the first-instance proceedings before the EGC in the examined period: each year on average between 12.9 and 17.1 months.[526] Ongoing procedural developments at the ECJ suggest that it increasingly focuses on upholding case law uniformity rather than maximising every contested ruling's correctness, let alone offering additional opportunities for deliberation.[527] The ECJ has recently been experimenting with a case-filtering device to concentrate its resources on what it considers the most critical cases.

[521] Article 76(2) RPCJ. Allan Rosas, 'Oral Hearings Before the European Court of Justice' (2014) 21 *Maastricht Journal of Comparative and European Law* 596, 599.

[522] Article 76 RPCJ.

[523] ECJ (n 421), 66. Practice directions to parties concerning cases brought before the Court [2014] OJ L31/1, para 46.

[524] Article 61(2) RPCJ.

[525] The procedural practice is similar in validity reference proceedings. Practice directions (n 523), para 50. Rosas (n 521), 609. Article 96 RPCJ provide for a single opportunity for the parties to the main proceedings to submit written observations.

[526] ECJ (n 265), 134.

[527] Article 62 of the Statute, regarding the procedure for extraordinary review of the EGC's appellate or preliminary rulings, suggests that the main task of the ECJ is to maintain the 'unity and consistency of Union law'. Niilo Jaaskinen and Alicja Sikora, 'The Exclusive Jurisdiction of the Court of Justice of the European Union and the Unity of the EU Legal Order' in Marise Cremona, Anne Thies and Ramses A Wessel (eds), *The European Union and International Dispute Settlement* (Oxford University Press 2017), 103. On the so-called 'revision model' of supreme courts, Michal Bobek, 'Quantity or Quality? Reassessing the Role of Supreme Jurisdictions in Central Europe' (2009) 57 *American Journal of Comparative Law* 33, 36.

From January 2016, the ECJ introduced through internal procedural guidelines a preliminary examination of appeals in the areas of intellectual property, public procurement, and access to documents.[528] Under these guidelines, the internal Directorate for Research and Documentation (DRD) is to single out appeals which can be dismissed as manifestly unfounded on top of the appeals that are singled out by the Registry to be dismissed as manifestly inadmissible. Both entities provide proposals for the reasoning used to dismiss an appeal.[529] Only if at least one member of the ECJ believes that a case should go through the full appellate procedure will the case be discussed at a weekly general assembly of the ECJ members; the discussion cannot relate to the motives of the order dismissing an appeal only.[530] Third, the advocate general drafts an opinion based on the Directorate's proposals, which the reporting judge integrates into the order. Finally, the draft is subject to deliberation by a chamber of three judges.[531] One might have doubts about whether the chamber's members would carry out fully independent scrutiny of the contested first-instance ruling, having already been offered the draft of an order.

These developments have given rise to doubts due to moving away from the original idea of two-tier annulment proceedings that should warrant a stronger judicial protection of private parties and employing an internal research service to scrutinise contested rulings.[532] Finally, the question of whether actual decision-making could be transferred to advocates general should be considered, as the Treaties give them a different task.[533] The reasoning provided by advocates general often seems more concise than that provided in standard orders drafted by reporting judges. Moreover, reporting judges tend not to contribute anything that goes beyond the advocate general's opinion.[534]

The ECJ took a further step by requesting an amendment to the Statute to introduce a fully fledged filtering device for cases in which the dispute has already been considered by one of four BoAs: EUIPO, CPVO, ECHA or EASA.[535] It is unclear why the BoAs of ESAs, ERA and ACER were not included in this list. The ECJ's underlying assumption seems to be that such bodies are quasi-judicial; by the time the ECJ adjudicates in such a dispute with one of the said agencies, it is

[528] ECJ President (n 513).

[529] ibid, paras 2, 7–8, 13 and 39.

[530] ibid, para 45.

[531] ibid, paras 49–52.

[532] As pointed out by one of the interviewees.

[533] Article 252 TFEU.

[534] For instance, Case C-570/17 P, *Lackmann v EUIPO*, ECLI:EU:C:2018:11.

[535] ECJ, 'Amendments to Protocol No 3 on the Statute of the Court of Justice of the European Union' (26.3.2018, Council doc. 7586/18). Under Article 256(1), para 2, TEU, the rulings of the EGC '*may be* subject to a right of appeal … *under the conditions and within the limits* laid down by the Statute' (emphasis added). However, in the course of the amendment process, committees of the Parliament were concerned about the impact of the selection device on the right to effective judicial protection. Committee on Constitutional Affairs of the European Parliament, 'Draft Opinion of 20 September 2018 on the Regulation amending Protocol no 3' (02360/2018 – C8-0132/2018 – 2018/0900(COD).

already the third independent instance to do so.[536] Following the amendment,[537] the ECJ can now select only appeals that raise significant issues regarding the 'unity, consistency and development of EU law'.[538] It is necessary for the party challenging the decision of the EGC to establish, through a document annexed to the appeal, its interest in light of the importance of the issue that it raises concerning the 'unity, consistency or development of EU law'.[539] Further details about the filtering device have been hammered out in the RPCJ. The decision on accepting the appeal is taken, on a proposal from the reporting judge and after hearing the advocate general, by a chamber specially established for that purpose.[540] In 2019 no appeal falling into this category was allowed to proceed.[541] Most recently, the ECJ suggested that the use of the filtering device should be expanded in the near future to allow the ECJ to focus on the preliminary reference procedure as its main task.[542]

V. Conclusion

Is the one-size-fits-all model of EU judicial review still capable of enhancing the authority of contemporary EU law-, rule- and decision-making in such diverse fields as public procurement, competition law, financial supervision, the risk regulation of chemicals, pharmaceuticals and food safety? The flexible notions of 'acts producing legal effects' and 'legality' review have allowed the EU Courts to adjust the EU judicial review remit and technique to novel challenges. By dint of growing institutional experience, the EU judicature has managed to apply a more incisive review technique in complex competition law cases. However, a challenge is continuously posed by legal acts marked with empirical and normative epistemic uncertainty due to their technical, scientific and political complexity, as well as the vagueness of EU substantive legal frameworks, in the fields such as the risk regulation of chemicals, pharmaceuticals or food safety.

Although the rate of successful annulment actions is significant and relatively steady, the EU judicial review hinges upon legal arguments and evidence presented by the litigants. With the EU judicature not engaging in independent fact-finding, the litigants are shouldered with the burden of obtaining and persuasively presenting enough evidence to refute a strong presumption of correctness

[536] A board of appeal – the EGC – the ECJ.

[537] Council, 'Amendment of Protocol No 3 on the Statute of the Court of Justice of the European Union – Confirmation of the final compromise text with a view to agreement' (Council doc. 5190/19 received on 1.4.2019).

[538] Article 58a of the Statute.

[539] Article 170a RPCJ.

[540] Article 170b RPCJ.

[541] ECJ (n 484), 178.

[542] ECJ (n 464), 54.

assigned to technical and scientific findings accepted by the EU institutions and bodies. During judicial review proceedings, the EGC judges' activity concentrates on making the exchange of arguments more efficient by clarifying contentious issues and steering the deliberation. The EU Courts seek increased discretion to tailor the parties' procedural activity on a case-by-case basis, thus gaining more control on the allocation of limited resources, increasing productivity and further decreasing the time of proceedings.

With the ECJ focussed on its increasing preliminary reference docket, the EGC bears the responsibility for the correctness and uniformity of case law in legality challenges against multifarious EU rule-making and decision-making acts. It is unclear, however, whether the institutionally non-specialised and procedurally uniform model of judicial review relying on partisan legal arguments and evidence across the board will in the future meet the challenge of growing empirical and normative uncertainty and the corresponding elevating expectation of judicial ability to uncover 'objective truth'. When the required degree of empirical proof as to the existence or absence of risk to society is intrinsically linked to the essentially political view on the acceptable degree of risk, and obfuscated by abstruse scientific and technical issues, the judges may need not only time, but also procedural tools to obtain non-partisan expertise and, perhaps, even the possibility to clarify or redefine the subject matter of the legal problem before them in the public interest. A fundamental question is whether the judicial legitimacy assets, stemming from complete independence although decoupled from specialist expertise, and those stemming from adversarial proceedings implying an ample right to be heard but imposing on the applicants the burden of proof, especially in empirically uncertain cases, are sufficient to uphold the authority of contemporary EU law-, rule- and decision-making.

Should the EU Courts liberalise the access rules to encourage more litigation regarding normatively and empirically controversial cases? When it comes to the annulment procedure, the EU judicature retains a narrower 'administrative' profile, dealing mostly with individual economic operators and individual administrative decisions, rather than a broader 'constitutional' profile, in which it could engage with social actors and civil society to hammer out value judgements binding upon the EU institutions and bodies. The limited accessibility of EU judicial review is intrinsically linked to its limited institutional and procedural assets. Arguably, the EU judicature is not well equipped in terms of organisational resources and precise higher-order legal frameworks to undertake more responsibility for EU law-, rule- and decision-making; something that might be changed by the political EU institutions rather than the ECJ itself. Contentious normative assumptions underpin the discussion about the rule of law and what it should imply in terms of the accessibility and thoroughness of EU judicial review. Such assumptions may need to be discussed and settled in a political rather than purely juridical process.

5

Administrative Review: Cheaper, Quicker and More Thorough?

The hodgepodge of legal frameworks governing individual BoAs is a source of confusion regarding their essentially administrative or judicial nature. The BoAs are supposed to keep the bulk of technically and scientifically complex cases away from the EU Courts, providing cheaper, faster and more thorough review of complex and epistemically uncertain appraisals requiring specialist knowledge. However, due to the lack of full organisational independence from the agencies, the BoAs may simultaneously be perceived as inferior forms of legal protection. In this view, administrative review by BoAs would be more thorough, cheaper and faster but, at the same time, more biased towards the agencies' policy goals. The confusion persists because we know little about how the BoAs operate in practice.

This chapter examines the practical operation of the ECHA BoA, fleshing out the legitimacy assets it offers. It also takes account of available data regarding the BoAs to establish whether the findings relating to the ECHA BoA are representative of broader problems faced by the BoAs. The overarching objective is to critically evaluate whether and in what way the BoAs' legitimacy assets constitute an added value in relation to the legitimacy assets offered by the EU Courts, or vice versa. The relative authority approach, adopted in this book, is interested not so much in formal labels such as 'judicial' or 'administrative' review, but rather, as far as possible, in the practical operation of the institutional and procedural features of specific mechanisms.

This chapter focusses on the ECHA BoA because its output is the most substantial among those dealing with empirically uncertain and voluminous cases.[543] Unlike other BoAs, such as those of the EUIPO and CPVO, the ECHA BoA is burdened with striking a delicate normative balance between the powerful chemical industry's economic interests and fundamental public interest goals: the protection of public health and the environment. For this reason, its experience is likely to prove particularly valuable in discussions about ways of resolving a proliferating number of public law disputes involving advanced technical or scientific knowledge and controversial normative choices, and about the role of specialist adjudication at the EU level.

[543] For an overview of the BoAs, see De Lucia (n 23) and Chirulli and De Lucia (n 5).

Section I discusses practical problems with ensuring the ECHA BoA independence and, at the same time, letting its members benefit from agency expertise. Section II examines how the ECHA BoA has been exercising its powers in practice and especially if it and other BoAs have indeed managed to develop a more thorough review technique. Section III examines the problem of accessibility, and especially the profile of appellants and third-party interveners before the ECHA BoA in recent years. Section IV examines the parties' activity and the BoA members during appeal proceedings, drawing especially from available data on written submissions and internal documents of the ECHA BoA. Section V presents this chapter's conclusions.

I. Reconciling Independence and Proximity

A. Protection from External Influence

The ECHA BoA's experience illustrates how difficult it is to secure independence and impartiality of a relatively small adjudication unit, whose workload is difficult to predict. To avoid unnecessary expenses, the majority of the BoAs operate in an ad hoc manner. Only the BoAs of the EUIPO, having a steady workload, are permanent bodies with full-time staff. The ECHA BoA remains in between. Formally, it is a permanent body composed of three members (the Chair and a technically and legally qualified member).[544] However, it is occasionally assisted by alternate members, appointed for a term of office but working on an ad hoc basis in the temporary absence of permanent members.

The founding regulations proclaim that the BoAs shall not be bound by any instructions and that they shall be independent. The BoAs do not enjoy safeguards as elevated as those bestowed upon the EU judges. The BoAs' safeguards may nonetheless be far reaching, effectively ruling out pressure from the agencies. Some unavoidable organisational links to the agencies may still unfavourably affect the public appearance of BoAs' independence, giving rise to not unreasonable suspicions of possible influence. However, the proximity to the agencies is one of BoAs' assets as it enables them to build up their own expertise.

EU law does not favour a specific judicial appointment model, considering a great variety of national solutions in this respect. However, the appointment procedure plays a vital role in choosing the candidate with relevant

[544] Regulation 1907/2006 of the Parliament and the Council concerning the Registration, Evaluation, Authorisation and Restriction of Chemicals (REACH) [2006] OJ L396/1. Article 89(1) REACH specifies only that the BoA is composed of the Chairman and two other members. Article 1 of Commission Regulation 771/2008 laying down the rules of organisation and procedure of the Board of Appeal of the European Chemicals Agency [2008] OJ L206/5 (RPBoA) further specifies that at least one member of the Board must be technically qualified and at least one must be legally qualified. More members can be appointed to the BoA if a high number of appeals so requires.

expertise and internal independence; hence, it matters for the public appearance of independence.[545] There is no uniform procedure for the appointment of BoA members, although they are most often appointed by the management boards of the respective agencies (from a list of qualified candidates submitted by the Commission)[546] or by the Council.[547] There is usually an open call for applications or expressions of interest. A common trait is a fixed term of office with possible reappointments.

The ECHA BoA members are appointed for a term of office of five years (one reappointment is possible) by the ECHA Management Board, the majority of which are representatives of Member States, the Commission, the Parliament and stakeholders.[548] Legal criteria only loosely constrain the selection of ECHA BoA members. Following a public call for applications, the Commission performs an eligibility check.[549] A Commission implementing regulation[550] and an ECHA Management Board decision[551] describe the required qualifications and eligibility criteria in rather open-ended terms. It has been decided that a more precise specification might impair the recruitment of qualified candidates. In the past, the Commission reported a limited response to the call for applications. Relaxation of requirements was even considered.[552] The interviews of candidates precede the selection by the delegated members of the Management Board. An assessment centre run by external recruitment consultants may also be organised.[553]

The appointment by the Management Board, the majority of which is formed by representatives of Member States, does not deprive the ECHA BoA of independence, in and of itself. The members of EU Courts are also appointed by a common accord of the Member States, which enjoy great latitude in the selection of candidates.[554] Problems may arise if candidates for BoA permanent or ad hoc members are at the same time officials of other EU institutions or bodies. In that

[545] Krajewski and Ziółkowski (n 260).

[546] EASA, ECHA, ACER, ESAs, ESAs, ERA.

[547] The Council appoints the EUIPO and CPVO Presidents, who then appoint the BoA members.

[548] Article 79 REACH.

[549] Article 89(3) REACH.

[550] Commission Regulation 1238/2007 on laying down rules on the qualifications of the members of the Board of Appeal of the European Chemicals Agency [2007] OJ L280/10.

[551] ECHA, 'Eligibility criteria for the Executive Director, the Accounting Officer and of the members of the Board of Appeal' (MB/45/2013 final), 3–4.

[552] ECHA, 'Minutes of the Meeting of ECHA's Management Board 18/19 June 2008' (MB/M/03/2008 final), 7–8.

[553] ECHA, 'Appointment of a (alternate and additional) Chairman(s) of the Board of Appeal and decision on a staff request pursuant to Article 90(1) of the Staff Regulations' (14.3.2019, MB/08/2019, internal document received on 5.8.2019, request ATD-52-2019), 2.

[554] The candidates are now scrutinised in terms of their expertise and experience by an expert panel, but the specific assessment criteria are elaborated by the panel itself and its opinions are not made public. The selection of candidates at the national level is not always transparent. Tomáš Dumbrovský, Bilyana Petkova and Marijn van der Sluis, 'Judicial Appointments: The Article 255 TFEU Advisory Panel and Selection Procedures in the Member States' (2014) 51 *Common Market Law Review* 455.

case, inter-institutional agreements must be signed to rule out giving instructions to BoA members by their parent institutions.[555]

The possibility of removing BoA members during their term of office is the most likely to prove problematic. The ECJ has elaborated bottom-line rules, applicable to domestic judges, according to which removal from office must be constrained by clear legislative criteria and subject to judicial review.[556] The ECHA BoA members, similarly to the members of other BoAs, may be removed from office by the Commission (or the respective Management Board in some cases) on somewhat nebulous 'serious grounds'.[557] However, dismissed BoA members could arguably challenge the Commission decisions before the EU Courts, which seems to protect them from arbitrary dismissals.[558] A straightforward way to enhance the independence of BoAs would be to specify the grounds for dismissal and to confirm the right to judicial review explicitly. The safeguards enjoyed in this respect by the members of EUIPO and CPVO are stronger as they may be dismissed only by the ECJ.[559] The safeguards enjoyed by the EU judges themselves in this respect are even more elevated as they can be dismissed only by the ECJ members' common accord.[560]

The ECHA BoA members and their Registry staff are employed as temporary officials of the ECHA.[561] The REACH Regulation explicitly obliges the ECHA BoA members to remain independent in their decision-making[562] and not to perform any other duties in the ECHA.[563] However, it is still possible to discern some links between the BoA members and the ECHA Management Board, although not the ECHA as such or its Executive Director. Even though the Management Board does not issue any decisions that might later be subject to review, any links to it undoubtedly influence the overall appearance of BoA independence. The ECHA BoA generally reports on its work to the ECHA Management Board. The BoA members, like any temporary agents, must undergo a probation period and annual performance appraisals. Delegated members of the Management Board carry out

[555] A draft service-level agreement was disclosed by the ECHA on 4.11.2020, request ATD/069/2020.

[556] Case C-619/18, *Commission v Poland*, ECLI:EU:C:2019:531, paras 111ff.

[557] Article 90(4) REACH.

[558] Case C-192/18 PPU, *Commission v Poland*, ECLI:EU:C:2019:924, paras 112–15.

[559] Article 166(1) and (6) of Regulation 2017/1001 of the European Parliament and the Council of 14.6.2017 on the European Union trade mark. Article 47(5) of Council Regulation (EC) No 2100/94 of 27 July 1994 on Community plant variety rights. The members of other BoAs may be dismissed for disciplinary offences by the Commission or the Management Boards of the respective agencies.

[560] Article 6 of Protocol no 3 on the Statute of the Court of Justice.

[561] They enjoy privileges and immunities provided for the EU officials in Protocol 7 to the TFEU. The ad hoc members of the BoAs, who are not at the same time employed by other EU institutions or bodies, may not enjoy even these general privileges and immunities. See, for instance, Call for expression of interest for the post of Member of the Board of Appeal of the Community Plant Variety Office [2019] OJ C142A/1.

[562] Article 90(2) REACH.

[563] Article 90(3) REACH.

these appraisals.[564] According to the rules governing the appraisals, they should not relate to particular appeal cases or the substance of ECHA BoA decision-making but only to the 'ability, efficiency, and conduct in the service' based on 'the Board of Appeal work programme, adopted each year by the Board of Appeal'.[565] The BoA members may also be assessed by the Management Board when applying for the second term of office. The Management Board members delegated for the appraisal of BoA members make proposals in this respect.[566]

The ECHA BoA, as well as other BoAs, are also equipped with safeguards of impartiality assessed with regard to individual proceedings. The ECHA BoA and the staff of its Registry are currently subjected to elevated duties that aim to ensure their impartiality, as a result of proposals submitted by the European Court of Auditors[567] and the European Ombudsman.[568] These duties may be deemed even more precisely defined than those to which the EU judges and their *référendaires* are subjected.[569] Not only are the ECHA BoA members and the staff of its Registry obliged to submit annual declarations of interest,[570] but they must also submit more specific declarations when allocated work on a particular case.[571] If suspected of partiality, a member of the ECHA BoA may be also objected to by any party to the appeal proceedings. The decision in this respect is to be taken by the BoA, whereas the member objected to is then replaced by an alternate.[572]

[564] For instance, ECHA 'Minutes of the 53rd meeting of the Management Board' (MB/M/01/2019), 13. ECHA, 'Minutes of the 38th meeting of the Management Board' (MB/M/02/2015), 9.

[565] Articles 5(1), 6(4)(b) and 13(1) of the ECHA Decision concerning the probationary period appraisal, managerial trial appraisal and annual performance appraisal of the Executive Director and the members of the Board of Appeal (…) (MB/36/2018). An examination of the practice of these assessments for the purpose of this book has been prevented by data protection considerations. On these grounds, the ECHA refused access to specific probationary period and annual performance appraisals, which would allow examination of their actual content. Email from the ECHA's Governance, Strategy and Relations Unit of 20.12.2019, request ATD/95/2019.

[566] Point 3.6.2.6. of the Guidelines on the selection and appointment procedure of the Chairman, two other members of the Board of Appeal (BoA) of the European Chemical Agency, their alternates and additional members and their alternates (Ares(2018)5743847, received on 31.1.2020, request ATD/03/2020).

[567] ECHA, 'Annex 1: European Chemicals Agency Report for the Financial Year 2010 Pursuant Article 96(2) of the Framework Financial Regulation: ECHA follow-up actions in response to the special report of the Court of Auditors', 3–4 (annex).

[568] Ombudsman, Case OI/12/2012/EIS, *European Chemicals Agency*, paras 20–23.

[569] The *référendaires* have only a general duty to inform a member of the Court on a possible conflict of interest. Article 2 of Décision de la Cour de Justice du 12 novembre 2018 portant adoption de règles de bonne conduite des référendaires (internal document received on 22.7.2019, request 0008/2019D). Importantly, the *référendaires* are also employed as temporary agents, and there are frequently 'revolving doors' between the EU Courts and the private legal sector.

[570] Also, the current Technically Qualified Member of the BoA provided to the Chairman of the Board of Appeal a list of the clients advised in his previous capacity as consultant. See ECHA (n 567), 4.

[571] The declaration of the BoA Chairman is checked by the longer-serving BoA members, those of the BoA members and the Registrar are checked by the Chairman, and those of the legal advisers are checked by the Registrar. ECHA, 'Appeal proceedings before the Board of Appeal' (PRO-BOA-001.07, 22.6.2017, internal procedural guidelines received on 6.5.2019, request ATD/029/2019).

[572] Article 90(5)–(7) REACH.

Analogous provisions are also contained in the rules of procedure of other BoAs. As regards the EU Courts, surprisingly, the RPGC and RPCJ do not even specify the procedure for objecting to a member of court formation by a party to judicial proceedings (*iudex suspectus* or *iudex inhabilis*).[573]

The strict conflict of interest policies at the BoAs is justified because BoA members and staff might previously have worked (or in the case of ad hoc BoAs and alternate members, they may simultaneously work)[574] in private sectors falling within the jurisdictional remit of the respective BoAs.[575] The strict conflict of interest policy may become all the more important now that alternate members may be called to support the ECHA BoA in an ad hoc manner due to the changes in its composition and increased workload.[576] Nonetheless, even the most rigorous conflict of interest policy may not succeed in removing the structural problem, which is the permanent links of ad hoc BoA members to either the private sector concerned or the EU administration. Such permanent links may undoubtedly result in a bias towards specific kind of private interests or administration's policy goals, and thus affect the public appearance of BoA independence.

B. Organisational Proximity: Risks and Opportunities

The organisational proximity to the agency is, arguably, less problematic in case of relatively large adjudicatory bodies such as the EUIPO BoAs. Thanks to the steady workload, these BoAs have been equipped with a permanent structure, their own resources and supporting staff, including specialist research, training and alternative dispute resolution services.[577] Conversely, the ad hoc BoAs may not be allocated with sufficient specialist support (such as scientific or technical advisers) necessary to develop a thorough standard of review.[578]

573 Such a situation has recently occurred before the ECJ. The decision not to recuse the judge objected to was taken by the *réunion général* of judges and advocates general but a statement of reasons for this decision was not published. The decision is mentioned by AG Tanchev, Joined Cases C-585/18, C-624/18 and C-625/18, *A.K. v Krajowa Rada Sądownictwa*, ECLI:EU:C:2019:551, para 49.

574 See also, ECHA, 'Decision of the Board of Appeal of the European Chemicals Agency adopting the Code of Conduct of the (Regular/Alternate/Additional) Members of the Board of Appeal' (22.6.2010, BoA/02/2010).

575 For instance, ECHA, 'Advice of the Conflict of Interest Advisory Committee' (Advice 5/19, 4.12.2019, received on 31.1.2020, request ATD/03/2020).

576 ECHA, 'Annual report from the Chair of the Board of Appeal and exchange of views' (MB/32/2020 final). Hence, an increase in the reimbursement rates and training opportunities for alternate members has been proposed. ECHA, 'Revision of the Decision on the remuneration of alternate and additional members of the Board of Appeal' (MB/50/2020 final, internal document received on 4.11.2020, request ATD/069/2020).

577 EUIPO BoAs, 'Annual Report 2018', 5.

578 The ACER BoA has consistently invoked legal deadlines imposed upon its review proceedings and the complexity of cases to justify deferential review. ACER BoA, Case A-001-2019, *Amprion & Transnet*, paras 74–81. Moreover, the ACER BoA has highlighted that 'whereas the Agency's director has a full-time staff of technical experts and his disposal, the members of the Board of Appeal exercise these functions on a part-time basis, and they are selected precisely because of their current or former

The initial doubts as to the ECHA BoA's precise range of tasks coincided with uncertainty as to the expected number of appeals. As a result, the ECHA Management Board hesitated as to whether a permanent structure of the ECHA BoA was justified,[579] given that the BoA members were prohibited from performing other functions in the ECHA.[580] The Commission had probably foreseen in its staff model and Revised Financial Legislative Statement for REACH[581] that the ECHA BoA would work on an ad hoc basis with reimbursement of its members for their actual work instead of permanent employment in the ECHA.[582]

Ultimately, the Management Board decided to set up one full-time BoA of three members for the first five years. It was also prepared for the eventuality of a larger number of appeals, by appointing alternate members that could either replace a permanent member temporarily unable to work or support the BoA temporarily in times of increased workload.[583] In 2012 the Working Group revised the structure of the BoA. It observed that

> the number of appeals was significantly lower than estimated … [the] workload of the BoA is very difficult to predict as it depends solely on factors outside of its control, i.e. the decision of companies subject to REACH whether to appeal against an ECHA decision or not … [Certain cases] have proven more complicated than anticipated both in terms of the issues raised and in the management of the process, including the number of procedural and other decisions. This has meant that the appeals have taken more man hours to consider than was anticipated.[584]

The Working Group recommended that the Management Board maintain the permanent structure of the BoA, and the Management Board agreed. The main reasons were that an ad hoc structure could generate problems with regard to impartiality. The ad hoc BoA members would need to have their main employment outside the ECHA, most likely in the private sector (with potential appellants), which might generate serious conflicts of interests. It could, moreover, compromise the quality of review considering the complexity of appeals which is 'greater and more critical' than in other BoAs.[585]

experience as staff of national or EU authorities in the energy sector. A Board of Appeal thus composed cannot be expected, nor was it intended, to replicate the in-depth assessment of highly complex technical issues …'. ACER BoA, Case A-006-2019, *Gaz-System*, para 14. Recently, the members of the ESAs BoA and the SRB Appeal Panel opined that more training and access to relevant expertise would be necessary for them to develop a more thorough standard of review. Marco Lamandini and David Ramos Munoz, 'Law and Practice of financial Appeal Bodies (ESAs' Board of Appeal, SRB Appeal Panel): A View from the Inside' (2019) 57 *Common Market Law Review* 119.

[579] ECHA, 'Financial Regulation of the European Chemical Agency and its Implementing Rules' (MB/WP/03/2014 and MB/55/2014).

[580] Article 90(3) REACH. The 2007 discussion has been reported in ECHA, 'Structure and Composition of the Board of Appeal: Meeting of the Management Board 13–14 December 2012' (MB/64/2012, 3.12.2012, internal document received on 6.5.2019, request ATD/029/2019).

[581] Commission, 'REACH Revised Financial Legislative Statement' (SEC(2006)924, 12.7.2006).

[582] ECHA (n 580), 4.

[583] ibid, 1 (reference to an earlier document MB/17/2007).

[584] The document states at the same time that 'the average annual gross salary costs for the three members total to ca. 530.000 EUR, excl. overhead costs such as office rent or IT equipment', ibid, 3.

[585] ibid, 7.

The caution with which the Management Board approached the ECHA BoA's status demonstrates a problem inherently related to any small adjudicatory body operating in a newly emerging field of complex decision-making. On the one hand, the comprehensive review of extremely complex scientific appraisals requires significant resources (for instance, more members of the BoA, more legal and scientific assistants or advisers, the possibility to appoint ad hoc experts). On the other hand, the co-legislators were not ready to secure such resources so as not to increase the overall cost of the REACH system, especially given that they were not even sure about the precise range of the BoA's tasks.

At present, the BoA Registry is the *smallest* unit in the ECHA, composed of the Registrar a few legal advisers, and legal and administrative assistants, besides the three permanent BoA members. A scientific adviser was recently hired, only 10 years after the BoA was set up.[586] In the past, Registry staff used to be redeployed to perform other tasks in the ECHA to ensure the efficient use of its resources.[587] However, this practice engendered doubts regarding the BoA's actual independence from the rest of the ECHA. The problem of organisational resources relates to the other BoAs which operate in an ad hoc manner. Such BoAs noted a link between their limited resources and the intensity of review they are able to develop.[588]

Uncertainty surrounding the level of the BoA's workload and permanent structure led to another controversy. The ECHA and the BoA held different views as to the possibility of separating the BoA Registry from the organisational structure of the ECHA in order to better ensure the public perception of its independence. Prior to 2016, the BoA Registry was fully attached to the ECHA Secretariat.[589] The Rules of Procedure of the Board of Appeal (RPBoA) provided that the Registrar was appointed by the Executive Director upon a proposal by the BoA Chairwoman. Thus, the Executive Director, being the head of one of the parties in appeal proceedings, could also appraise the work undertaken in appeal proceedings by legal advisers and assistants working in the Registry and affect their remuneration or promotion. He could also temporarily or permanently redeploy the Registry staff to other parts of the ECHA or make other staffing changes, although internal administrative arrangements required consultation with the BoA Chairwoman to do so.[590]

[586] ECHA, 'Annual report from the Chairman of the Board of Appeal 50th Meeting of the Management Board 20–21 June 2018' (MB/28/2018 final), 10.

[587] ECHA (n 580), 3.

[588] See n 578. The thoroughness of review depends also on the complexity of cases. For instance, the ad hoc CPVO BoA fully reconsiders the contested decisions, the latter, however, being less voluminous than those of the ECHA BoA.

[589] ECHA, 'Structure of the Board of Appeal and its Registry – considerations for improved independence' (MB/26/2014, received on 10.4.2019, request ATD-25-2019).

[590] ECHA, 'Administrative Arrangement for Safeguarding the Independence of the Board of Appeal' (MB/51/2009). See also the current version, 'Revised administrative arrangements for safeguarding the independence of the Board of Appeal and delegation of powers' (MB/21/2016).

The point of contention was whether the administrative arrangements between the ECHA Executive Director and the BoA Chairwoman were sufficient to ensure the BoA's appearance of independence. An organisational link between the ECHA Registry and the ECHA was necessary for efficient resource management when the number of appeals was low.[591] But the Working Group on the BoA finally took the view that such an arrangement could impair the appearance of the BoA's independence.[592] On the Management Board's recommendation, the Commission amended the RPBoA so it is now the BoA Chair who appoints the Registrar and manages the Registry's work.[593]

Yet another struggle that the BoA had to face concerned access to expertise. This is somewhat surprising since the very purpose of establishing a BoA is to ensure review of complex acts by both legally and technically qualified adjudicators. As it has turned out, the Commission and co-legislators wrongly assumed that just *one* technically qualified member is capable of guaranteeing the necessary level of expertise. The ECHA deals with a great variety of chemical substances. Each of them may display completely different chemical properties and necessitate different studies. It is simply impossible for one technically qualified member to have the knowledge necessary to review decisions relating to such a great variety of scientific data.[594] Insufficient access to expertise may also hamper the mission of ad hoc BoAs. Members of the ESAs BoA and the SRB Appeal Panel, operating in the sector of financial supervision, recently reported several problems in capacity-building, such as insufficient research support due to budgetary constraints.[595]

To gain the necessary expertise, the ECHA BoA members requested to be included – by default – in the activities of ECHA's scientific bodies: the Enforcement Forum,[596] the Risk Assessment Committee and the Socio-Economic Analysis Committee.[597] Thus, they could develop knowledge about the scientific and decision-making processes at the ECHA. A Technically Qualified Member specifically addressed the Management Board, suggesting that the ECHA could

[591] ECHA (n 589), 4.

[592] ECHA (n 580), 6.

[593] This change went hand in hand with internal administrative arrangements regarding the appraisal of the performance of temporary and contract staff of the Registry. Due to provisions of the EU staff regulations and an atypical status of the Board, certain decisions of the Chairman or Registrar with regard to the staff of the Registry must still be countersigned by the HR Director or Executive Director of the ECHA. However, no problems in this respect were reported. See ECHA, 'Administrative arrangements for safeguarding the independence of the Board of Appeal' (26.7.2016, I(2016)0143).

[594] As observed by one of the interviewees.

[595] They also pointed out that the BoA members rarely meet with each other and the members of other BoAs, which hinders the development of collective memory and consistency of review practices. Lamandini and Munoz (n 578).

[596] Composed of national enforcement officials and experts tasked with identifying and disseminating good enforcement strategies and practices. Article 76(1)(f) REACH.

[597] The Committees issue scientific opinions to support science-based decision-making, Article 76(1)(c) and (d) REACH.

increase training activities and information provision to the BoA to facilitate 'capacity building'.[598]

However, the ECHA was concerned about the public perception of the BoA's independence and impartiality. Members of the chemical industry participated in the discussions within the aforementioned bodies.[599] The Commission opined that the BoA

> should not be seen too much as 'sitting' with the ECHA Secretariat. The involvement [of the BoA] can therefore not go into policy questions and has to be considered very carefully, also with regard to the outward appearance and the necessary safeguarding of the Board of Appeal's impartiality and autonomy.[600]

In her 2018 report, the ECHA BoA Chairwoman 'welcomed' the appointment of the new Executive Director and declared that the BoA

> is hopeful that a new spirit of cooperation will characterise the relations between the BoA and the ECHA Secretariat. In particular, BoA and its Registry's staff should in future be provided with the necessary resources for fulfilling its tasks. Without prejudice to the independence of the BoA, exchanges of the latest information on technical and legal aspects of the implementation of REACH and the BPR [Biocidal Product Regulation] should in the future take place on a regular basis between BoA and different units in ECHA.[601]

Could a wall around the BoA be aimed at neutralising its potential interference with the ECHA decision-making? Such a strategy might be counterproductive. It is in the agency's own interest to raise prospective appellants' confidence in the impartiality of appeal proceedings. In this way, unsuccessful appellants will be discouraged from continuing litigation before the EU Courts, which will save the agency's resources and effort. This is why the ECHA Executive Director and the BoA have made an effort to ensure the public perception of the BoA's independence and impartiality by publishing detailed administrative arrangements regarding the organisational aspects of the BoA's work.[602]

In 2017 the ECHA Chairwoman continued to caution that 'the scientific complexity of many cases means that the limited scientific expertise in the BoA is sometimes insufficient to deal with a large number of decisions … at the

[598] ECHA, 'Minutes of the 26th Meeting of the Management Board' (20–21.6.2012, MB/M/02/2012 final), 11.

[599] ECHA, 'Minutes of the 18th Meeting of the Management Board' (22–23.6.2010, MB/M/02/2010 final), 12–13.

[600] ECHA, 'Minutes of the 22nd Meeting of the Management Board' (21–22.6.2011, MB/M/02/2011 final), 13.

[601] ECHA (n 586), 13. Regulation 528/2012 of the European Parliament and of the Council concerning the making available on the market and use of biocidal products [2012] OJ L167/1.

[602] ECHA (n 590).

same time'.[603] The Commission also highlighted the issue of limited resources in its 2018 REACH Review report, concluding that the Board

> is a vulnerable body, depending on the solid performance of its members …[604] [since] there can only be one technically qualified member in the Board, it has become clear that the assistance provided by the Registrar to the Board should be strengthened to cover scientific aspects, and not be limited as it is today to legal research and drafting.[605]

Overall, the experience of the ECHA BoA shows that, in case of narrow and highly specialised regulatory fields, the classical legal safeguards of independence must be complemented by a strict conflict of interest policy, to avoid a regulatory capture of the adjudicatory body. At the same time, some of the problematic links between the ECHA BoA and its appointing authority could arguably be severed through legislative amendments. Being the organisational part of the agency does not seem to be a problem in and of itself, provided that additional legislative safeguards are put in place which could be 'seen' by the BoA's audience. Quite the contrary, the organisational proximity of the agency and its decision-making processes may be a legitimacy asset for a BoA in need of developing its capacity to apply a thorough standard of administrative review, especially in fields requiring highly specialist knowledge. Inclusion of a single or, arguably, even a few technically qualified members in the BoA's composition proves insufficient to secure meaningful review of voluminous, variegated and empirically complex cases; proactive capacity-building and institutional memory play a crucial role. However, the small size of an adjudicatory body and its uncertain workload leads to multiple organisational problems considering the overarching need of EU institutions and bodies to demonstrate efficient use of limited resources.

II. The Reach of Law and Science

A. Blind Spots in the Legislative Design

Unlike the EU Courts, the BoAs do not have a universal competence to review all decision-making acts adopted by the respective agencies. Their jurisdiction is

[603] ECHA, 'Annual report from the Chairman of the Board of Appeal: 46th Meeting of the Management Board 21–22 June 2017' (MB/29/2017 final), 4.

[604] An important factor in this respect might have been the relative continuity of the BoA membership. The Chairwoman and technically qualified members have served on the Board for the last ten years, just like the majority of alternate members, whereas the legally qualified member previously worked at the Board as its Registrar. ECHA, 'Annex III Table of BoA members: "full-time" and alternate and additional members (June 2018)', 28.

[605] Commission, 'Commission Staff Working Document Accompanying the Document Communication from the Commission to the European Parliament, the Council and the European Economic and Social Committee "Commission General Report on the operation of REACH and review of certain elements: Conclusions and Actions"' (SWD(2018)58 final), 21.

usually clearly defined by law-makers regarding particular types of individual decisions producing legal effects vis-à-vis private parties. For instance, the ECHA BoA can only review decisions by which the ECHA itself imposes duties on chemical operators (to provide additional scientific data, perform tests, share the data with other operators), but not the preparatory acts, which only form part of broader rule- or decision-making by the Commission.[606] Neither do the BoAs play a role in reviewing agency soft law measures. Such measures may produce significant practical effects on the conduct of private parties and decision-making by national authorities. However, the EU judicature has not considered them as legal acts amenable to judicial review.[607]

A normative discussion on extending the jurisdictional remit of the BoAs should be based on a precise evaluation of how well they have handled their current tasks. Have they managed to engage with voluminous and abstruse empirical appraisals to a greater extent than the EU Courts, as arguably intended by their designers, thereby bestowing the reviewed legal acts with stronger legitimacy assets and greater authority? In principle, the EUIPO and CPVO BoAs, dealing with intellectual property rights, fully reconsider the impugned decisions. The remaining BoAs adopt review techniques that are limited to a lesser or greater extent to detecting 'errors'. They do not offer a comprehensive re-examination of the case from scratch. Several litigants recently challenged this approach, demanding a more in-depth engagement with impugned empirical considerations.[608]

The mixed composition of the BoAs, involving scientific and technical specialists, might suggest that the BoAs are to perform not only 'legality' review, but also more exhaustive 'merits' review, encompassing in particular scientific and technical assessment criteria. This view corresponds to a distinction between legality and merits review known from comparative law literature.[609] However, this distinction does not entirely clarify the tasks of the EU Courts and the BoAs. Over the last decades, the normative reach of what is formally still 'legality' review drastically expanded, owing to the *Tetra Laval*, *Pfizer* and *Technische Universität München* lines of case law. At the same time, EU legislation often incorporates scientific or technical criteria. Since the requirement to consider all 'relevant'

[606] This asymmetry of legal remedies (the lack of specialised review of Commission acts underpinned by ECHA preparatory acts) was criticised in Marco Bronckers and Yves van Gerven, 'Legal Remedies Under the EC's New Chemicals Legislation REACH: Testing a New Model of European Governance' (2009) 46 *Common Market Law Review* 1823.

[607] Eliantonio and Stefan (n 40).

[608] Case T-125/17, *BASF v ECHA*, ECLI:EU:T:2019:638. Case T-133/08, *Schräder v CPVO*, ECLI:EU:T:2012:430. Case C-546/12 P, *Schräder v CPVO*, ECLI:EU:C:2015:332. ACER BoA, Case A-001-2019, *Amprion & Transnet*, paras 74–81. Merijn Chamon and Annalisa Volpato, 'Sketching Out the Role and Function of the ECHA Board of Appeal: Germany v ECHA and BASF v ECHA' (2020) 45 *European Law Review* 840.

[609] Peter Cane, 'Judicial Review and Merits Review: Comparing Administrative Adjudication by Courts and Tribunals' in Ssusan-Rose Ackerman and Peter Lindseth (eds), *Comparative Administrative Law* (Edward Elgar 2018).

factors – ie both legal and technical or scientific – in a 'careful and impartial way' is now a *legal* requirement, amenable to judicial review, a distinction between legality and merits fades away.

Ideally, the law-makers should first specify the intended powers and impact of the BoA on the agency decision-making and adjust the BoA's composition, available resources, jurisdiction, specific powers, and procedure accordingly. However, BoAs seem to have been rather conceived of as 'experiments'. The law-makers have not specified their criteria or technique of review, relegating this task to the Commission, the agencies or the BoAs themselves. On the one hand, thanks to this wait-and-see strategy, the practice of BoAs has unfolded organically and incrementally. On the other hand, in the absence of legislative coordination and, arguably, due to path dependency, the BoA may partly replicate the technique of judicial review, as best matching their constrained resources.

The law-makers devoted several provisions of the REACH Regulation[610] to the ECHA BoA's independence and impartiality.[611] They also meticulously indicated the categories of ECHA decisions amenable to administrative review.[612] However, they paid relatively little attention to the details of the BoA's powers and technique of review. REACH only stipulates that 'the Board of Appeal may exercise any power which lies within the competence of the Agency or remit the case to the competent body of the Agency for further action'.[613] Similar provisions may be found in other founding regulations, although – besides the ECHA BoA – only the EUIPO and CPVO BoAs are authorised to rectify the substance of unlawful decisions by themselves.[614] The remaining BoAs can only confirm the impugned decisions or remit the cases to the agencies for re-examination in light of the BoA's findings. The founding regulations usually oblige the BoAs to examine if the appeal is 'well-founded' without specifying the criteria of review: a thinner notion of legality or thicker technical standards.[615]

[610] REACH (n 544).

[611] Articles 89 and 90 REACH.

[612] Article 91(1) REACH. Moreover, the BoA has accepted the possibility of reviewing even simple communications which, however, produce legal effects, ie a distinct change in a legal situation of the appellant, and the substance of which is equivalent to the substance of decisions amenable to the BoA review. Therefore, the ECHA cannot avoid the Board's review by manipulating the form of its decisions. In this respect, the BoA is clearly inspired by the approach of EU Courts to the concept of 'legal acts'. ECHA BoA, Case A-005-2017, *Thor GmbH*, paras 38–50. The BoA did not, however, try to extend its jurisdiction beyond that provided for in the REACH. ECHA BoA, Case A-015-2015, *Evonik Degussa GmbH and Others*, paras 63–71. Case A-011-2017, *REACheck Solutions v ECHA*.

[613] On the contrary, Article 263(2) TFEU is somewhat more precise by specifying that judicial review consists in identifying a breach of competence, procedural or substantive law, or an abuse of power.

[614] Regarding the EUIPO BoAs, Article 71 of Regulation 2017/1001 [2017] OJ L154/1. Regarding the CPVO BoA, Article 72 Council Regulation 2100/94 [1994] OJ L227/1.

[615] Article 60(3)–(4) of the ESAs regulations. Regulation 1093/2010 [2010] OJ L331/12. Regulation 1095/2010 [2010] OJ L331/84. Regulation 1094/2010 [2010] OJ L331/48. Regarding the SRB Appeal Panel, Article 85(7)–(8) of Regulation 806/2014 [2014] OJ L225/1. Regarding the ACER BoA, Article 28(4)–(5) of Regulation 2019/942 [2019] OJ L158/22. Regarding the EASA BoA, Article 113 of Regulation 2018/1139 [2018] OJ L212/1. Regarding the ERA BoA, Article 62(3) of Regulation 2016/796 [2016] L138/1.

Based on the provision authorising the ECHA BoA to exercise any of the ECHA's powers and the case-law concept of 'continuity in terms of function' between an agency and its BoA,[616] it might be expected that the ECHA BoA would act following a more inquisitorial procedural logic, raising on its own motion all relevant pleas in law and obtaining new evidence. However, neighbouring provisions of REACH, as well as the regulations governing other BoAs, suggest a more adversarial court-like adjudicatory framework. They require that the appellant bring an appeal together with 'the statements of the grounds thereof'. Said 'grounds' are subsequently examined by the BoA,[617] and they seem to be synonymous with 'pleas in law'.

Should the ECHA BoA fully reconsider scientific issues, or should it confine itself to examining the pleas in law, arguments and evidence brought by the appellant? An answer to this question is crucial from the point of view of appellants' rights, the necessary resources, the expected time of appeal proceedings, and the power of the BoA vis-à-vis the agency. Therefore, it may come as a surprise that the specific range of tasks allocated to the ECHA BoA was not unambiguously determined by the co-legislators or possibly even thoroughly discussed during the legislative work on REACH.[618] REACH largely copied provisions relating to other BoAs, which deal with much less voluminous and less critical instances of empirical and normative uncertainty. Several Member States raised doubts regarding the scarce REACH provisions on the ECHA BoA during the legislative proceedings:

> What type of decisions will the Board of Appeal take? Is the Board of Appeal expected to deal with substance matter, e.g. whether a certain test or modification of test is scientifically justified or not or shall the Board of Appeal only ensure that rules of procedure have been followed correctly? If they were to deal with e.g. scientific issues, they would probably also need a secretariat and funding for the use of external expertise, e.g. the Board of Appeal's own expert committee(s). If the Board of Appeal shall only ensure that rules of procedure have been followed, then [the envisaged provisions on the Board of Appeal] should be amended. What budget does the Board of Appeal get?[619]

[616] Case T-308/01, *Henkel KGaA v OHIM*, EU:T:2003:241, para 29.

[617] Articles 92(2) and 93(2) REACH stipulate that the appeal will be lodged 'together with the statements of the grounds thereof' and 'the appeal will be remitted … for examination of the grounds …'. See also analogous provisions regarding ESAs BoA in Article 60(2) and (4) of Regulation 1093/2010, Regulation 1095/2010, Regulation 1094/2010. Regarding the SRB Appeal Panel, Article 85(3) and (7) of Regulation 806/2014. Regarding the ACER BoA, Article 28(2) and (4) of Regulation 2019/942. Regarding the latter two BoAs, the legislative provisions only require them to verify if the appeal is 'well-founded'. Regarding the EASA BoA, Articles 110 and 112 of Regulation 2018/1139 stipulate that 'where the Board of Appeal finds … that the grounds for appeal are founded …, it shall remit the case to the agency'. Conversely, the legislative provisions governing the EUIPO BoAs explicitly authorises them to raise certain substantive pleas, which are considered to be of public interest, on their own motion. Article 27 of Commission Delegated Regulation 2018/625 [2018] OJ L104/1.

[618] This was stated by an ECHA agent before the EGC during an oral hearing in case T-125/17, *BASF v ECHA*, ECLI:EU:T:2019:638 on 12.12.2018. This agent declared previously working in the Council Legal Service (the author's own notes from this oral hearing, on file with the author).

[619] Questions submitted by Denmark, supported by Malta and Portugal, as reported in Council, 'Title IX – Agency: Proposal for a Regulation of the European Parliament and of the Council concerning

Raising these doubts did not result in a clarification of the provisions. Nor is there any written record of an answer to these questions.[620] Similar doubts as to the range of the ECHA BoA's tasks were repeated in the course of the preparatory works[621] on the Commission implementing regulation laying down the ECHA RPBoA.[622] However, the Commission did not resolve these doubts unequivocally either, reiterating instead the provisions of REACH and copying the procedural rules of other BoAs.[623] Analysis of preparatory works on the RPBoA suggests that the Commission and the Member States were mostly concerned with secondary issues such as the linguistic regime of appellate proceedings.

B. Review or Second-guessing Expert 'Gut Feeling'?

Despite the blind spots in its legislative design, the ECHA BoA has indeed hammered out an astute review technique with a hands-on approach to learning by doing. It has still not eliminated deference to some of the ECHA's empirically uncertain appraisals. The review technique by the ECHA BoA and the remaining BoAs, just like the technique of judicial review, hinges upon the evidence and arguments advanced by the appellants. The BoAs' modest resources and composition cannot possibly guarantee in-depth knowledge of all intricacies of chemistry, aviation safety, the energy market or financial services. The experience of the ECHA BoA demonstrates, however, that the BoAs may adopt a relatively active and less formalist problem-solving approach, situating themselves in a broad interstice between the ideal-type inquisitorial and adversarial procedural paradigms. This pragmatic approach allows the ECHA BoA to thoroughly discuss contentious technical or scientific issues in order to reduce, as much as possible, the level of empirical and normative uncertainty involved in the agency decision-making.[624]

The scientific complexity and uncertainty of ECHA decisions vary. The problems of epistemic uncertainty are arguably the most pressing in compliance check and substance evaluation cases. The REACH Regulation's key objective was to make the chemical industry responsible for demonstrating the safe use of chemical substances. A chemical producer must register a dossier at the ECHA, showing

the Registration, Evaluation, Authorisation and Restriction of Chemicals (REACH) (...)' (26.9.2005, Council doc. 11337/1/05), 34.

[620] Such answer could have been provided by a Commission representative orally at the Council's meeting. Reply by email from the Council Transparency Unit received on 24.7.2019 in response to a request for public access to documents (19/1516-em/mf).

[621] 'Hungarian Comments to the Commission regulation laying down the rules of organisation and procedure of the Board of Appeal of the ECHA' (4.4.2008), as part of the preparatory works on the said regulation, received on 14.3.2019, request GestDem 2018/6961.

[622] Commission Regulation 771/2008 laying down the rules of organisation and procedure of the Board of Appeal of the European Chemicals Agency [2008] OJ L206/5.

[623] See, in particular, Articles 6 and 18 RPBoA.

[624] Section IV below.

how responsibilities to ensure safe use are implemented. The submitted data are later communicated downstream to further users in the supply chain. The mere act of registering a complete dossier grants market access. The ECHA verifies the *compliance* of selected dossiers with the requirements specified in the Annexes to REACH. Normative and empirical uncertainty may relate to whether there is a concern to be clarified and what studies would be adequate in this respect. Both issues may be far from unambiguous in practice, due to conflicting scientific findings, unclear data and uncertain research methodologies. The ECHA may also proceed to the evaluation of a substance of concern, selected through a complex procedure involving national authorities and the Commission. In this procedure, the ECHA imposes costly testing obligations, the only limit to its discretion being the principle of proportionality.[625]

Epistemic uncertainty involved in the ECHA decision-making is reflected in the composition of its main decision-making body – the Member State Committee – composed of experts delegated and assisted by resourceful domestic authorities. The body adopts its decisions unanimously. Representative composition, organisational resources, and consensus-building procedure secure substantial legitimacy assets, which contrast with the not equally robust assets of the ECHA BoA.

In practice, the ECHA BoA – similarly to the remaining BoAs – has adopted the same grounds of review as the EU Courts in annulment proceedings:[626] breach of competence; breach of an essential procedural requirement; breach of a substantive rule or misuse of powers.[627] It did not back away from strictly enforcing the registrants' procedural rights before the ECHA, even beyond the standard explicitly enshrined in REACH in the name of the fundamental right to be heard.[628] It also settled several contentious issues regarding the application of substantive REACH provisions, where the case law of the EU Courts was not providing clear answers.[629] Most recently, it settled a highly controversial matter of the relationship between the REACH Regulation and Cosmetics Regulation, with potentially far-reaching consequences for the industry and animal welfare.[630]

When it comes to the review of empirical determinations and their legal assessment, the ECHA BoA in its rhetoric refers to the process-oriented review

[625] Lucas Bergkamp, *The European Union REACH Regulation for Chemicals: Law and Practice* (Oxford University Press 2013), 82ff.

[626] Article 263(2) TFEU.

[627] As regards breaches of competence, see, for instance, ECHA BoA, Case A-023-2015, *S.A. Akzo Nobel Chemicals et al. v ECHA*, paras 182–87. Case A-011-2014, *Huntsman P&A UK Limited et al. v ECHA*. As regards the misuse of powers see, ibid, paras 156–62.

[628] ECHA BoA, Case A-009-2014, *Albemarle Europe et al*, paras 225 and 229. Case A-009-2016, *Symrise* (the contested decision was annulled due to multiple breaches of the right to be heard not provided in REACH). Case A-001-2010, *N.V. Elektriciteits Produktiemaatschappij Zuid-Nederland*. Case A-002-2013, *Distillerie de la Tour*. Case A-005-2012, *SEI EPC Italia*. Case A-005-2015, *Thor GmbH*. As regards the duty to state reasons, see, for instance, Case A-013-2016, *BASF Personal Care and Nutrition v ECHA*.

[629] See, ECHA, 'Overview of 10 years of BoA work and its findings', Annex II to ECHA (n 586).

[630] ECHA BoA, Case A-010-2018 and A-009-2018, *Symrise AG Germany*.

technique, well known from the practice of the EU Courts.[631] However, while the EU Courts shy away from second-guessing scientific opinions underpinning the contested acts,[632] the ECHA BoA is directly called upon to scrutinise them to detect 'errors'. According to its own rhetoric, it can sanction a simple 'error of assessment', whereas the EGC may sanction only a '*manifest* error of assessment'. It should be kept in mind, however, that similar references often make a purely semantic difference.[633]

A closer look at decisions issued in 2014–18[634] reveals that the ECHA BoA did delve into issues that the EU Courts would be likely to subject to a rather superficial intelligibility analysis. In principle, the appellant bears the responsibility for presenting persuasive evidence and arguments and for elucidating the BoA members as to why a specific element of the contested decision should be deemed as containing an error.[635] However, a specialisation of BoA members in chemical litigation, as well as some technical expertise of one of the members and supporting staff, may help the appellants with a potentially good case.

In the examined period, the review technique by the BoA appeared more thorough than that applied by the EU Courts in scientifically uncertain cases. The BoA undertook a searching review of the quality of submitted data in light of potential methodological flaws and the importance of resulting data gaps to be filled by the appellants,[636] the reliability of inferences from the available data proposed by the appellants,[637] or the seriousness of newly identified concerns.[638] The motives

[631] ECHA BoA, Case A-005-2011, *Honeywell*, paras 76ff, referring to ECJ case law. Case A-006-2017, *Climax Molybdenum*, para 38.

[632] Chapter 3, Section II.B.

[633] See, accordingly, Castillo de la Torre and Gippini Fournier (n 71), 268 and 284.

[634] Twenty decisions were identified in which a definitive decision was issued by the ECHA BoA between 1.1.2014 and 31.12.2018 (where no court action against the decision was lodged) in which the ECHA BoA dealt with pleas in law relating to the legal assessment of empirically uncertain data or uncertain normative appraisals pertaining to the adequacy or proportionality of the scientific studies requested by the ECHA from the appellants.

[635] ECHA BoA, Case A-013-2014, *BASF SE*, para 160.

[636] For instance, in ECHA BoA, Case A-006-2017, *Climax Molybdenum*, paras 54–77, the ECHA BoA opined that, in the previous studies, the tested animals were insufficiently and inadequately exposed to the substance (including a lack of coordination with their mating period), considering relevant Organisation for Economic Co-operation and Development (OECD) guidelines, which distorted the results. In Case A-005-2016, *Cheminova*, paras 95–97, the ECHA BoA came to the conclusion that the proposed, so-called, read-across adaptation (a prediction of the properties of a substance based on a comparison with a different, similar substance) was not sufficiently justified as the appellant's justification relied on yet another predictive rather than evidence-based tool.

[637] In Case A-005-2016, *Cheminova*, paras 95–97, the ECHA BoA opined that the proposed, so-called, read-across adaptation (a prediction of the properties of a substance based on a comparison with a similar substance) did not support sufficiently certain conclusions as the appellant's justification relied on yet another predictive rather than evidence-based tool. In Case A-004-2015, *Polynt*, paras 129–38, the BoA pointed out in a very detailed manner differences between the two substances based on which the ECHA had had to reject the read-across adaptation proposed by the appellant.

[638] In Case A-009-2014, *Albemarle Europe et al*, paras 99–105, the BoA noted that, in the course of proceedings, the Agency itself as well as the supporting intervener admitted having doubts regarding the reliability of a scientific publication constituting the basis for the contested request for further studies, which led to a partial annulment of the contested decision. At the same time, other concerns were

of BoA decisions demonstrate a careful and profound scrabbling around in the detailed design of scientific tests and methodological issues, their compliance with international standards, and the reliability of conclusions drawn from the scientific literature. Moreover, the ECHA BoA provided specific arguments as to why it considered specific studies, requested by the ECHA, to be adequate to clarify the points of concern,[639] and proportionate.[640] While confronted with scientific opinions of specialised committees, the EGC usually confines its analysis to the rather superficial intelligibility check, whereas the BoA directly considers the correctness or at least persuasiveness of scientific reasoning.

If the ECHA BoA disagrees with the first-instance decision-makers on any issue pertaining to the scientific methodology or data analysis, it formally identifies an 'error of assessment'. An ECHA BoA's decision to state an error is not merely 'objective' and value-neutral (it is not just a matter of cognition). For instance, in one case the ECHA BoA had to decide whether a concern resulting from inhalation toxicity studies of one type of the substance in question could justify the request of further studies with regard to this substance's other types, whereas there were multiple doubts regarding all these substances' intrinsic properties.[641] A normatively discretionary assessment underpins a decision as to what counts as sufficient proof of potential risk to public health or the environment (it is a matter of volition).[642] How one understands 'sufficient proof' of product safety results from one's subjective or implicit axiological choice as to the relative priority between, for instance, the economic rights of the industry (and related social issues) and the protection of public health and the environment. Similar problems with the concept of proof pertain to any regulatory fields marked with epistemic empirical and normative uncertainty.

The entanglement of empirical and normative uncertainty is further illustrated by the ECHA BoA's approach to the proportionality analysis of chemical studies requested from the operators by the ECHA. For instance, the ECHA BoA quashed a scientific test prescribed by the first-instance decision-makers since it considered that this test had contained too many onerous specifications potentially increasing the chance of success and, overall, aimed at generating an excessive amount of scientific data by the operator in question.[643] The ECHA BoA had to

deemed duly justified. Ibid, para 81. See also Case A-014-2015, *Grace and Advanced Refining Technologies*, paras 55ff.

639 In Case A-004-2014, *Altair Chimica*, paras 49–56, the BoA carefully explained why the testing approach followed by the ECHA was justified considering specific properties of the substance in question. See also ECHA BoA, Case A-018-2014, *BASF Grenzach*, paras 42–45. Case A-013-2014, *BASF SE*, paras 159–62.

640 ECHA BoA, Case A-006-2017, *Climax Molybendum*, para 140, suggesting that the BoA can by itself consider different feasible versions of the requested study to assess if the study is proportionate. See also Case A-015-2015, *Evonik Degussa GmbH and Others*, paras 210–18.

641 Case A-014-2015, *Grace and Advanced Refining Technologies*.

642 The conceptual distinction between matters of cognition/volition is noted by Mendes (n 85).

643 ECHA BoA, Case A-008-2017, *SI Group UK and Osiris Chemicals*, paras 126–29. The specifications were two different temperatures, a duration of at least six months, an assessment of transformation products formed at level of 1 or even 0.1%.

subjectively assess the chances of success of these studies and to what extent the chemical industry should bear potentially futile costs in the name of precaution for public health and the environment. In another case, the ECHA BoA considered that concern about a substance in question had led the first-instance decision-makers to order the carrying out of a chemical study which had little chances of success, so the ECHA had effectively burdened the chemical operator with the task of improving available scientific methods.[644] In yet another case, the ECHA BoA held that the contested decision was disproportionate as it requested an excessive amount of data on many different types of the registered substance. In contrast, the available evidence suggested a potential risk concerning only one type, and the ECHA could not specifically explain in what specific way the data would be used. The ECHA counterargued that the unexplained differences in toxicity between the different types of the substance, many of which were marketed by the appellants, were in themselves a potential concern that required clarification.[645] In each of these cases, the ECHA had to strike *in concreto* a normative balance between the rights of the industry and the public interest, while at the same time interpreting intricate empirical problems.

In some cases, the degree of uncertainty may lead the ECHA BoA to defer to the first-instance assessments, either explicitly – invoking a 'difference of scientific opinion'[646] – or by only making a declaration that an 'error' has not been detected.[647] For instance, the ECHA BoA upheld a specific first-instance assessment of what counts as a slight, moderate or severe maternal toxicity, based on assumptions in available literature rather than precise and rigorous justification, because the applicable legislation itself left the interpretation of these terms open.[648] In some cases, the ECHA BoA simply ascertained whether the appellant's claims had already been addressed at first instance.[649]

Likewise, other BoAs face problems of empirical and normative uncertainty. Evidently, they tend to transplant the largely adversarial procedural setting, in which the appellant shoulders the burden of proof, and the process-oriented

[644] For instance, in ECHA BoA, Case A-026-2015, *Envigo Consulting and DJChem Chemicals Poland*, paras 122–25 and 136–40.

[645] ECHA BoA, Case A-015-2015, *Evonik Degussa GmbH and Others*, paras 210–18.

[646] For instance, in ECHA BoA, Case A-015-2015, *Evonik Degussa et al*, para 174, the BoA observed: 'the data available for substance evaluations is in some cases inconsistent or indeed contradictory and in other leave questions open. It is therefore not surprising that there is often a difference of opinion between experts when assessing the available data'. See also, Case A-018-2014, *BASF Grenzach*, paras 134 and 155–56.

[647] Interestingly, the ESAs' BoA style their reasoning in a somewhat different way, suggesting an autonomous reconsideration (different view) rather than detection of errors. For instance, 'in the Board of Appeal's view, this was a sensible approach …' (ESAs BoA, Joined Cases BoA-D-2019-1 to 4, *Svenska Handelsbanken et al v ESMA*, para 225) or 'although the position is less than clear, the Board *prefers* the appellant's contention in this regard …' (ESAs BoA, Case BoA 2013–14, *Global Standard Rating v ESMA*, paras 137 and 111 (emphasis added); see also, for instance, paras 101–02, 112).

[648] For instance, in ECHA BoA, Case A-023-2015, *Akzo Novel Chemicals et al*, paras 67–68 and 74–76.

[649] For instance, ECHA BoA, Case A-015-2015, *Evonik Degussa et al*, paras 170–74; Case A-018-2014, *BASF Grenzach*, paras 57–64, 163–65.

review technique of the EU Courts. The ACER BoA invokes even the concept of a '*manifest* error of assessment'.[650] These BoAs also tend to explicitly defer to uncertain assessments of first-instance decision-makers, where the degree of uncertainty is high.[651] The legitimacy assets of first-instance decision-makers in the respective agencies are clearly superior. The BoA of ESAs or the EASA, just like the ECHA BoA, deal with regulatory fields in which there are no unfailing methodologies. Having got to the very root of a contentious scientific or technical issue, we must content ourselves with what is ultimately a value-laden gut feeling or 'professional judgment' of someone who is considered an expert. If this feeling is to be reviewed in a meaningful way, an expanded structure of expert adjudicators seem indispensable.

The rate of successful appeals provides a picture of the BoA's interference with the ECHA decision-making.[652] From 2009 until the end of 2018, the ECHA BoA ruled in 50 per cent of appeals brought to it. As many as 34 per cent of appeals were withdrawn. In 16 per cent of cases, the contested decision was ultimately rectified by the ECHA Executive Director.[653] More specifically, in 2014–18 the ECHA BoA annulled the impugned decision and remitted the case for reconsideration in 24 out of 45 cases (53.3%).[654] Such a high rate of at least partially successful appeals, especially if coupled with the more in-depth study of the ECHA BoA's case law – does not seem to raise concerns about excessive deference to the ECHA or the BoA's added value.

However, the ECHA BoA has used its competence to modify the decision's substance in only one case relating to a data-sharing dispute. These kinds of cases do not raise empirically uncertain issues, and the ECHA BoA held that the documentation available to it was sufficiently complete to allow it to indicate the list of scientific studies to which the appellant sought access.[655] Conversely, in a recent substance evaluation case, the ECHA BoA refused to replace the unlawful decision with its own as it considered that the many actors participating in the first-instance proceedings must be given an opportunity to make supplementary

[650] ACER BoA, Case A-002-2018, *PRISMA European Capacity Platform GmbH*, para 16 (emphasis added). See also, Case A-001-2017, *Energie Control Austria et al*, paras 104–11. Case A-001-2018, *AQUIND*, paras 46 and 51–53.

[651] See, in particular, ESAs BoA, Case BoA 2017 01, *Financial Craft Analytics v ESMA*, para 87. SRB Appeal Panel, Case 8/18, *anonymised*, para 30. EASA BoA, Case AP/01/2012, *Heli-Flight GmbH*, paras 62–63. See, however, ESAs BoA, Case BoA 2013–14, *Global Standard Rating v ESMA*.

[652] It is difficult to present numbers regarding other BoAs dealing with complex matters as their output has been very modest until now.

[653] The possibility of rectification by the Executive Director is provided for by Article 93(1) REACH.

[654] A similar rate of successful appeals was obtained with regard to the whole period of the ECHA BoA's operation from 2009 until the end of 2018. See, ECHA, 'Final report from the outgoing Chairman of the Board of Appeal' (MB/10/2019 final of 29.3.2019). The rate of success is therefore higher than before the GC, where it amounts to approximately 40% (partially or fully successful actions for annulment).

[655] ECHA BoA, Case A-013-2018, *Tecnofluid*, para 58. See also, Cases A-014-2018 to A-021-2018, *Tecnofluid*, para 98.

scientific appraisals.[656] In all other successful cases, the ECHA BoA annulled the impugned decisions and remitted the case to the ECHA for further consideration, which from the perspective of the appellants prolongs the overall time of proceedings before the ECHA.

C. Who Should Demonstrate Added Value?

Overall, the review by the ECHA BoA tends to be more thorough than the review by the EGC regarding uncertain empirical issues. Neither did the ECHA BoA shy away from settling controversial interpretive issues. Moreover, the ECHA and its BoA members have put considerable effort into improving the public appearance of BoA independence. In this context, what is the added value of the two- or three-tier system of extra-judicial and judicial review (a BoA, the EGC and the ECJ)?[657] What role should be played by the BoAs in relation to the EU judicial review, and vice versa, especially in cases characterised by normative and empirical uncertainty?

Recent litigation before the BoAs and the EGC prompts raising this question. In particular, a chemical operator contested what it considered an inadequately intense standard of review by the ECHA BoA in a case in which the ECHA had applied deference.[658] It raised several arguments. It stressed 'functional continuity' between the agency and its BoA, a concept introduced by the EGC to clarify the duties of the BoAs given a lack of clear legislative guidance. It also invoked the legislative provision authorising the BoA to exercise any power of the agency, inferring therefrom that the BoA should fully reinvestigate every case.[659]

The ECHA argued before the EGC that its BoA performs 'quasi-judicial review' as it relies on the parties' evidence. The ECHA also stressed the institutional context and the resource gap between the ECHA Member States Committee (which must reach its decisions unanimously) and the BoA.[660] The ECHA tried to clarify the BoA's role by disentangling the scientific and political layers of decision-making. In the ECHA's view, the determination of an acceptable degree of risk to human health and the environment, to protect, among other things, the interests of the chemical industry, involves 'political choices' that are for the ECHA and national

[656] ECHA BoA, Case A-008-2020, *Taminco*, para 101.

[657] The question is equally valid for the other BoAs replicating the deferential standard of judicial review (EASA, ACER, ESAs and SRB Appeal Panel), as well as those which fully reconsider the submitted cases on both legal and factual points (EUIPO, CPVO).

[658] Case T-125/17, *BASF v ECHA*, ECLI:EU:T:2019:638. Germany, conversely, claimed that the scope of review by the ECHA BoA is too thorough. Case T-755/17, *Germany v ECHA*, ECLI:EU:T:2019:647.

[659] The report for the hearing in the Case T-125/17, *BASF v ECHA*, ECLI:EU:T:2019:638, paras 36–40 (personally obtained at the EGC on the day of the hearing, on file with the author).

[660] If the Member States fail to reach a unanimous agreement on the matter, it falls to the Commission to adopt the final decision in a procedure in which, however, the Member States may still exercise control over the Commission's powers. Articles 51(7) and 59(9) REACH.

authorities to make.[661] Meanwhile, the appeal process does not even provide for the involvement of the Member States other than as simple interveners,[662] so the BoA must confine itself to the detection of errors.

Interestingly, EGC judges' questions at the oral hearing suggested that they had difficulty seeing efficiency in the current structure for several tiers of broadly similar review. At the same time, they implicitly acknowledged that imposing on the ECHA BoA a duty to reinvestigate every case would bring catastrophe upon it due to the unforeseen level of additional resources.[663] It was no surprise that the EGC ultimately endorsed the ECHA BoA's review technique, mostly referring to the institutional considerations. It emphasised that certain ECHA decisions are made in the inescapable context of scientific uncertainty and that the ECHA BoA does not have the same resources as the first-instance decision-makers to repeat the full investigation of every case. It also pointed to the ECHA BoA's procedural scheme, according to which the applicants must discharge the burden of proof and flesh out the ECHA's errors.[664]

Similar allegations were presented before other BoAs. The ACER BoA held that it could not be expected to fully reinvestigate the cases due to its limited resources and time to complete the proceedings.[665] The EU Courts, however, adopted a different solution with regard to the CPVO BoA. The latter was under a duty to fully reinvestigate the cases due to an explicit legislative provision imposing upon it the same procedural obligations as those imposed on the first-instance decision-makers.[666] Nonetheless, although requiring scientific knowledge, the cases before the CPVO are arguably not equally complex in terms of the number of empirical factors and normative choices to consider.[667]

The fact that a specialist adjudicative body ventures into the areas of science from which judges prefer to stay away may lead to some problems. Specialised

[661] The report for the hearing (n 659), paras 53ff. As argued by the ECHA Chairwoman in her extra-'judicial' statements, the doctrine of functional continuity may need to be applied to the ECHA BoA with caution. 'If the [EU] legislator intended to have a second tier of scientific evaluation, the composition and size of the BoA should have been entirely different'. Mercedes Ortuño, 'The standard of review by the Board of Appeal' (Seminar on 10 years of REACH Litigation, Helsinki, 24.5.2017, available at echa.europa.eu), 9.

[662] The report for the hearing (n 659), paras 53ff. Germany argued that the Member States Committee is not even a body of the ECHA but rather an emanation of Member States' sovereign powers. This interpretation would not only further limit the ambit of ECHA BoA review (to procedural matters only) but would even shield the ECHA's substantive decisions from the BoA's scrutiny.

[663] The author's own notes from the oral hearing on 12.12.2018 in Case T-125/17, *BASF v ECHA*, ECLI:EU:T:2019:638.

[664] Case T-125/17, *BASF v ECHA*, ECLI:EU:T:2019:638, paras 62–65 and 85. In this respect, the EGC mainly relied on the implementing provisions of the RPBoA and not the legislative provisions of the REACH itself. A question then arises as to whether the Commission enjoys leeway to introduce a more inquisitorial model of proceedings before the ECHA BoA.

[665] ACER BoA, Case A-001-2019 *Amprion & Transnet*, paras 74–81.

[666] Case T-133/08 *Schräder v CPVO*, ECLI:EU:T:2012:430 and Case C-546/12 P *Schräder v CPVO*, ECLI:EU:C:2015:332.

[667] The EGC mentioned in the ruling relating to the ECHA BoA a different 'regulatory context'. Case T-125/17, *BASF v ECHA*, ECLI:EU:T:2019:638, paras 101ff.

adjudication may foster the emergence of narrow epistemic communities, in which specialised adjudicators and litigators lose sight of horizontal issues and, consequently, unwittingly reproduce systemic mistakes. A related risk is regulatory capture. The members and staff of a specialised adjudicative body, recruited from private sector experts, may favour this sector's perspective rather than the public interest. This risk applies in particular to ad hoc BoA members. Higher-instance generalist courts may bring an external perspective, detect systemic mistakes and maintain horizontal consistency between specialised administrative law branches.

In an efficient several-tier judicial and extra-judicial review system, each tier should arguably bring a distinctive added value or set of legitimacy assets. The EU system architects enjoy broad leeway in reshaping institutional and procedural features of the BoAs and the EU Courts alike. They might broaden the composition of BoAs and provide them with more resources to enable them to develop an even more thorough review technique, including perhaps more inquisitorial adjudicatory practices. Importantly, Article 263(5) TFEU authorises the EU co-legislators to lay down specific arrangements for private court actions against agency acts. Should the BoAs play a more significant role in the legal protection of individuals, and were their independence safeguards reinforced to comply with the 'judicial standard', the co-legislators might consider a filtering device to enable the EGC to review only selected cases against the BoAs. The co-legislators might as well, quite to the contrary, choose to invest public resources in a further expansion of the EGC and, perhaps, provide it with specialist support, a system of expert witnesses or the like. In this scenario, the added value of the BoAs could be called into question. Overall, a decision regarding the specific shape of EU judicial and extra-judicial architecture pertains to the political sphere.

III. The Long Shadow of *Plaumann*

A. A Specialised Tribunal for Chemical Operators

The instrumental and deliberative functions of a review mechanism hinge upon its accessibility, especially in cases regarding legal acts that may adversely affect its formal addressees and a wide range of third parties or society in general. The ECHA decisions, although addressed to individual chemical operators, affect a whole array of public interest goals: public health, the environment and animal welfare. Notably, frequent applications for intervention by environmental and animal welfare organisations express interest-aggregation and deliberative expectations towards the ECHA appeal process.

In drafting the REACH Regulation, the Commission aimed to secure the new system's reasonable costs and the prerogatives of the ECHA decision-making committee.[668] Initially, it proposed granting the right of appeal only to the formal addressees of ECHA decisions. Some Parliament members proposed granting access to 'all those having a legal interest' or 'any party having a legal interest'. These proposals, however, were not ultimately accepted.[669] Instead, the co-legislators copy-pasted the Article 263(4) TFEU admissibility criteria for annulment actions. Thus, as in the cases of other BoAs, the right to appeal is granted to the addressees of ECHA decisions and those 'directly and individually concerned' by such decisions.[670]

In interpreting its access rules, the ECHA BoA has generally followed the case law of EU Courts and their restrictive *Plaumann* doctrine.[671] As a result, in the examined period all of the appellants before the ECHA BoA were chemical operators. When it comes to admissible cases, 84 per cent of the applicants were the intended addressees of contested decisions. The cases in which the appeals were accepted based on the 'direct and individual concern' criterion concerned joint registrations of the same substance. The decisions directly affected joint registrants and their cost-sharing obligation.

For instance, the appeal in *REACheck Solutions* was brought by a lead registrant of the substance 'charcoal' against a decision by which the ECHA found a separate registration of the same substance submitted by another registrant to be complete. The appellant claimed that, pursuant to REACH, the second registrant should have joined the first registration and reimbursed the appellant for a part of its registration costs. The BoA found that the contested decision concerned the appellant directly as the contested decision had deprived it of the *right* to demand the reimbursement.[672] The contested decision also concerned the appellant individually; since it had been the lead registrant of the substance – known to the ECHA – it clearly formed part of a 'closed class' of persons affected by the contested decision.[673]

[668] There is an appeal fee but, at the same time, a system of reductions and waivers is provided. Articles 10 and 13 of Commission Regulation 340/2008 on the fees and charges payable to the European Chemicals Agency [2006] OJ L107/6. Even though there are no formal fees at the EGC and the ECJ, the cost of litigation before the EU Courts is considered significant due to the costs of professional legal representation (by independent lawyers, representation by in-house lawyers being precluded).

[669] Parliament, 'Report on the proposal for a regulation of the European Parliament and of the Council on the Registration, Evaluation, Authorisation and Restriction of Chemicals (REACH)' (A6-0315/2005 final, 24.10.2005), 29, 483 and 853.

[670] Otherwise, given that the lodging of an administrative appeal is a precondition of a subsequent action for annulment before the EU Courts, the access rules of a BoA could effectively narrow down (or broaden) access to the EU Courts. See Council (n 619), 36 (Article 88(1)).

[671] ECHA BoA, Case A-022-2013, *REACheck Solutions*, paras 69, 83 and 91, referring to the ECJ case law on the restrictive standing criteria. See also, ECHA BoA, Case A-022-2015, *Manufacture Française des Pneumatiques Michelin v ECHA*, para 116. It has been argued in the literature that a BoA could depart from the restrictive interpretation of the EU Courts and, thus, widen access to justice at the EU level. According to case law, discussed in Chapter 4, a prior procedural involvement is one of the means to meet the *Plaumann* test. Being an applicant before the BoA is undoubtedly a procedural involvement even if the final decision is formally addressed to another person. See Andreas Witte, 'Standing and Judicial Review in the New EU Financial Markets Architecture' (2015) 1 *Journal of Financial Regulation* 226, 247–253.

[672] Case A-022-2013, *REACheck Solutions*, para 86.

[673] ibid, para 92.

Occasionally, the BoA's interpretation of 'direct and individual concern' seemed stricter than that applied by the EGC. As already discussed, the EGC sometimes adopts a more liberal approach. It accepts actions from applicants whose *economic interests* (market position) rather than *legal situation*, strictly speaking, are particularly adversely affected by the contested decision. This occurs in particular when the applicant has participated in the administrative proceedings leading to the adoption of the contested act or has some contractual links to the formal addressee. However, the BoA has not endorsed an analogous approach to the non-addressees of contested decisions who have had business links to the addressees. In *Manufacture Française des Pneumatiques Michelin* the BoA did not recognise the standing of a downstream user to challenge a decision regarding substance evaluation addressed to this substance's producer. The *economic* interests of the downstream user could undoubtedly be significantly affected by the contested decision. But the BoA found that REACH did not grant any rights regarding substance evaluation to the downstream users.[674]

The *Plaumann* doctrine, governing the direct access of private parties to the EU Courts, in principle excludes legality challenges by public interest organisations and social actors. As a result of its application to the ECHA BoA, the ECHA BoA is called to scrutinise the ECHA decisions almost exclusively from the perspective of chemical operators' private economic interests, just like the EU Courts. The appeal process cannot be triggered by environmental organisations wishing the act as the ECHA's watchdogs. Although a different interpretation of 'direct and individual concern' by a BoA is not inconceivable, hitherto there have been no attempts by an NGO to appeal to the ECHA BoA. An important argument favouring a more liberal interpretation of the admissibility criteria by the ECHA BoA would undoubtedly be offered by the Aarhus Convention, which promotes access to justice in environment-related cases by the members of civil society.[675]

B. Environmental Interventions

Notably, the ECHA BoA's approach to intervention is distinctly more liberal than that of the EU Courts.[676] The BoA has maintained this despite the ECHA's consistent opposition. A possible explanation could be that interveners provide the BoA with useful data, which facilitates correct decision-making. Moreover, in its rhetoric, the ECHA BoA also advances deliberative justifications pertaining to

[674] ibid, paras 123–29. It held that the downstream user was not directly concerned regardless of its status as a participant in an information exchange forum regarding this particular substance – a form of data sharing provided for by REACH – or the fact that it had contractual data-sharing and cost-sharing obligations towards the lead registrant. Ibid, paras 130–46.

[675] Aarhus Convention (n 125).

[676] However, when seized to interpret the conditions of intervention before the ACER BoA, the EGC tended to apply the reasoning applicable to interventions in its own proceedings. Case T-146/17, *Mondi v ACER*, ECLI:EU T:2018:570.

the inclusion of environmental organisations as stakeholders, in the public debate about the implementation of REACH, as well as the already mentioned Aarhus Convention.

Pursuant to the RPBoA, any person establishing an *interest* in the result of an appeal may intervene in that case.[677] What constitutes sufficient 'interest' is evidently indeterminate and subject to interpretation by the BoA just as before the EU Courts. Intervention does not grant the same procedural rights as the status of the appellant. It is limited to supporting or opposing the remedy sought and pleas in law formulated by one of the parties. It nonetheless offers meaningful opportunities to influence the outcome of appeal proceedings. Interveners receive the copies of all written submissions and they can submit their own written observations and actively participate in the oral hearing.[678]

Often, applications for intervention come from co-registrants of the substance to which the appellate proceedings relate,[679] and national chemical safety authorities.[680] Importantly, in the examined period, intervention by an environmental or animal welfare organisation was admitted in as many as 11 proceedings (25% of admissible proceedings). In most cases, the intervener organisations sided with the appellants and opposed animal testing.

The admissibility criteria of interventions by environmental organisations as conceived by the BoA has raised opposition from the ECHA. In its early practice, the ECHA BoA relied on the case law on intervention before the EU Courts, which set up easier conditions for intervention by 'representative organisations', ie those representing a certain group of operators in a given market. Such organisations, whose object is to protect their members' interests, may intervene in cases raising questions of principle liable to affect those members. In practice, the BoA checks whether the organisation is an accredited stakeholder, whether its goals encompass animal welfare (or other environmental goals),[681] whether it has indeed been active in its field of interest including within the ECHA's stakeholder committees,[682] and whether the subject matter of appeal proceedings concerns animal welfare.[683]

The ECHA was right to point out that the said case law referred to organisations of economic operators rather than public interest organisations. However, the

[677] Article 8 RPBoA.

[678] Although they do not have a right to demand the oral hearing be held.

[679] See ECHA BoA, Case A-010-2017 (intervention), *Colorex et al.* Conversely, the BoA held that being the registrant of a *similar* substance does not constitute a sufficient interest, Case A-006-2017 (intervention), *Plansee SE*.

[680] See ECHA BoA, Case A-019-2013 (intervention), *Solutia Europe*. Regarding the difficulties of Member States in establishing their interest in the result of the case, see Case A-004-2014 (intervention), *Altair Chimica*.

[681] ECHA BoA, Case A-014-2015 (intervention), *Grace GmbH et al v ECHA*.

[682] For instance, Case A-001-2012 (intervention), *Dow Benelux*, paras 26–27. For a positive outcome, see Case A-001-2014 (intervention by PETA), *Clinic Chemicals*.

[683] See, for instance, a case in which the link was too remote, ECHA BoA, Case A-005-2013 (intervention), *Vanadium R.E.A.C.H. Forschungs- und Entwicklungsverein*, para 22.

BoA stated that this case law is applicable to appeal proceedings due to REACH's objectives.[684] More specifically, REACH seeks to promote various interests, including the protection of human health and the environment, ensuring competitiveness and innovation, the protection of workers' health, and to replace, reduce or refine animal testing. To this effect, the REACH Regulation foresees the involvement of stakeholders in the Agency's work … This involvement is to help ensure that the different interests are considered in the Agency's decision making.[685]

The BoA also added that 'accredited stakeholders may be considered to satisfy more readily the required interest for intervening in proceedings before the Board of Appeal'.[686]

Since then, the BoA has clung to its liberal interpretation of intervention criteria, notwithstanding continuous though waning opposition from the ECHA. The ECHA again opposed the liberal practice, once the EGC had clarified the criteria for intervention by environmental organisations in court proceedings. Contradicting the BoA's liberal practice, the EGC stated that the requirement for an 'interest' in the result of the case means that the scope of the organisation's activities must coincide with the specific 'sector' to which the case relates. In practice, the 'sector' meant the specific chemical substance. Where the scope of an organisation's activities is wider, it should at least be actively involved in protection programmes or studies relating to the sector/substance concerned.[687] The ECHA BoA found these criteria 'unduly restrictive' and maintained its previous approach with reference to the objectives of REACH and the need to involve stakeholders in the ECHA decision-making.[688] However, as discussed in the previous chapter, the ECJ most recently tended to abandon the requirement of prior activity relating to a specific sector or substance, and general campaigns against pesticides or animal testing sufficed to intervene in cases related to those matters.[689]

IV. Procedural Activity in an Administrative Trial

A. Mimicking a Court

Proceedings before the ECHA BoA and other BoAs deliver instrumental and deliberative legitimacy assets similar to those delivered by the EGC,[690] as the

[684] ECHA BoA, Case A-001-2012 (intervention), *Dow Benelux B.V.*, para 22.

[685] ECHA BoA, Case A-005-2011 (intervention), *Honeywell*, para 22.

[686] ibid, para 30.

[687] Case T-429/13, *Bayer CropScience v Commission*, ECLI:EU:T:2018:280.

[688] ECHA BoA, Case A-013-2016 (intervention), *BASF Personal Care and Nutrition GmbH.* Case A-001-2018 (intervention), *BrüggemannChemical.*

[689] Chapter 4, Section III.B. *in fine*.

[690] In the course of preparatory works on the ECHA BoA's rules of procedure, the fair trial standards under Article 6(1) ECHR were invoked, which would suggest that the appeal proceedings were somehow conceived of as akin to judicial proceedings. The preparatory works (doc. 4_071126) (n 621).

structure of the BoA procedure is usually modelled upon that of the EGC.[691] The ECHA BoA offers the parties ample opportunities for participation as its operation depends entirely on the data provided by them. The REACH Regulation is ambiguous on the degree of procedural activity expected of the ECHA BoA. The co-legislators delegated the power to lay down the specific procedural rules in this respect to the Commission. However, the first draft of the RPBoA was elaborated and forwarded to the Commission by the ECHA itself.[692] Hence, the ECHA had a meaningful say on the BoA's tasks and powers, its own procedural rights, and the appeal system's overall cost.

Neither the ECHA nor later the Commission unequivocally determined the adversarial or the inquisitorial character of appeal proceedings. Arguably, they left the matter to incrementally and organically unfold in practice. On the one hand, the RPBoA require the appellant to set out specific pleas in law and offer relevant evidence. In principle, no new plea in law or new pieces of evidence may be introduced after the first exchange of written pleadings. On the other hand, no provision in the RPBoA specifies that the BoA has to confine itself to examining only the pleas and evidence adduced by the appellant.[693] Moreover, the ECHA BoA's own rules on allocating the costs for taking evidence provide for a possibility of the ECHA BoA's commissioning new evidence on its initiative.[694] The ECHA, Commission and Member States did not seem to have any clear vision regarding the procedural activity of the parties and the BoA. During the drafting process they were concerned about how to split the costs of new evidence, were new evidence taken before the BoA.[695] They concentrated on keeping the level of the costs of proceedings as low as possible. Unable to find common ground, they ultimately authorised the BoA itself to adopt procedural rules regarding the cost of taking evidence.[696]

[691] The rules of procedure of the BoAs are adopted by the Commission (CPVO, ECHA) or the BoAs themselves (EUIPO, ESAs, EASA, SRB Appeal Panel).

[692] The preparatory works (doc. 1_071113) (n 621).

[693] Articles 6 and 19 RPBoA. The adversarial or inquisitorial nature of proceedings before the BoA may cause confusion. At the oral hearing in the pending BASF case (T-125/17, *BASF v ECHA*, 12.12.2018) regarding the BoA's responsibilities, the judges entertained doubts as to whether 'functional continuity', as conceived of by BASF, implied that the BoA would be obliged to raise on behalf of the appellant all relevant pleas in law. The BASF representative clarified that the BoA should fully review the contested decision (intensity of review) 'in the context of' grounds of review set out by the appellant (the author's own notes from the oral hearing, on file with the author).

[694] Article 2(2) of the Decision of the ECHA BoA on implementing rules on costs relating to the taking of evidence in appeal proceedings.

[695] Draft Commission Regulation [RPBoA] with comments by the Commission services and the ECHA, at 14–15. Email from the Commission to the ECHA of 28.12.2007 (comments to draft Article 21). Lithuania's comments of 4.4.2008 (preparatory documents received from the Commission on 14.3.2019, request GROW/D1/CK/nt; grow.ddgl.d.l(2019)1271411).

[696] Article 17(4) RPBoA. Some controversies surrounded this issue as well. Germany expressed doubts as to whether the BoA should be authorised to concretise its own tasks and powers by adopting general and abstract procedural norms. 'Opinion of the German Federal Government on the Commission Regulation laying down the rules of organisation and procedure of the Board of Appeal of the European Chemical Agency' (Bonn, 1.4.2008), 3. Ibid.

Considering the unprecedented scientific complexity and epistemic uncertainty involved in the REACH system, a small adjudicatory unit such as the ECHA BoA had no choice but to adopt in practice the adversarial system of pleas. In its early days, it was not quite sure of the actual scope of its duties. Interestingly, in its first substantive decision, it had to decide whether an FAQ published on the ECHA's website had misled the appellant, who, as a result, had not paid a registration fee on time. The BoA needed to compare the successive versions of the FAQ, whereas the appellant had only referred to the latest version in its notice of appeal. The ECHA contested the examination of previous versions as the BoA obtained them on their own initiative. The ECHA claimed that 'it would be inappropriate for the Board of Appeal to raise new grounds for a possible annulment of the contested decision which have not been invoked by the appellant'.[697]

In response, the BoA held that REACH authorises it to exercise any power which lies in the competence of the ECHA. It also invoked the case law of the EGC under which 'continuity in terms of functions' exists between an agency and its BoA. The EGC explained, with regard to the EUIPO BoAs, that

> the examination which the Board [of EUIPO] must conduct is not, in principle, determined by the grounds relied on by the party who has brought the appeal. Accordingly, even if the party who has brought the appeal has not raised a specific ground of appeal, the Board of Appeal is none the less bound to examine whether or not, in the light of all relevant matters of fact and of law, a new decision with the same operative part as the decision under appeal may be lawfully adopted at the time of the appeal ruling.[698]

The ECHA BoA held that the same concept of functional continuity should apply to itself and that it must, therefore, carry out a full re-examination of the case's merits, regardless of the arguments raised by the appellant.[699]

In its subsequent practice, the BoA has not followed this path. It has confined itself to examining the pleas in law set out by the appellant, in the same way as the EU Courts do. Nor does it allow new pleas in law to be raised after the expiry of the deadline for lodging the appeal,[700] let alone modify the form of order (remedy) sought.[701] Only once has it applied the EU Courts' case law regarding public policy pleas, raising on its own motion a plea relating to the breach of an essential procedural requirement.[702] Even though the rules on evidence adopted by the ECHA BoA foresee the possibility that it would take evidence on its own initiative,[703] it has not used this option. In practice, it entirely relies on the evidence

[697] ECHA BoA, Case A-001-2010, *N.V. Elektriciteits*, para 30.

[698] ibid, paras 30–34 referring to Case T-308/01, *Henkel KGaA v OHIM*, ECLI:EU:T:2003:241, para 29.

[699] ibid, paras 35–37.

[700] ECHA BoA, Case A-004-2011, *Kronochem*, para 43; Case A-023-2015, *S.A. Akzo Nobel Chemicals NV*, paras 191–97.

[701] ECHA BoA, Case A-018-2014, *BASF Grenzach*, paras 29–32.

[702] ECHA BoA, Case A-020-2013, *Ullrich Biodiesel v ECHA*, paras 23–25.

[703] Article 2(2) cf the Decision of the ECHA BoA on implementing rules on costs relating to the taking of evidence in appeal proceedings.

presented by the parties.[704] It does not even have access to the full first-instance case file, even though they are stored in the same building.[705]

In a public interview, a member of the ECHA BoA, while explaining the functioning of the appeal system, emphasised the importance of the appellant's procedural activity and responsibility to set out compelling pleas in law, advance relevant arguments and adduce pertinent evidence so that the overall task of not-so-specialist members of the ECHA BoA be facilitated.

> And the clearer they can make those arguments and the clearer they can make the evidence supporting those arguments, the easier is for us to really consider their case carefully, and properly, and fully … So be clear what your grounds are, and make your points as straightforwardly as you can.[706]

The ECHA BoA imposes on the appellant a large part of procedural responsibility for demonstrating and proving the impugned act's unlawfulness. Although appellants' well-prepared procedural activity increases the chances of success, the ECHA BoA has at the same time been inclined to enforce the system of pleas in a not so rigorous way, especially since there is no obligation to be represented before the ECHA BoA by an independent lawyer, unlike before the EU Courts.[707] The ECHA BoA has proven active in clarifying ambiguous pleas in the course of proceedings by carefully analysing the content of appeals to reconstruct the intended pleas in law, the scope of the challenge and the form of order (remedy) sought, even if these are improperly formulated.[708]

In one case the BoA applied a procedural measure requesting clarification of the pleas in law. 'The Board of Appeal underlined that it had found it extremely difficult to identify clearly the precise pleas in law raised by the Appellants in their submissions, and what facts were invoked in support of each plea'. The BoA requested 'a clear, precise and exhaustive list of all pleas raised in [the] Notice

[704] As the REACH shoulders the registrant with the burden of proof regarding the safety of the substance, the registrant cannot submit to the ECHA BoA new evidence that it has failed to submit within the registration dossier. Case A-018-2014, *BASF Grenzach v ECHA*, paras 123–24 and the earlier case law cited therein. However, in substance evaluation cases, where the burden of proof is shifted back onto the ECHA, the appellant can provide new evidence together with the notice of appeal. See, ibid, paras 125–31.

[705] The latter information was provided by the ECHA's agents at the oral hearing on 12.12.2018 in the Case T-125/17, *BASF v ECHA* (the author's own notes from the oral hearing). In one of the cases the BoA emphasised the procedural duties of the appellants to set out and prove the relevant facts by holding that it 'cannot be assumed to have any prior knowledge of the specific facts and circumstances of the case brought before it'. Case A-004-2011, *Kronochem v ECHA*, para 48.

[706] 'CIR 2015: An interview with Andrew Fasey, ECHA' (available at www.youtube.com/watch?v=eZGDtObk_uo). See also on the effort required from the appellant, Christina Bramante, 'Launching and Participating in Proceedings Before the ECHA Board of Appeal: An Industry Perspective' (2018) 1 *International Chemical Regulatory and Law Review* 114–18.

[707] Article 9 RPBoA. An interviewee also informed that small and medium companies could obtain clarification from the Registry as to the required contents of the appeal.

[708] For instance, ibid, para 51. Case A-003-2012, *THOR v ECHA*, paras 45–46 and 59–62.

of Appeal'.[709] When it comes to the EGC, the pleas in law are considered to form part of the essence of the application so they must be contained in the original application submitted in due time. As confirmed by interviewees, the ECHA BoA tries to adopt a proactive and flexible approach to help the appellants voice their grievances. However, problems with unclear appeals have not in practice been so severe as to engender ECHA concerns on account of the former's rights of defence.[710]

B. Seeing the Agency's Faces

The largely adversarial system of pleas – even in its 'lighter' form as adopted by the ECHA BoA – charges the applicant with significant responsibility for the case's outcome. Hence, procedural tools fostering the parties' active participation in the proceedings become crucial to instil legitimacy assets in the ECHA appeal process. From the instrumental perspective, the parties' active participation is the only way for the BoA to obtain the scientific and legal data necessary to make the correct ruling, given the great variety of chemical substances with which the ECHA deals. From the deliberative perspective, the appeal process is often the first occasion for the appellants to see the agency's faces and discuss their cases with the actual people.[711] The first-instance proceedings occur through an IT remote application and in writing.

Even though it is not enshrined in the RPBoA, the BoA's goal is to ensure that the parties have had an opportunity to comment on all the elements which will inform the ruling, which is quite a challenge since a notice of appeal with all the attached annexes (containing scientific studies) has, on average, over 500 pages.[712] Therefore, it comes as no surprise that the procedural opportunities for party participation before the ECHA BoA are at least as generous as those of the EGC. The structure of proceedings before the ECHA BoA is analogous to those before the EU Courts: exchanges of written pleadings followed by an optional oral hearing. Unlike the RPGC and RPCJ, the RPBoA are silent about the second exchange of written pleadings. However, the ECHA BoA is authorised to request, where appropriate, additional written submissions on specific questions or issues raised by the other party and use 'procedural measures' for the same purpose, such

[709] The BoA also requested, however, that the appellants 'indicate, for each of these pleas, the paragraph(s) of the Notice of Appeal and of the subsequent observations on the Defence that contain the arguments raised in support … this request is not an opportunity to expand on your arguments or to add new arguments'. ECHA BoA, Case A-004-2014, *Altair Chimica et al*, paras 23–24.

[710] Most recently, the ECHA BoA examined substantive pleas of error of assessment, even though it had noted that the pleas were raised only during the proceedings. However, the pleas were ultimately declared unfounded, so this move could not have breached the rights of the agency. Case A-011-2020, *Clariant Plastics & Coatings*, paras 32ff and 68ff.

[711] As observed by one of the interviewees.

[712] ECHA (n 586), 14.

as sending to the parties a list of questions.[713] In the cases closed between 2014 and 2018, the BoA requested further written submissions in all cases, sometimes several rounds thereof. By requesting answers to specific questions, the ECHA BoA actively steers the parties' discussion during the proceedings.[714]

Due to the volume and uncertainty of legal and scientific issues involved in a case, the possibility of holding the oral hearing is crucial to confront the data and arguments collected within the written procedure. At the beginning of a hearing, the BoA Chair advises the parties to express themselves in possibly simple words and to avoid scientific jargon. It is in the parties' best interests to make their arguments intelligible and convincing to the BoA members, who are not all scientists or specialists on a given chemical substance. Importantly, before the ECHA BoA an appellant may be represented by a whole group of lawyers and scientists, which may all directly address the BoA, unlike before the EGC, where in principle only the indicated lawyers are authorised to address the court.[715] The ECHA BoA allows videoconferences, an option which is often used by scientific experts employed by the parties.

The hearings have a mixed adversarial-inquisitorial character. The Chair leads the discussion and the respective BoA members are very active during the whole hearing by asking very specific questions and requesting subsequent clarifications. The ECHA BoA does not wield the authority of EU Courts. Consequently, it is not burdened with the formalist and solemn atmosphere of majestic courtrooms in Luxembourg. The members of the ECHA BoA, who hold oral hearings in a relatively simple conference room, may allow themselves to use more casual and blunt expressions for the benefit of the precision and veracity of the responses. The deliberation revolves around the questions addressed by BoA members. However, the parties are generally allowed to comment on each other's responses. The oral hearings may even take on the character of negotiations, mediation or scientific discussion on the intricacies of respective substances and testing methodologies.[716] It may become evident in the course of face-to-face exchanges between the parties that one of them becomes aware of its mistake.[717]

[713] Articles 12(3) and 16 ROBoA.

[714] At the time of writing, the BoA does not have procedural instruments, such as those offered by the procedural framework of EU Courts, by means of which it could force the appellants to produce concise written submissions and thus increase procedural economy. Nor can it request their regularisation, but only clarification (Article 6(3) RPBoA). The Practice Directions recommend the parties limit the length of their written submissions to 20 pages. But these are only soft rules that cannot be enforced by, for instance, rejecting lengthy written submissions or charging the appellant with the procedural costs of their processing or translation. As informed by an interviewee, in practice, the ECHA BoA does not send back lengthy submissions for regularisation.

[715] According to the EGC practice rules, 'in order to assist the Court in relation to certain technical issues, the President of the formation may authorise the parties' representatives to give the floor to individuals who, despite not having the status of representative, are best placed to comment'. EGC (n 496), para 161.

[716] This description is based also on the author's own observations of the audio recordings of 10 oral hearings provided by the ECHA on 7.3.2019, request ATD_017_2019, and on 12.6.2020, request ATD/41/2020.

[717] Recording of the oral hearing in the case A-004-2017. Ibid.

The direct interaction of scientific experts during the oral hearing enables the verification and clarification of evidence and contentious issues by the BoA. The experts are presumed to speak on behalf of their principals, rather than as neutral court experts. However, a confrontation of their scientific assessments helps detect potential errors in the contested decisions by identifying more compelling arguments. The ECHA BoA acknowledges the instrumental and deliberative rationale of the broad participation opportunities in appeal proceedings. The BoA Chairwoman stressed the importance of the right to be heard, especially in the course of oral hearings, and of interacting face to face with the ECHA to bolster the industry's trust in the REACH processes and avoid litigation before the EU Courts.[718]

The importance of oral hearings also results from certain shortcomings of first-instance administrative proceedings before the ECHA.[719] The ECHA adopts hundreds of decisions each year. Geared towards efficiency, the administrative proceedings are standardised and digitalised. The registrants interact with the ECHA through online applications. They have relatively few opportunities to interact with the ECHA directly and influence its decision-making even by submitting written comments. The registrant is usually invited to comment only on the draft decision and proposals for amendments, if any, submitted by national chemical safety authorities. Nor are there face-to-face meetings.[720] In practice, registrants may feel surprised by the content of the final decision in their cases.

The appellate proceedings may provide the appellant with the 'first and only opportunity … to get in touch with real human beings at the Agency'[721] and comment on some aspects of the case. The oral hearing plays a crucial role in raising applicants' confidence that their arguments have been genuinely heard and their case dealt with carefully and impartially. The appearance of impartiality is strengthened by the fact that the ECHA acts before the BoA on an equal footing with the appellant.[722] The ECHA Chairwoman also stressed in her reports that – arguably thanks to this strategy – only a handful of BoA rulings out of over 120 have hitherto been challenged before the EGC.[723]

Under the current interpretation of the RPBoA, the BoA is bound by the party's request to hold the oral hearing.[724] Out of 41 admissible cases closed between 2014 and 2018, an oral hearing was organised at the initiative of both parties in 11 cases (26.8%) and at the appellant's initiative only in 23 cases (56%).

[718] ECHA, 'Annual Reports from the Chairman of the Board of Appeal: 42nd Meeting of the Management Board 22–23 June 2016' (MB/22/2016), 1 and 5.

[719] As observed by one of the interviewees.

[720] The members of the industry may participate in the Member States Committee (the main decision-making body of the ECHA) but without the right to intervene at these meetings.

[721] In the words of one of the interviewees.

[722] For instance, a late written defence by the ECHA cannot be accepted. BoA ECHA, Case 022-2015, *Manufacture Française des Pneumatiques Michelin*, paras 49–56.

[723] ECHA (n 586).

[724] As confirmed by one of the interviewees.

In the remaining seven cases (17%), neither the appellant nor the ECHA requested the oral hearing and the ECHA BoA did not decide to hold it on its own motion. These rates generally demonstrate the subjective importance of the oral hearings for the parties.

Last but not least, the proceedings before the ECHA BoA appear to be quicker than those before the EGC. In recent years, the average duration of appeal proceedings is close to 15 months,[725] whereas that of annulment proceedings before the EGC has varied between 19.5 and 28.4 months, but in the most complex competition law cases, it could even amount to 51.5 months.[726] This difference cannot be explained by, for instance, fundamental differences in the respective authorities' rules of procedure, as they are practically very similar. The difference could perhaps be explained by the workload level, with an EGC judge hearing, on average, several times more cases per year than a member of the ECHA BoA. However, it is difficult to compare the workloads of the two bodies. The complexities of cases vary. At the EGC, the phases of actual decision-making before and after the oral hearing (the drafting of preliminary reports, chamber conferences and deliberation) are becoming shorter but can still take up to several months.[727] Regarding the duration of proceedings before the ECHA BoA in the same period, the phases of actual decision-making following the closure of written procedure or the oral hearing took in principle only three months.[728] Overall, from the appellants' or applicants' perspective, the justice delivered by the BoA is quicker than the justice delivered by the EU Courts.

V. Conclusion

Has the ECHA BoA successfully fashioned an institutional and procedural framework for adjudication in EU law areas requiring specialist knowledge and marked by a high degree of epistemic uncertainty? Have the BoAs fulfilled their designers' promise of cheaper, quicker and more thorough administrative review? The answer must be nuanced. The ECHA management's priority is to keep the appeal system cost-effective.[729] There is strong evidence suggesting that the

[725] ECHA (n 586), 5.

[726] ECJ (n 265), 242.

[727] For instance, in 2018 the drafting of a preliminary report in the annulment proceedings settled by a ruling took 5.8 months on average, the preliminary deliberation took 1.1 months, and the deliberation after the oral hearing took 3.5 months. EGC, 'Durée de l'instance par stade de procédure (en mois) – Affaires réglées par arrêt (avec audience)' (internal document disclosed by email of 4.9.2020 upon request 17/2020D), 1.

[728] ECHA, 'Annual Report from the Chairman of the Board of Appeal 2014' (18.6.2015, MB/24/2015), 1. By the end of 2018, the duration of the phase of decision-making before the ECHA BoA decreased to the extent that only 60% of cases were closed within 3 months following the closure of written or oral procedure, but the overall duration of proceedings was still 15 months. ECHA (n 586), 6.

[729] ECHA, 'Minutes of the 28th Meeting of the Management Board' (13–14.10.2012, MB/M/04/2012 final), 11.

appellants obtain justice at the ECHA BoA more quickly than at the EU Courts. However, the expectations of litigants towards the BoAs increase just like the expectations of the EU Courts. The outstanding issue is whether the BoAs should seek no more than to reduce the number of complex cases reaching the EU Courts, or whether they play a more significant role in the EU system of judicial and extra-judicial review as first-tier specialist adjudicators. Depending on available resources, the BoAs could instil more authority in the normatively and empirically uncertain decision-making, primarily through more thorough review techniques.

However, the designers of the ECHA BoA did not seem to have a clear vision of specific legitimacy assets this BoA was supposed to deliver. They had not unambiguously determined the range of its tasks or even contours of the technique of review. Nor had they adjusted the composition of BoAs or secured resources that might have enabled the BoAs to exert a more meaningful impact on the agency decision-making. The ECHA BoA, just like other relatively young BoAs, had to build up its capacity and seek access to expertise. It has managed to develop an astute review technique, allowing it to delve into the intricacies of scientific methodologies and the interpretation of complex data from which the EU Courts tend to stay away. In some of the most complex cases, the ECHA BoA has deferred to the empirical and normative appraisals by first-instance decision-makers. Nonetheless, it has turned the relative informality of its proceedings into an advantage, actively steering the legal and scientific debate between the multiple legal and scientific representatives of the parties, demanding an in-depth but straightforward explanation of scientific problems, perspicuous to non-specialists. It has also moderately broadened access to the appeal process for environmental and animal welfare organisations through the right to intervene. Conversely, it has not engaged in independent supplementary fact-finding owing to limited resources.

The experience of the ECHA BoA demonstrates that the setting up of specialised adjudicators in the most complex areas of EU law encounters an inherent difficulty. Faced with uncertainty as to whether the actual number of appeals will justify the financing of a permanent BoA, the co-legislators or agencies may opt for an ad hoc BoA. However, it is more challenging to secure an independent registry and staff of an ad hoc BoA and manage more likely conflicts of interest.

A more significant role of the BoAs depends on a political vision regarding the judicial and extra-judicial review system's shape. How should the legitimacy assets offered by the BoAs relate to those offered by the EU Courts? A mere replication of judicial legitimacy assets serves no purpose unless the BoAs are merely intended to ease the overburdened EU Courts randomly, ie without a conscious selection of cases which should subsequently be reheard by the EU Courts due to a presence of systemic or horizontal issues.[730] Assuming that an appeal before the BoAs could

[730] The agencies have no right to challenge the decisions of their BoAs. Quite the contrary, their legal services have to defend these decisions before the EU Courts, even if they have previously advanced an opposing view before the BoAs.

satisfy the right to effective judicial protection, thanks to, for instance, a reinforcement of their independence safeguards, should the EU co-legislators equip the EGC with the right to select cases against BoA decisions it wishes to hear?[731] A discussion regarding the role of BoAs within a broader architecture of judicial and extra-judicial review might foster more efficient use of limited resources.

[731] Under Article 263(5) TFEU, 'acts setting up bodies, offices and agencies of the Union may lay down *specific conditions and arrangements* concerning actions brought by natural or legal persons against acts of these bodies, offices or agencies …' (emphasis added). Such specific conditions and arrangements have been a requirement to first institute appeal proceedings before a BoA prior to lodging an action for annulment with the EGC. Arguably, specific conditions and arrangements could also be a filtering of incoming cases directed against BoA decisions by the EGC, to select only those raising systemic issues, on condition that the right to an effective remedy and a fair trial (Article 47 of the EU Charter) is considered satisfied by the BoA.

6

Ombuds-review: Justice without Binding Powers

With the EU Courts epitomising the rule of law, the Ombudsman attracts comparatively little attention.[732] However, a few comprehensive academic works have revealed her role in improving the accountability of EU institutions and bodies,[733] and good administration standards.[734] In the lack of binding powers may lie her greatest strength. It has opened up the possibility of the Ombudsman's broad and flexible jurisdictional remit, accessible proceedings and the creative development of normative standards. Through convincing arguments and soft pressure, she may induce the EU institutions and bodies to comply with her recommendations and proposals. By dint of these characteristics, the ombuds-review may potentially instil into the EU legal acts and processes valuable legitimacy assets.

How much complementarity is there in practice between the judicial and ombuds-review? Could the ombuds-review fill some gaps in the judicial review? This chapter sheds light on the part of the Ombudsman's docket which pertains to review of EU law, rule- and decision-making acts and processes. It pays particular attention to the ombuds-review of normatively and empirically uncertain appraisals.

Section I discusses polemics surrounding the duty of the Ombudsman's independence and how it relates to the idea of political neutrality. Section II examines which kind of rule- and decision-making acts fell inside the Ombudsman's net in 2014–18, what kind of review technique she employed and what results she reported. Section III analyses the profile of complainants and the kinds of cases they bring. Section IV explores the Ombudsman's evolving procedural scheme

[732] Regarding the relationship between the rule of law and ombudsmen in general, see, Benny YT Tai, 'The Ombudsman and the Rule of Law' in Marc Hertogh and Richard Kirkham (eds), *Research Handbook on the Ombudsman* (Edward Elgar 2018). Alex Brenninkmeijer and Emma van Gelder, 'The Rule of Law in the European Union: Standards of the Ombudsman, Judge, and Auditor' in Marc Hertogh and Richard Kirkham (eds), *Research Handbook on the Ombudsman* (Edward Elgar 2018).

[733] Busuioc (n 6).

[734] Vogiatzis (n 6). Tom Binder, Marco Inglese and Frans van Waarden, *The European Ombudsman: Democratic Empowerment or Democratic Deficit?* (BEUCITIZEN: Barriers Towards EU Citizenship 2017). Paola Chirulli, 'La denuncia al Mediatore Europeo' in Paola Chirulli and Luca de Lucia (eds), *Rimedi amministrativi ed esecuzione diretta del diritto europeo* (Giappichelli Editore 2018). See also an overview of literature, Richard Kirkham, 'Review of Herwig Hofmann and Jacques Ziller (eds.), Accountability in the EU: The Role of the European Ombudsman, Cheltenham: Edward Elgar Publishing 2017' (2018) 11 *Review of European Administrative Law* 84.

in terms of the importance of the parties' active participation, and some controversies surrounding recent changes geared towards enhancing the Ombudsman's procedural discretion. Section V presents conclusions.

I. Independence and Political Neutrality

There are different ideas across the EU regarding ombudsman or ombudsman-like institutions, their specific tasks, jurisdictional remit, and what their independence entails specifically. In some Member States, an ombudsman-like institution is a *médiateur*, settling disputes between administration and individuals in an impartial although proactive way, following the applicable legislation. Elsewhere, she may act like a *rzecznik* (advocate or spokesman) for constitutional rights, with power to scrutinise even parliamentary legislation in the public interest. Ideas also vary regarding the extent to which an ombudsman creatively develops and promotes good administration standards.[735] Therefore, it comes as no surprise that there have been different expectations regarding the European Ombudsman's interaction with the EU institutions and bodies or even the scope of her jurisdiction.

The first European Ombudsman was elected in 1995 but the establishment of this office had been discussed for 20 years.[736] The original Spanish proposal envisaged an ombudsman equipped with powers to scrutinise EU law implementation at both the EU and domestic level.[737] Ultimately, the Ombudsman obtained a much narrower jurisdictional remit limited to the EU administration, modelled upon the remit of the Danish ombudsman, an independent authority appointed and accountable to the Parliament, whose primary objective is the control of public administration.[738] The Ombudsman was intended to remedy the Union's democratic deficit by bringing it closer to its citizens and to control the EU executive better,[739] give each citizen 'the psychological reassurance … regarding his right in the apparatus of the Community bureaucracy',[740] and 'give the European administration a more human face'.[741] The Ombudsman was supposed to form

[735] Jacques Ziller, 'Variations Around the O-word: The European Ombudsman from Médiateur to Garante? Some Concluding Remarks' in Jacques Ziller and Herwig Hofmann (eds), *Accountability in the EU: The Role of the European Ombudsman* (Edward Elgar 2018). Gabriele Kucsko-Stadlmayer, *European Ombudsman-Institutions: A Comparative Legal Analysis Regarding the Multifaceted Realisation of an Idea* (Springer 2008).

[736] Jean-Pierre Jarry, *The European Parliament and the Establishment of a European Ombudsman: Twenty Years of Debate (1974–1995)* (European Parliamentary Research Service 2015).

[737] Carlos Moreira Gonzales, 'The Spanish Proposal to the Intergovernmental Conference on Political Union', in European Ombudsman, *The European Ombudsman, Origins, Establishment, Evolution* (Office for Official Publications of the European Communities 2005).

[738] Constantino Nassis, *Good Administration in the European Union – The Role of the European Ombudsman and the European Network of Ombudsmen* (Esperia Publications 2009), 20–27.

[739] ibid, 484.

[740] Debates of the European Parliament No 249 (Sitting of 10.12.1979), 23.

[741] Ombudsman, 'Annual Report 1995'. See for a historical analysis, Nikos Vogiatzis, 'One Ombudsman (EU) or Many (UK)? Interpreting the Singularity of Actors in the EU' (2013) 19 *European Public Law* 739.

part of 'a more comprehensive system of protection of [citizens'] rights outside the courts',[742] while adopting a more flexible problem-solving approach and providing individual redress to the complainants.

The Ombudsman's impact on the EU authorities is secured, first and foremost, by a legal safeguard of independence through irremovability during the term of office.[743] The Ombudsman is legally obliged to act with complete independence and is forbidden from seeking or taking instructions from any government, institution, body, office or entity. She must refrain from exercising any other professional activity, gainful or not, just like the EU judges.[744] She can be dismissed only by the ECJ, upon the Parliament's request, where she no longer fulfils the conditions required for the performance of her duties or is guilty of serious misconduct.[745] She may be held accountable for the course of individual inquiries before the EU Courts within the action for damages.[746] The same person may be reappointed as the Ombudsman for another term of office. A desire to be re-elected may theoretically encourage an office holder not to take action against the Parliament's political preferences. Empirical research has generally confirmed the Ombudsman's decision-making independence, but she has recently been criticised for allegedly refraining from taking actions against the Parliament where the political stakes were high.[747] A separate budget and organisational structure undoubtedly enhance the Ombudsman's de facto independence.[748]

The Ombudsman may seek to impact the decision-making by EU institutions and bodies by a myriad of soft tools, depending on the matter's seriousness. The first two Ombudsmen – Söderman (the former Finnish Ombudsman) and Diamandouros (the former Greek Ombudsman) – in principle employed in their dealings with EU authorities a conciliatory and amicable strategy oriented towards finding 'win-win' solutions. They adopted a more serious tone only occasionally.[749] The inquiries were conceptualised as 'flexible, good-faith efforts to achieve equitable solutions … rather than as rigid disciplinary procedures whose

[742] Parliament Committee on Institutional Affairs, 'Report on the regulations and conditions governing the performance of the European Ombudsman's duties (Rosy Bindi)', 12.

[743] The Ombudsman can be dismissed only by the ECJ at the request of the Parliament. The Ombudsman and her staff enjoy all the privileges and immunities of the EU civil servants. Articles 8–10 of the decision of the European Parliament on the regulations and general conditions governing the performance of the Ombudsman's duties (the Ombudsman's Statute) [1994] OJ L113/15.

[744] Article 228(3) TFEU; Article 9 of the Ombudsman's Statute.

[745] Article 228(2) TFEU.

[746] Case T-217/11, *Staelen v Ombudsman*, ECLI:EU:T:2015:238. Case C-337/15 P, *Ombudsman v Staelen*, ECLI:EU:C:2017:256.

[747] Christine Neuhold and Andreea Năstase, 'Transparency Watchdog: Guarding the Law and Independent from Politics? The Relationship between the European Ombudsman and the European Parliament' (2017) 5 *Politics and Governance* 40–50. Giorgio Grasso, 'The European Ombudsman as an Insurmountable Roadblock?' (*Verfassungsblog*, 15.10.2019, available at https://verfassungsblog.de/the-european-ombudsman-as-an-insurmountable-roadblock/). Ombudsman, Case 900/2010/(MF)RT, *Parliament*, paras 49 and 54.

[748] In the past, the Ombudsman's resources were more dependent on the Parliament, Alexander Tsadiras, 'Of Celestial Motions and Gravitational Attractions: The Institutional Symbiosis between the European Ombudsman and the European Parliament' (2009) 28 *Yearbook of European Law* 435, 443.

[749] Magnette (n 6), 113.

objective is the attribution of blame'.[750] Söderman and Diamandouros arguably saw the Ombudsman as first and foremost a dispute-settlement body. By carefully selecting cases raising public interest concerns, however, they were able to tackle systemic issues.[751]

Söderman was even accused of adopting too legalistic an approach[752] and of replicating the grounds and technique of judicial review.[753] This is why he used the power of own-initiative inquiry sparingly, mainly in response to a series of complaints regarding the same subject matter. The basis of his proposals and recommendations were legal arguments.[754] The Ombudsman embarked upon a step-by-step crystallisation of soft norms, used precedents to build up a quasi-judicial 'case law' or 'ombudsprudence', verified consistency in answers provided by the authorities in different cases, and referred to the authorities' public image or sought the support of other institutions.[755] This approach might have been characteristic of the Ombudsman's fledgling period, during which this new institution needed to build the trust of its interlocutors.

Over time, the Ombudsman's position evolved 'from that of an *ex-post* redresser of disputes between administrators and individuals to a more ambitious strategy of reform … through the careful selection of cases which [the Ombudsman] sees as symbolically important'.[756] Diamandouros emphasised that good administration standards may be normatively more demanding than the standards of legality as enforced by the EU Courts.[757] In his view, good administration also included 'the principle of service' of administration towards the citizens. Many specific elements of this principle were legal principles, the justiciability of which might, however, be limited (transparency, equal treatment, avoiding unnecessary delay).[758]

[750] A Tsadiras, 'The European Ombudsman's Remedial Powers: An Empirical Analysis in Context' (2013) 38 *European Law Review* 52, 57.

[751] Magnette (n 6).

[752] Richard Rawlings, 'Engaged Elites: Citizen Action and Institutional Attitudes in Commission Enforcement' (2000) 6 *European Law Journal* 4. Peter Bonnor, 'Institutional Attitudes in Context: A Comment on Rawlings' "Engaged Elites" – Citizen Action and Institutional Attitudes in Commission Enforcement' (2001) 7 *European Law Journal* 114.

[753] Konstantinos D Magliveras, 'Best Intentions But Empty Words: The European Ombudsman' (1995) 20 *European Law Review* 401–08. Adam Tomkins, 'Transparency and the Emergence of a European Administrative Law' (1999–2000) 19 *Yearbook of European Law* 217. Paivi Leino, 'The Wind is in the North: The First European Ombudsman (1995–2003)' (2005) 10 *European Public Law* 333.

[754] Vogiatzis (n 6), 141.

[755] Peter Bonnor, 'The European Ombudsman: A Novel Source of Soft Law in the European Union' (2000) 25 *European Law Review* 39, 45–47. For instance, Busuioc explained the higher compliance rate of agencies as being prompted by a concern that their maladministration would be reported by the Ombudsman to the Parliament, which can hold the management of agencies to account, Busuioc (n 6).

[756] Magnette (n 6), 684.

[757] Herwig CH Hofmann, 'The Developing Role of the European Ombudsman' in Herwig HC Hofmann and Jacques Ziller (eds), *Accountability in the EU: The Role of the European Ombudsman* (Edward Elgar 2017), 4.

[758] Nikiforos Diamandouros, 'The Relationship Between the Principle of Good Administration and Legal Obligations' in Carl Baudenbacher, Claus Gulmann, Koen Lenaerts, Emmanuel Coulon and Emmanuel Barbier de la Serre (eds), *Liber Amicorum en l'honneur de/in honour of Bo Vesterdorf* (Bruylant 2007).

O'Reilly's strategy is to tackle systemic issues head on. She held that 'a narrow description of this institution as a complaint handling body fails ... to give adequate expression to its deeper role as an embedder of democracy, as a driver of change in a culture that still lacks the requisite levels of accountability and transparency appropriate to institutions crafted from the finest European ideals'.[759] This more 'political' role of the Ombudsman, first and foremost, relates to more frequent own-initiative inquiries into high-profile political issues.[760] In this respect, O'Reilly's approach has been met with severe criticism,[761] but at the same time, it has received some support from the Parliament. The power to initiate strategic inquiries – 'to identify repeated or particularly serious instances of maladministration, promote best administrative practices and proactively address structural issues of public interest' – is highlighted in the 2019 draft of the new Ombudsman Statute, adopted by the Parliament but still awaiting Council's approval at the time of writing.[762]

A more political role may also relate to the way in which the Ombudsman exercises pressure on the institutions, for instance by means of social media. Currently, simple language is promoted in drafting inquiry documents as more appropriate to communicating with the complainant and the public.[763] But simple language may also make it more difficult to present to the institutions convincing legal arguments and induce their compliance with the Ombudsman's proposals.[764] Changes in drafting and communication style stirred up controversies inside the Office, according to some interviewees, but have also received positive assessment.[765]

A political role may also relate to the setting of the Ombudsman's priorities, such as the transparency of EU institutions. However, by setting clear priorities and devoting more attention and resources to selected issues, the Ombudsman may come too close to being perceived as a political body.[766] The setting of priorities might be considered an objective need in an institution receiving

[759] Speech by Ombudsman Emily O'Reilly at the Conference at the occasion of the 20 years of the European Ombudsman (22 June 2015, Brussels). See also the assessment in Roberto Mastroianni, 'New Perspectives for the European Ombudsman Opened by the Lisbon Treaty' in Herwig CH Hofmann and Jacques Ziller (eds), *Accountability in the EU: The Role of the European Ombudsman* (Edward Elgar 2017).

[760] Ian Harden, 'The European Ombudsman and Good Administration in the European Union, by Nikos Vogiatzis (Book Review)' (2018) 24 *European Public Law* 365, 367.

[761] Torsten Stein, 'A Supervisory Agency of Its Own Making?' (*Verfassungsblog*, 1.9.2019, available at https://verfassungsblog.de/a-supervisory-agency-of-its-own-making/).

[762] Regulation of the Parliament laying down the regulations and general conditions governing the performance of the Ombudsman's duties (Statute of the European Ombudsman) and repealing Decision 94/262 [2019], not yet approved by the Council.

[763] Ombudsman, 'New Implementing Provisions – Questions and Answers' (internal document received on 16.1.2019, request Ares(2018)6490466), 2, para D.1.

[764] I am grateful to an interviewee for this observation.

[765] Mastroianni (n 759).

[766] Jarle Trondal and Anchrit Wille, 'The European Ombudsman: A Resilient Institution in a Turbulent, Evolving Administrative Order' in Herwig CH Hofmann and Jacques Ziller (eds), *Accountability in the EU: The Role of the European Ombudsman* (Edward Elgar 2017), 47. Hofmann (n 757), 26–27.

hundreds of admissible complaints but having at its disposal only a few dozen case handlers. As already noted, case-selection procedural devices are also known in many apex courts across Europe and elsewhere. Such a device was recently introduced at the ECJ.

Finally, the Ombudsman's political discretion can manifest itself in autonomous and creative interpretation of EU legislation and concretisation of good administration standards in the absence of relevant case law from the EU Courts. As will be further discussed, the Ombudsman may present specific proposals as to how the EU institutions should strike a balance between different normative goals when the relevant EU legislation is drafted in open-ended terms. Although mentioned in the applicable legislation, specific substantive values or public interest goals may end up overshadowed in the rule- or decision-making by other considerations. Where the EU judges should recognise the political discretion of EU institutions and bodies, due to the binary and binding nature of their rulings, the Ombudsman may allow herself to be more 'political' and encouraging rather than assertive. By promoting public interest goals in the interpretation of EU legislation, the Ombudsman may seek to fill its substantive value-related gaps. However, it should be kept in mind that the Ombudsman does not have extensive legal services, such as those of the Commission or the Council, so the independent standard-setting should be undertaken with caution. A mistaken public allegation that an institution has breached the law could impair the public confidence in the Ombudsman's impartiality and objectivity.[767]

II. Taking the Ombudsman Seriously

A. Flexible Jurisdictional Remit

One way to restrain the tremendous power of the EU Courts vis-à-vis other EU institutions is to enumerate the kinds of legal acts they deal with.[768] However, as already noted, the concept of 'acts producing legal effects vis-à-vis third parties' is interpreted flexibly to account for changing trends in the EU law-, rule- and

[767] I am grateful for this observation to an interviewee, who gave the example of Joint Cases 488/2018/KR and 514/2018/KR (recommendation), *Commission* (regarding the appointment of the Commission's new Secretary General), and the Commission's firm and negative reply, Commission, 'Opinion of the European Commission on the European Ombudsman's recommendation – Complaint by delegations of the European Parliament (ref. 488/2018/KR and 514/2018/KR', available at https://g8fip1kplyr33r3krz5b97d1-wpengine.netdna-ssl.com/wp-content/uploads/2018/12/488-2018_and_514-2018_reply.pdf). The interviewee also referred to Ombudsman, Case 1697/2016/ANA, *ECB* (the ECB President's membership in the 'Group of 30') and the ECB's negative reply, ECB, 'The European Central Bank's (ECB) detailed opinion on the European Ombudsman's Recommendations in Case 1697/2016/ANA' (LSNC/18/10, 18.4.2018).

[768] Article 263(1) TFEU. In the Article 267 TFEU validity reference procedure, the ECJ's jurisdiction is potentially broader. See Chapter 4, Section II.A.

decision-making. The EU Courts have still not accepted that their jurisdiction should be broadened to account for the proliferation of various 'soft' measures, which may exert a tangible impact on the rights, obligations or interests of private parties.[769] Another limitation upon courts is that they act primarily as 'firefighters' rather than 'firewatchers'.[770] They may be called upon to scrutinise an incredibly complex and potentially long decision-making process only after its definite completion, ie the adoption of a final act.[771]

By dint of the lack of binding powers, the Ombudsman's powers do not require rigorous jurisdictional constraints. In practice, the concept an 'instance of maladministration', which defines the Ombudsman's jurisdiction, has turned out broad enough to encompass the substance and different stages of the process of EU rule-making and decision-making. The Ombudsman may interfere in a rule-making or decision-making process prior to its completion. She may inquire into single procedural stages[772] (such as the process of carrying out a scientific opinion or a risk or impact assessment, which forms the basis of a subsequent decision, rule-making[773] or even law-making acts[774]) or recurrent decision-making practices[775] (such as resulting from scientific guidelines,[776] or established practices of applying certain scientific tools[777]). The Ombudsman's jurisdiction partly overlaps with that of the EU Courts inasmuch as legal acts, processes, procedural stages or administrative practices subject to ombuds-review could also – at an appropriate time and at the initiative of an appropriate applicant – be subject to judicial review.

Some EU bodies were trying to oppose the expanding 'firewatcher' function of the Ombudsman and the trend of incrementally broadening the range of measures and processes amenable to ombuds-review. Wishing to keep the Ombudsman at a distance from ongoing processes, they favoured the judicial model of reviewing only definitive measures. One of the agencies argued that the Ombudsman

[769] Gentile (n 10).

[770] Carol Harlow and Richard Rawlings, 'Firefighting and Fire-watching: Courts and Ombudsmen', *Process and Procedure in EU Administration* (Hart Publishing 2014).

[771] The EU Courts may also try to discharge the 'firewatcher' function by developing general administrative and constitutional law principles to be observed in the law-, rule- or decision-making procedures, but nonetheless, they can verify their observance only after the completion of a process.

[772] For instance, Ombudsman, Case 1409/2014/MHZ, *Commission*. Case 952/2014/OV, *EFSA*. This applies even to very early stages of decision-making, Ombudsman, Case 1693/2015/PD, *ECB*.

[773] For instance, Ombudsman, Case 916/2018/ANA, *NARGC v Commission*. The challenged letter in that case ordering a risk assessment was a first step in a procedure that might lead to the adoption of an implementing regulation restricting the use of lead in bullets.

[774] Ombudsman, Case 1842/2016/CEC, *Commission*.

[775] Ombudsman, Case 12/2013/MDC, *ECHA*. Case 1568/2012/(FOR)AN, *ECHA*. Case 2000/2015/ANA, *Commission*. In Case 735/2017/MDC, *European Center for Constitutional and Human Rights v EASO*, the point of contention was a potentially recurrent practice of EU officials which might have affected decision-making in asylum cases by domestic authorities. Ombudsman, Case 1179/2014/LP, *Commission* (access to State aid case files).

[776] Ombudsman, Case 2018/2/KR, *EMA* (in this case, the Ombudsman engaged with the process of making the guidelines, although the complainant also made substantive allegations).

[777] Ombudsman, Case 747/2016/PL, *EFSA* (Threshold of Toxicological Concern).

can review 'only complaints concerning concrete instances of maladministration' as only in this way can she assess 'in retrospect how the EU administration has acted [and], where appropriate, express recommendations or critical remarks on concrete administrative practices'. Otherwise, the agency claimed, the Ombudsman would be called on to consider prospectively 'abstract legal questions', acting more like a regulatory body.[778] In response, the Ombudsman stressed that she must 'act proactively to prevent maladministration from occurring in the first place', intervening in ongoing processes and scrutinising recurrent administrative practices.[779]

In the examined period 2014–18, the Ombudsman dealt with a variety of decision-making or soft rule-making acts, which produced different forms of 'weak' or indirect legal effects, such as scientific guidelines,[780] scientific reports,[781] interpretive guidelines pertaining to EU legislation,[782] or investigation reports.[783] Instances of such decision-making or rule-making might not easily be brought before the EU Courts and, even if they are, the judicial review is incidental and indirect. The most important in quantitative terms were the cases concerning the handling of individual complaints by the Commission relating to potential infringements of EU law by Member States. Since the basis of the right to lodge such a complaint is the Commission's communication[784] rather than a binding legal act, the right to having one's complaint handled in a proper way is not enforceable before the EU Courts.[785] It is, however, amenable to ombuds-review.[786] In the past, the Ombudsman did not shy away from thoroughly scrutinising the Commission's reasoning in support of the rejection of an infringement complaint.[787] The Commission's choice as to which infringement case to pursue involves a political choice nonetheless. Under the current 2020 internal guidelines of the Ombudsman, 'if the essence of an infringement complaint is that the complainant questions the

[778] Ombudsman, Case 1568/2012/(RT)AN (friendly solution proposal), *ECHA*, para 10.

[779] ibid, para 11. Ombudsman, Case 2469/2011/VL, *ECHA*, paras 14–15.

[780] For instance, Ombudsman, Case 747/2016/PL, *EFSA* (regarding a scientific report describing the general use by the EFSA – in the process of preparing individual opinions submitted to the Commission for the final decision-making – of a specific and controversial scientific assessment tool).

[781] For instance, Ombudsman, Case 174/2015/FOR, *PIP Action Campaign v Commission* (regarding a report on the safety of breast implants by the Commission's scientific committee).

[782] For instance, Ombudsman, Case 1581/2013/ANA, *Commission* (regarding guidelines interpreting the EU transport legislation).

[783] For instance, Ombudsman, Case, 1239/2014/JAS, *OLAF*. Case 246/2017/DR, *OLAF*. Court actions against OLAF investigations and reports are likely to be inadmissible as not producing immediately legal effects but being subject to an assessment by domestic authorities, Case T-289/16, *Inox Mare v Commission*, ECLI:EU:T:2017:414.

[784] Communication from the Commission – EU law: Better results through better application [2017] OJ C18/10.

[785] Case C-317/19 P, *ND and OE v Commission*, ECLI:EU:C:2019:688, paras 20–24.

[786] For a case of similar infringement complaints to other EU bodies. See Ombudsman, Case 618/2017/CEC, *ESMA*. The action against a decision dismissing a complaint is available, on procedural grounds, if the right to complain is confirmed by legislation, as in State aid cases. Such cases may also be directed to the Ombudsman. See Case 1773/2016/JAP, *Commission*.

[787] For instance, Ombudsman, Case 1689/2016/MDC, *Commission*.

Commission's political choice in the matter, the Committee of Petitions will, all things being equal, be better placed to deal with the matter'.[788]

Legal acts and processes that the Ombudsman has been dealing with are most often individual administrative decisions and decision-making processes regarding, among other issues, public access to documents, the award of grants and tenders, and even the registration of chemical, pesticide and medicinal products.[789] Moreover, on several occasions, the Ombudsman was dealing with different aspects of processes leading to the adoption of acts of general application, such as implementing regulations, or even with preparatory stages of legislative law-making.[790] In a case regarding the Common Agricultural Policy, the Ombudsman even examined the substance of an implementing regulation for manifest errors of assessment in the mathematical method for calculating the subsidies due to farmers.[791] In an earlier case, the Ombudsman withdrew from the review of an implementing regulation's substance in light of the principle of proportionality. Although the previous Ombudsman did not exclude the ombuds-review of such acts as a matter of principle, he noted that 'an inquiry … into this allegation would serve no useful purpose since the Implementing Regulation is a measure of general application that must be presumed to be valid unless and until annulled by the Court of Justice'.[792] In her most recent internal guidelines, the current Ombudsman stated she 'can review the implementing acts to verify that there is uniform implementation of a legally binding act'.[793] It seems that while being cautious, the Ombudsman is open to legality challenges against implementing acts of general application.

The Ombudsman's jurisdiction is at the same time narrower than that of the EU Courts inasmuch as it excludes challenges against the substance of legislative and quasi-legislative acts.[794] This limitation is seen as inherent in the concept of 'mal-*administration*'.[795] In 2015 the Ombudsman entered into a debate with the

[788] Ombudsman, 'Manual on case handling procedures – Final version – June 2020' (internal document received on 2.10.2020, request Ares(2020)1169876), para 97.

[789] See the examples discussed in the following subsection.

[790] Ombudsman, Case 1171/2013/(RA)TN, *EASA* (an update to EU rules on rules on flight and duty time limitations and rest requirements for commercial airline transport). Case 2018/2/KR, *EMA* (scientific guidelines concerning the use of 'normal human immunoglobulin'). Cases 432/2017/AMF, 505/2017/AMF and 878/2017/AMF, *Commission* (review of a legislative directive on the protection of animals used for scientific purposes). Case 428/2016/LM, *Commission* (an implementing decision regarding a genetically modified organism – GMO). Case 952/2014/OV, *EFSA* (a regulation for the renewal of the authorisation of glyphosate). Case 23/2018/SRS, *Commission* (Council testing methods regulation – animal testing).

[791] Ombudsman, Case 1348/2013/EIS, *Commission.*

[792] Ombudsman, Case 1047/2013/BEH, *Commission*, para 12.

[793] Ombudsman (n 788), para 42.

[794] Ombudsman, Case 541/2014/PMC, *Olive Oil Producers v Commission*, para 30.

[795] In this context, some doubts surround the scope of the EU Courts' 'judicial activities', which remain outside the Ombudsman's mandate. At present, the Ombudsman favours a narrower definition of 'judicial activities' than the ECJ President, Ombudsman, Case 2006/2017/CEC, *Court of Justice* (letter opening inquiry and the Court's response). The EGC has proposed a middle ground option, Case T-433/17, *Dehousse v Court of Justice*, ECLI:EU:T:2019:632.

Council regarding the scope of the latter's legislative function, which remains outside the Ombudsman's jurisdictional ambit. In that year the Ombudsman launched an own-initiative inquiry regarding the transparency of trilogues:[796] trilateral, informal and closed meetings organised between the representatives of the Parliament, the Council and the Commission with a view to agreeing on joint positions on legislative proposals. The trilogues have given rise to controversies for a long time due to the principle of transparency of legislative proceedings.[797] In the Ombudsman's view, the technical organisation of legislative proceedings, the flow and transparency of documents, are administrative rather than political.

The Council, and its Legal Service in particular, at first opposed this inquiry.[798] The Legal Service provided its own detailed interpretation of the Ombudsman's mandate.[799] According to the linguistic argument, 'limitations have to be inferred from the very notion of maladministration which clearly refers to an inappropriate exercise of an *administrative* activity'.[800] According to the historical argument, this understanding lay at the foundation of the Ombudsman. According to the comparative argument, the different types of ombudsmen across the EU share the same essential role of monitoring the functioning of *administration*.[801]

The institution of the European Ombudsman is indeed based on the Danish model of a parliamentary ombudsman who scrutinises the functioning of administration on behalf of the parliament. However, at the time the Ombudsman was established the EU legal order did not know the concept of EU legislative acts or procedures. This idea came only with the Constitutional Treaty and was then partially transferred to the Treaty of Lisbon. What today are formally labelled as 'legislative acts' used to be understood as a form of *sui generis* executive rule-making, with some involvement of the European Parliament through the old co-decision procedure. Even today, the practical effects of the formal distinction between regulatory and legislative acts as regards the ease with which they can be challenged before the EU Courts give rise to serious doubts, considering the democratic deficiencies of EU legislative processes. As regards the comparative argument, suffice it to note that the role of ombudsmen across the EU varies significantly, and it does not always exclude the constitutional scrutiny of legislation.[802]

[796] Ombudsman, Own-Initiative Inquiry OI/2/2017/AB, *Council* (access to documents relating to Council preparatory bodies when discussing draft EU legislative acts).

[797] Deirdre Curtin, 'Legal Acts and the Challenges of Democratic Accountability' in Marise Cremona and Claire Kilpatrick (eds), *EU Legal Acts: Challenges and Transformations* (Oxford University Press 2018), 17–19.

[798] Council, 'Opinion of the Legal Service: European Ombudsman's Own Initiative Inquiry OI/8/2015/FOR against the Council concerning transparency of trilogues – Scope of the Ombudsman's mandate' (11440/15, document received on 11.1.2019, request Ref. 18/2308-mj/jg).

[799] ibid, para 3.

[800] ibid, para 9 (original emphasis).

[801] ibid, para 10 with reference to the *travaux préparatoires* of the Maastricht Treaty and the Ombudsman Statute in the European Parliament.

[802] In Poland the Ombudsman may scrutinise the compliance of parliamentary legislation with constitutional rights and freedoms. She may challenge legislation – without being constrained by any

Ultimately, the Council and the Commission accepted the inquiry but expressed major reservations regarding the Ombudsman's mandate to assess the very organisation of legislative proceedings in the form of trilogues, which, they believed, is a legislative prerogative.[803] Indeed, in order to ensure the Parliament's support, the first Ombudsman, Söderman, drew a distinction between *administration* and *politics*. He ruled out the ombuds-review of the 'political work of the European Parliament or its organs' or of 'the merits of legislative acts of the Communities'.[804] The Ombudsman recently held that post-Lisbon delegated acts adopted by the Commission[805] – as opposed to implementing acts[806] – qualify as essentially 'political', even though formally they are infra-legislative. She noted that the EU legislature has the power to veto a Commission delegated act. Consequently, once the legislature endorses such an act, it begins to express the legislature's own political choice, and hence it falls outside the Ombudsman's mandate.[807]

However, the Ombudsman's jurisdiction over legislative or quasi-legislative proceedings is still a controversial and dynamic issue. Although the Ombudsman has excluded the possibility of inquiring into the substance of legislation or legislative proposals,[808] she claimed competence to 'check that correct procedures were followed and that there was no manifest error of appraisal'.[809] She has in fact inquired into the carrying out of impact assessments prior to legislative proposals,[810] and into the elaboration and negotiation process regarding a trade agreement, which if approved by the Council with the Parliament's consent, would qualify as a legislative act,[811] as well as to the organisation of public consultations

time limits – before the Constitutional Tribunal, and without the need to show any particular 'legal interest' (like a 'privileged applicant').

[803] Council, 'Reply to the Own-Initiative Inquiry OI/2/2017/AB' (29.10.2015). Commission, 'Reply to the Own-Initiative Inquiry OI/2/2017/AB'.

[804] Ombudsman, 'Annual Report 1995', 23. Case 875/2011/JF, *Commission*, para 20, where the Ombudsman considered that the adoption of the Rules of Procedure and the conduct of plenary sessions are part of the political work of the Parliament and therefore refused to deal with complaints concerning penalties imposed on MEPs by the President of the Parliament. In Ombudsman, Case 296/2009/OV, *Council*, the Ombudsman further considered that a complaint concerning the merits of the Conclusions adopted by the Council at an Ecofin meeting did not concern a possible instance of maladministration, but rather the exercise of a political activity. Conversely, in Ombudsman, Case 2395/2003/GG (special report), *Council*, the Ombudsman inquired into the transparency of the Council's meeting when acting in its legislative capacity. See also, Ombudsman, Case 107/2009/(JD)OV, *Commission*.

[805] Article 290 TFEU.

[806] Article 291 TFEU.

[807] Ombudsman, Case 417/2015/NF, *Commission*, paras 32–35.

[808] Ombudsman, Case 1317/2017/PB, *Commission*, para 19.

[809] Ombudsman, Case 875/2011/JF, *Commission*, para 20. Case 904/2014/OV, *European Competitive Telecommunications Association v Commission*.

[810] Case 904/2014/OV, *European Competitive Telecommunications Association v Commission*. Ombudsman, Case 1842/2016/CEC, *Secretary of 'Firearms United' v Commission*.

[811] Ombudsman, Case 1409/2014/MHZ, *Commission*. The decision does not disclose whether the Council objected to the inquiry on the grounds of the legislative nature of the negotiated act. Importantly, the Ombudsman *did* find an instance of maladministration, in this case consisting of the lack of a human rights impact assessment. Regarding the legislative status of international agreements ratified by the EU, see Case T-512/12, *Front Polisario v Council*, ECLI:EU:T:2015:953, para 71 (this finding was neither contested nor confirmed by the ECJ on appeal).

preceding a legislative proposal for a directive.[812] The Ombudsman's handling of complaints against acts of general application should be closely monitored to better assess her capacity to help close this important gap in the EU system of access to justice.

B. Review Technique: Catching Up with the Courts or Bringing in a Public Interest Perspective?

The Ombudsman's Statute and Implementing Provisions do not indicate specific criteria for ombuds-review. The concept of maladministration has proven to be sufficiently flexible to cover, in practical terms, similar ground of review as those applied by the EU Courts: lack of competence, a breach of a procedural requirement, a breach of a substantive norm.[813] Most often, the Ombudsman focuses on procedural requirements,[814] unless the complainant advances concrete substantive allegations.[815] In specific types of recurrent cases, like those relating to public procurement by EU institutions and bodies, the Ombudsman may more directly tackle substantive issues.[816] She may call the authorities to provide explanations as to how their broad discretionary ambit has been exercised.[817] She subsequently assesses whether the explanation is persuasive in discursive terms.[818] When a case specifically concerned the correct interpretation of a substantive legal norm, the Ombudsman ventured to provide an autonomous interpretation that she believed was the right one in the absence of relevant case law.[819] She even challenged the interpretation favoured by the interested institution.[820]

Faced with various rule-making and decision-making acts and processes, involving different levels of empirical and normative uncertainty, the Ombudsman reached for the review techniques that have already been hammered out by the EU judicature. Notably, the Ombudsman referred to the EU Courts' concept of

[812] Ombudsman, Case 1800/2016/JAP, *Committee of Regions*.

[813] For an example of case in which the Ombudsman found a lack of competence to adopt the measure, see Ombudsman, Case 1103/2006/BU, *EASA*. For examples of cases in which the Ombudsman found a breach of procedural or substantive norms, see the following paragraphs.

[814] For instance, Ombudsman, Case 1935/2008/FOR, *Commission* (the duty minutes during meetings in competition investigations linked to the duty to assess all relevant facts), paras 82ff.

[815] For instance, Ombudsman, Case 1047/2013/BEH, *Commission*.

[816] Ombudsman, Case 2400/2012/ANA, *Commission*, para 12. See also Case 1515/2015/DR, *European Monitoring Centre for Drugs and Drug Addiction*.

[817] For instance, Ombudsman, Case 536/2017/JN, *Commission* (making specific requirements in a call for tenders), para 10.

[818] See, for instance, cases regarding the Ombudsman's handling of infringement complaints against the Member States, Ombudsman, Case 503/2012/RA (draft recommendation), *Commission*, paras 44–46. Case 25/2013/ANA (draft recommendation), *Commission*, para 33. Case 539/2017/JAP, *Commission*, para 15.

[819] For instance, Ombudsman, Case 1130/2016/JAS, *Commission and ECHA*, paras 36–37 and 41.

[820] Ombudsman, Case 2093/2012/EIS (draft recommendation), *Commission*, para 36.

manifest error of assessment.[821] In principle, she could be expected to apply a lighter-touch standard of review than the EU Courts or the boards of appeals due to her limited resources and limited access to expertise. Based on this premise, one of the agencies questioned whether the substance of complex scientific or technical assessments might even amount to 'maladministration'. An agency suggested that, in the case of complex assessments, a complainant should lodge an action for annulment before the EU Courts instead.[822] Admitting she is not a scientific body, the Ombudsman asserted her capacity to review 'whether a procedural error has occurred or whether there is a manifest error in the reasoning of the contested decision'.[823] Nonetheless, she pointed out that in cases involving complex factual appraisals it was the complainant 'who shoulder[ed] the burden of proof'.[824] In this respect, the Ombudsman's technique of review resembles that of the EU Courts. This finding contrasts with the usual assumption of a more proactive role of the Ombudsman within her inquiries. Yet again, it demonstrates the principal difficulty encountered by review mechanisms equipped with only scarce resources to scrutinise the epistemically uncertain empirical determinations.

In several cases decided in the examined period, nonetheless, the Ombudsman visibly put much effort into a careful reconstruction of procedural requirements, steps and relevant factors indicated by the applicable legislation. Thus, she could thoroughly review the reasoning presented in the challenged act, as well as indirectly appraise its evidentiary foundation, taking full advantage of the process-oriented review technique. In a case against the European Medical Agency (EMA), a pharmaceutical company complained about an administrative decision by which it was denied a waiver of the duty to test the use of their cardiological product on children. Such tests generate high costs, so pharmaceutical companies try to avoid them. Meanwhile, two other companies were granted the waiver for very similar products registered around the same time. The complainant alleged maladministration consisting of arbitrary and discriminatory treatment.[825]

The Ombudsman painstakingly reconstructed the consecutive stages of the complex decision-making process prescribed by the applicable regulation. She verified whether the EMA had effectively considered all the potential benefits of the new product as compared to both the existing ones and the others newly registered around the same time. She finally determined that in the case of an unmet therapeutic need among a small population of patients, the EMA was obliged to select for testing only one product, which was preferable for any minimal although objective reason. The overarching goal was to avoid unnecessary clinical

[821] Ombudsman, Case 2015/2008/GG, *Commission*, para 81. Case 2575/2009/(TS)(TN)RA, *EMA*, para 83 (see also, footnote 68 referring to Case T-13/99, *Pfizer Animal v Council*, ECLI:EU:T:2002:209, para 169). Case 1348/2013/EIS, *Commission*, paras 25–26.

[822] Ombudsman, Case 2575/2009(TS)(TN)RA, *EMA*, paras 14–16.

[823] Ombudsman, Case 364/2013/(EIS)PMC, *EMA*, paras 38–41, 43 and 48.

[824] Ombudsman (draft recommendation), Case 2575/2009/(TS)(TN)RA, *EMA*, paras 83 and 95.

[825] ibid, paras 1–12.

tests on children.[826] Having examined the full versions of all decisions addressed both to the complainant and two other companies, the Ombudsman found such an objective reason, for which the complainant's product had been chosen, ie an optimal taste for children and low interference with food. She concluded that the problem lay in the fact that the EMA had not sufficiently documented the full comparative assessment in all three decisions, and this is why the complainant had not been in a position to understand the full reasoning.[827]

Moreover, the Ombudsman has proven capable of availing herself of the normative potential of law, and different public interest goals to which the law points, to orient the exercise of political discretion by EU bodies.[828] This point is well illustrated by a case brought by the Pesticide Action Network Europe, an environmental organisation. In this case, the Ombudsman inquired into the Commission's recurrent administrative practice regarding the approval of pesticides.[829] In general, the Commission approves a new active substance by adopting an implementing regulation, which in such a case is a hybrid act: a generally applicable regulation and at the same time, an administrative decision addressed to the applicant who wishes to market products containing the new substance. The decision-making procedure is complicated and involves submitting scientific assessments by competent national authorities and the European Food Safety Authority (EFSA). It takes from two-and-a-half to three-and-a-half years.

The complainant's main allegation was that the Commission had adopted a consistent practice of approving active substances without complete data which would allow it to exclude risks for human health, animal health, groundwater and the environment. Simultaneously, the Commission had regularly requested 'confirmatory' data to be delivered at a later stage in order not to compromise the economic interests of the pesticide industry. Thus, according to the complainant, the Commission had been in breach of the precautionary principle, which is the cornerstone of EU risk regulation and regularly committed maladministration.

The Ombudsman began her analysis by reconstructing the applicable EU legislation.[830] She first identified the values that the parent legislation pursued: the protection of the environment, human and animal health and the improvement of plant protection. She then noted that the EU legislature intended to reserve the use of the procedure for provisional approval and request for confirmatory data to exceptional cases, in which the probability that the risk assessment would

[826] ibid, paras 48–58, 60–62, 111.

[827] ibid, paras 120–25. For other examples of ombuds-review on competence-related and procedural grounds for compliance with the applicable legislation see, Ombudsman, Case 916/2018/ANA, *National Association of Regional Game Councils v Commission* (regarding the ECHA's risk assessment of led bullets), paras 25–35. Case 510/2018/NF, *EMA (Rituximab)* and the annex to the decision.

[828] Mendes (n 20).

[829] Ombudsman, Case 12/2013/MDC, *Commission*. See also Case 687/2018/TE, *Commission*.

[830] Regulation 1107/2009 of the Parliament and of the Council concerning the placing of plant protection products on the market and repealing Council Directives 79/117/EEC and 91/414/EEC [2009] OJ L309/1.

be changed was minor.[831] Meanwhile, statistical data presented by the complainant showed that the Commission uses the said procedure in nearly every case, despite the opinions of EFSA identifying issues of high concern.[832] Moreover, the complainant pointed out that the applicable legislation did not provide for the submission of confirmatory data to a full peer review by EFSA,[833] and that multiple confirmatory procedures had been pending for over a decade.[834] In the Ombudsman's view, such frequent use of the confirmatory procedure essentially meant that the Commission adopted an excessively lenient approach to the risk assessment of new substances – unduly prioritising the industry's economic interest over the protection of the environment, human and animal health.[835]

In a follow-up report, the Commission still claimed to act strictly in line with the applicable legislation. It argued that despite the precautionary principle, many incomplete applications cannot be rejected because new data requirements arise at later stages of decision-making procedures. Also, the approval process is lengthy and manufacture methods are being improved in the meantime, which requires submission of updated data.[836] Some of these assertions were questioned by the complainant.[837] In a follow-up inquiry, the Ombudsman was still concerned about the process for approving active substances. These substances could be approved without data on the impact of water treatment processes on residues present in surface and groundwater abstracted for drinking water production. In fact, a necessary guidance document by the Commission or relevant agencies had not yet been published, and the data provided by the registrants without specific guidance were considered insufficient by the EFSA in many cases.[838] The Commission argued that appropriate measures can be taken by the Member States which approve products for a specific use.[839] Bearing in mind the commitment of the new Commission to significantly reduce the use of chemical pesticides, the Ombudsman discontinued the inquiries. Irrespective of the case's final outcome, access to the ombuds-review enabled the complainant to question how the Commission introduces a hierarchy of public interest objectives enshrined by the EU legislature in the process of

[831] Ombudsman, Case 12/2013/MDC, *Commission*, para 10.
[832] ibid, para 18.
[833] ibid, para 40.
[834] ibid, para 30.
[835] ibid, para 44.
[836] Commission, 'Report in reply to a further remark from the European Ombudsman in her closing decision – Complaint 12/2013/MDC' (14.2.2018, published on the Ombudsman's website), 4–6.
[837] PAN Europe, 'Comments on DG SANTE's report of February 14, 2018 in reply to the Ombudsman's findings on confirmatory information' (17.4.2018, available at https://www.pan-europe.info/sites/pan-europe.info/files/public/resources/press-releases/letter-commiss-andriukaitis-report-ombudsman-ci-april-2018.doc).
[838] Ombudsman, Joint Cases 1570/2018/JF-JN and 1973/2018/JF-JN, *Commission* (Pesticides), paras 67–71.
[839] 'Comments of the Commission on the preliminary findings of the European Ombudsman – Complaints by Mr (…) on behalf of Pesticide Action Network, ref. 1570/2018/JF-JN and 1973/2018/JF-JN' (published on the Ombudsman's website), 7–8.

approving pesticides. The complainant was at least able to force the Commission to enter into some exchange of reasoned arguments on the matter.

Likewise, in a series of cases brought by animal welfare organisations against the ECHA, the Ombudsman inquired into a general administrative practice regarding the animal testing of chemical substances to be marketed in the EU in accordance with REACH. This administrative practice was a part of the ECHA decision-making procedures aimed at registering and evaluating chemical substances to be produced and marketed in the EU. The complainants challenged the ECHA's position that it could not reject animal testing proposals and suggest alternative methods instead.

The Ombudsman began her analysis by reconstructing the public interest objectives of REACH: the protection of the environment and public health through a high level of substance safety and the avoidance of animal testing. She admitted that the ECHA had not been given a power to impose upon the registrants the most appropriate testing methods. In the absence of relevant case law, she nevertheless suggested a reinterpretation of the REACH Regulation. She found a legal basis for the ECHA to require the registrants to show that they have made a genuine effort to obtain scientifically valid information allowing them to avoid animal testing. This legal basis could also allow the ECHA to reject inadequately justified testing proposals.[840] Thus, the ECHA could undertake specific actions to realise one of the REACH guiding values without compromising the other.

In a follow-up report, the ECHA confirmed that it now verifies the registrant's consideration of alternative testing methods by relying on publicly available scientific data, data provided by third parties and submitted within any ongoing procedures at the ECHA. This verification may lead to the conclusion that the animal testing proposed by the registrant is redundant.[841]

In some cases involving epistemically uncertain empirical appraisals, however, the process-oriented ombuds-review turned out to be as limited as the judicial review. The Ombudsman was only able to scrutinise the external and formal appearances of comprehensive and exhaustive empirical assessment. She pointed out references to various data coming from different sources, earlier replies to the complainant's arguments and consensus-based decision-making by scientific committees. She did not engage with the substantive accuracy or persuasiveness of scientific arguments.[842] The reasoning presented by the Ombudsman may give an

[840] Ombudsman, Case 1606/2013/AN, *ECHA*, paras 23–24. Case 1568/2012/(FOR)AN, *ECHA*, para 19.

[841] Ombudsman, 'Case 811/2016/MDC: Response to the European Ombudsman's request for further information regarding implementation of Decision 1606/2013/AN on how the European Chemicals Agency applies rules concerning animal testing' (20.3.2017, correspondence published by chemicalwatch.com). There is always a risk that, given a huge variety of chemical substances, the ECHA will mistakenly approve animal testing based on inaccurate data provided by the registrant. Ombudsman, Case 811/2016/MDC (review decision of 1.6.2017), *ECHA* (published by chemicalwatch.com).

[842] Ombudsman, Case 1475/2016/JAS, *European Medicines Agency* (HPV vaccines), paras 23–66 of the annex to the decision. Case 1769/2017/JAS, *European Chemical Agency* (glyphosate), paras 15–21, and a more detailed analysis in an internal case note (received on 12.6.2020, request Ares(2020)2526085).

impression that, in these complex cases, she had no choice but to look for a reason to uphold the contested decision-making. Without clear and persuasive material from the complainant,[843] the Ombudsman is unlikely to identify a substantive error of scientific assessment by herself[844] or to autonomously assess whether the decision-makers have taken all scientifically relevant factors into account.[845] Notably, the Ombudsman abstained from commissioning external expert reports, arguably in order not to increase the cost of inquiries and not to second-guess inherently uncertain empirical appraisals.[846]

An excellent example of the Ombudsman's struggles with uncertain empirical appraisals enmeshed with tough normative choices is provided by a case against the EFSA, brought by an organisation for the protection of public health and the environment, concerning a so-called Threshold of Toxicological Concern (TTC). The TTC is a tool for assessing chemicals, present at low concentrations in feed

[843] In Ombudsman, Case 1802/2016/CEC, *Global Cabin Air Quality Executive v Commission*, regarding a tender for research into aircraft cabin air quality, the Ombudsman decided not to open an inquiry into the complainant's allegations regarding substantive scientific errors. Instead, she opened an inquiry into procedural aspects of the case such as the timing and the notification of all interested parties to the tender procedure, as well as the transparency of prior consultations. Internal case note (received on 29.6.2020, request Ares(2020)2526085), 9. In her letter to the Commission, the Ombudsman held: 'The complainant's allegation about the content of the tender raises complex, scientific questions. We have informed the complainant that the Ombudsman does not have the scientific expertise to question such scientific evaluations and that she will not investigate this issue further unless the complainant provides convincing evidence that the relevant factual basis relied upon by the Commission was manifestly incorrect'. Letter of 8.2.2018 to the Commission (received on 29.6.2020, request Ares(2020)2526085), 2.

[844] Ombudsman, Case 176/2015/JF, *Groupe International d'Études Transdisciplinaires v EFSA*, paras 27–30 on whether the EFSA has chosen relevant comparators (non-genetically modified (GM) organisms) to assess the safety of genetically modified maize. Following a detailed scientific explanation, the EFSA concluded that the differences observed between the GM maize in question and its natural control were not biologically relevant, considering the natural variability of such organisms as estimated from available literature data. EFSA Executive Director, 'Re: Complaint 176/2015/JF' (3.8.2015 opinion of the complaint received upon request Ares(2020)2526085). It appears that to verify the veracity of this conclusion, it might have been necessary to simply repeat the whole examination.

[845] Ombudsman, Case 176/2015/JF, *Groupe International d'Études Transdisciplinaires v EFSA*, especially paras 7 and 19. Also in her reply to the complainant's request for the review of the Ombudsman's decision (5.6.2018, document received on 12.8.2020, request Ares(2020)2526085), she admitted that the EFSA had still not made clear whether the producer of the GMO in question had submitted only favourable scientific data. The EFSA mentioned multiple exchanges with the producer but did not explain what specific data gaps were problematic and what additional data had been taken into consideration. EFSA Executive Director, 'EFSA's Replies to the Ombudsman's Queries Outlined in the Proposal for a Solution' (28.2.2017, document received on 12.8.2020, request Ares(2020)2526085).

[846] The Ombudsman may hence seek to frame her inquiries as relating only to the comprehensiveness of information provided to the complainants by the EU institutions and bodies, rather than relating *directly* to the substance of decision-making underpinned by scientific appraisals. This was the case, for instance, in the Ombudsman's reply to the request for review of Case 176/2015/JF (5.6.2018, document received on 12.8.2020, request Ares(2020)2526085). However, the Ombudsman enjoys freedom (in the interest of complainants) from a court-like procedural formality, that would otherwise require her to strictly specify and observe the formal limits of her inquiries. Therefore, the boundary between the 'direct' review of replies to requests for information and the 'indirect' review of the substance of decision-making is blurred in practice.

and food, where little toxicological data regarding their properties exist, but it is nonetheless necessary to decide on their safety. Given the great variety of such substances, the limited capacities of public risk assessors, and the need to reduce animal testing, the TTC is also used to prioritise the assessment of the potentially most dangerous substances. The EFSA regularly uses it in the evaluation of flavouring substances used in food production and pesticide metabolites in groundwater. Moreover, the TTC reduces the costs of the industry.[847]

The complainant alleged that, due to the TTC approach, a risk assessment is not carried out in practice for all chemical compounds in all cases, as certain substances falling below the threshold are considered of no concern. Moreover, the complainant alleged that the exact value of the TTC is an essentially arbitrary (or political) decision as it does not strictly follow from available scientific data. One of the crucial points of contention was which data should be deemed relevant for setting the TTC. The complaint claimed that a statistical cut-off point adopted by the EFSA could not be considered an objective scientific benchmark but a political (risk management) choice, more suitable to be made by the Commission. The EFSA counterargued that the chosen threshold was a statistical convention used by specialists in the field, so it should not be considered arbitrary.[848]

The parties adduced an abundant amount of specialist literature and data, arguments, counterarguments and allegations as to the misunderstanding of scientific concepts or even manipulation of data. The normative question obfuscated by these abstruse and uncertain scientific details could be interpreted as whether the EFSA's practice of relying on the TTC – the specific value of which followed from an appreciable set of discretionary choices presented by 'scientific judgments' – expressed an appropriate balance of competing interests such as public health and the economic interests of the industry. The Ombudsman ultimately admitted that she was 'not a scientific body and [did] not have the expertise to evaluate the merits of the scientific opinions taken by specialised committees',[849] and that she did 'not have the expertise to assess whether EFSA's scientific analysis of the evidence dating from 2012 was correct and whether its ongoing monitoring of the latest scientific developments regarding the TTC [was] adequate'.[850]

In other words, a high concentration of empirical and normative problems urged the Ombudsman to take a step back. To be sure, the previous paragraphs have not covered the whole spectrum of possibly varying degrees of intensity in ombuds-review. Rather, they have aimed to demonstrate both the cutting edge and the epistemic limits of the Ombudsman's review technique. The depth of review

[847] Executive Director of EFSA, 'Re: complaint 747/2016/ANA …' (28.10.2016, opinion of the EFSA presented to the Ombudsman, part of case file received on 28.10.2020, request Ares(2020)2526085), 6.

[848] Executive Director of EFSA, 'Re: complaint 747/2016/ANA …' (27.4.2017, opinion of the EFSA presented to the Ombudsman, part of case file received on 30.9.2020, request Ares(2020)2526085), 4–5.

[849] Ombudsman, Case 747/2016/PL, *EFSA* (Threshold of Toxicological Concern), para 19.

[850] ibid, para 23. However, the Ombudsman has taken a stance on other institutional and procedural aspects of this case.

in a case depends on the character of allegations and the complainant's activity. If the facts of the case are sufficiently elucidated to the Ombudsman, or the case does not involve intricate empirical appraisals, the Ombudsman may find it legitimate to encourage the institution to take greater account of an undervalued public interest. However, in cases involving empirical uncertainty enmeshed with controversial normative choices, the Ombudsman clearly suffers from a comparative disadvantage in relation to the legitimacy assets of the primary decision-makers. She may therefore need to apply light-touch review. An additional hindrance to the Ombudsman is that she has no choice but to rely on the information and explanations provided by the institutions concerned. As will be further argued in Section IV devoted to the procedural activity, the institutions may seek to highlight in their responses any external and formal appearances of scrupulously followed procedure.

C. Measuring the Ombudsman's Impact

The rate of cases in which an instance of maladministration was identified should be considered in the ombuds-review's overall analysis. Although an ideal or desirable rate of such cases cannot be unequivocally fixed, a low rate of inquiries leading to a finding of maladministration, as well as a low rate of compliance with the Ombudsman's proposals, recommendations or suggestions, might suggest an overly cautious approach to the examined act or action, deference to the EU institutions and bodies, or otherwise insufficient inquiry tools and review techniques. A very high rate of identified instances of maladministration might, on the contrary, suggest a difference of values between the Ombudsman and the supervised institutions.

However, one needs to draw careful conclusions from the rate of successful inquiries. 'Maladministration' is arguably even more flexible a concept than 'legality' or 'error of assessment'. The Ombudsman's procedural framework gives her a lot of leeway in choosing between, for instance, a finding of maladministration or no maladministration, a statement of 'no grounds for further inquiries', or that the case has been settled or recommendation accepted. In choosing a form in which to conclude an inquiry, the Ombudsman looks beyond the specific case's confines. She must consider broader relations with the institution in question, the chances for fruitful collaboration in the future, and the public interest in insisting on resolving the individual case.[851] The interested institution's compliance with the Ombudsman's proposals regarding systemic improvement does not

[851] For instance, in Ombudsman, Joint Cases 1570/2018/JF-JN and 1973/2018/JF-JN, *Commission* (Pesticides), the Ombudsman stated 'no grounds for further inquiries', considering the new Commission President's public commitment to limit the use of pesticides in the EU, even though the Commission had practically admitted an irregularity (lack of a scientific guidance document resulting in pesticides being approved without complete safety data).

necessarily translate into appropriate personalised redress being provided to the complainant.[852]

The Ombudsman may influence decision-making by EU institutions and bodies in the course of the inquiry (through a 'proposal for a solution', a 'draft recommendation' or informal suggestions) or following its completion (through a public 'finding of maladministration', which in 2016 replaced the previous 'critical remark', or in the course of a follow-up inquiry).[853] If the institution accepts the proposal or recommendation, the operative part of the final decision classifies the case as 'settled' or states that the recommendation or proposal has been 'accepted'.[854] If, conversely, the institution reacts positively only to the public finding of maladministration, the Ombudsman may provide a brief summary of the institution's positive commitment in her annual 'Putting it Right' report.[855]

Less clear is the concept of 'no grounds for further inquiry/no further inquiries justified'. The use of this formula has recently changed. It was used in cases in which the individual instance of maladministration could no longer be remedied but the institution acknowledged an instance of maladministration.[856] This practice was intended to allow the institution to improve without risking a public finding of maladministration and to promote cooperation rather than defensive reactions.[857] The previous ombudsmen used to 'reserve' the 'critical remark' category for cases in which a public interest aspect was present. Currently, O'Reilly opts for clear statements that maladministration has or has not occurred,[858] which has attracted criticism of the Commission.[859]

[852] The Ombudsman can also make 'suggestions for improvement' (previously, 'further remarks'), which relate to more systemic improvements rather than to the individual case.

[853] The Ombudsman may also send a special report to the Parliament but she uses this 'nuclear option' very rarely.

[854] From 2016, the Ombudsman states also 'accepted proposals' while in the past such cases were categorised as 'settled'.

[855] From 2016, the report summarises only selected 'star cases', which makes the assessment of compliance more difficult for the public.

[856] For instance, Ombudsman, Joined Cases 562/2017/THH and 1069/2017/THH, *Commission*.

[857] Ian Harden, 'The European Ombudsman's role in promoting good governance' in Herwig C H Hofmann and Jacques Ziller (eds), *Accountability in the EU: The Role of the European Ombudsman* (Edward Elgar 2017), 207.

[858] Ombudsman, 'New Implementing Provisions – Questions and Answers' (a work-in-progress internal document received on 16.1.2019), 5, para F.6: 'The new case handling approach is expected to result in an increase in the recording of cases where no maladministration was found'. Ombudsman, 'Terminology specifically relevant to 2016 reform of EO complaint handling' (internal document received on 2.4.2019, request Ares(2019)1027373), 3.

[859] The Commission stressed that the previously used terms 'critical remark' and 'no grounds for further inquiry' would still be more appropriate than findings of maladministration and no maladministration in cases where the authorities concerned are not able to remedy the identified and acknowledged instances of maladministration. See, Commission, 'Revision of the Ombudsman's Implementing Provisions' (letter from the Secretary-General of the Commission to the Secretary-General of the Ombudsman, received on 2.4.2019, request Ares(2019)1027373).

Figure 6.1 The evolution of inquiry results as declared by the Ombudsman (% of all inquiries)

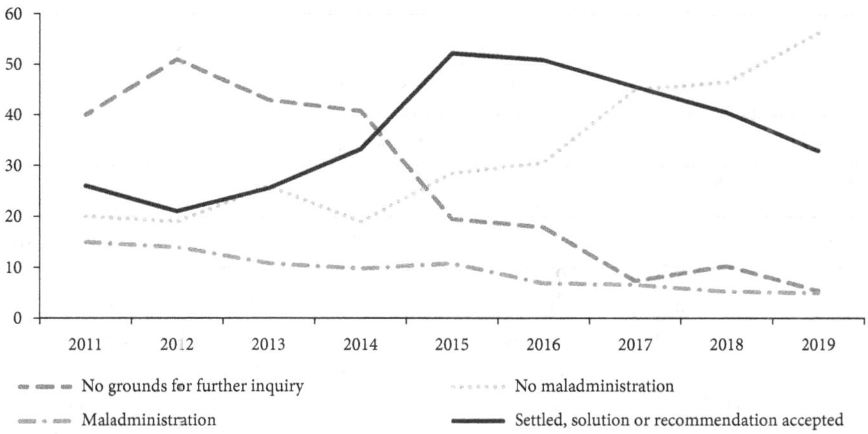

Figure 6.1 illustrates changes in the conclusions of inquiries declared by the Ombudsman.[860] The rate of cases in which 'no grounds for further inquiries' was stated fell from 40 per cent in 2011 to 5.4 per cent in 2019. At the same time, the number of cases in which *no* maladministration was stated radically increased: from 20 per cent in 2011 to 56.4 per cent in 2019. Moreover, the rate of inquiries in which an instance of maladministration was identified slowly but steadily decreased: from 15 per cent in 2011 to 5 per cent in 2019. Interestingly, the number of cases that the Ombudsman considers as 'settled' by the institution increased until 2015 and, subsequently, was steadily decreasing. The general trend of identifying fewer instances of maladministration may be linked to the fact that each year the Ombudsman closes more inquiries (277 inquiries closed in 2015 and 560 inquiries closed in 2019).[861] But is the quantity accompanied by quality? At any rate, any change in the rate of identified instances of maladministration may be linked to the attitude of the EU institutions and bodies towards the Ombudsman, and also to the way in which the Ombudsman assesses their submissions, which leads to the analysis of the Ombudsman's procedure in Section IV below.

A unique dataset has been compiled to account more specifically for the Ombudsman's impact on law-, rule- and decision-making measures and

[860] The data come from the Ombudsman's annual reports as published on the Ombudsman's website.
[861] Ombudsman, 'Annual Report 2019', 38.

processes, embodied in formally binding or non-binding forms, which might affect the rights, obligations and interests of private parties. The dataset included 430 complaint-based inquiries[862] closed in 2014–18[863] and relating to an act or action within law-, rule- or decision-making capable of affecting the rights and interests of private parties: legal acts,[864] acts producing some 'weak' legal effects by affecting the interests or expectations of individuals,[865] processes leading to the adoption of such acts (or specific stages or elements of these processes),[866] soft law acts,[867] recurrent decision-making practices, or administrative or scientific guidelines of general application framing rule-making or decision-making. The dataset included cases in which the Ombudsman intervened only at a preliminary stage of decision-making such as, for instance, in technical arrangements for public consultations of a draft policy measure,[868] or indirectly through a reply of an institution justifying its action towards a specific individual, such as going forward with a legislative proposal without a prior impact assessment.[869] The decisive criterion (the application of which, admittedly, required a modicum of subjective judgment) was whether the object of the Ombudsman's inquiry could be linked to a EU measure or process affecting the rights and interests of third parties (private parties).

Cases related to staff and recruitment matters,[870] contractual relationships,[871] purely factual problems, failures to provide requested information and to reply

[862] Including own-initiative inquiries based on a complaint from an individual, for instance a non-resident or an organisation not having a registered seat in the EU.

[863] The data were derived from the decisions closing the Ombudsman's inquiries published on the Ombudsman's website, as well as those unpublished and disclosed by the Ombudsman over the course of several months in 2018 and 2020 (requests ARES(2018)3431999 and Ares(2020)6868687). Some decisions were not disclosed as containing confidential or sensitive issues, as well as due to organisational limitations of the Ombudsman's office. Overall, 1,642 decisions were analysed for the inclusion in the dataset, which, according to the information provided by the Ombudsman, should account for more than 90% of all decisions issued in 2014–18. Also, the vast majority of undisclosed decisions are likely anyway to fall outside the scope of this study as relating to staff, recruitment, failure to reply or contractual cases. The number of decisions reported here is generally somewhat lower than the number of cases reported as closed in the Ombudsman's annual reports as the latter, according to the information provided by the Ombudsman, do not take account of joinders of cases or withdrawals by the complainant.

[864] Such as decisions pertaining to access to documents or public procurement.

[865] For instance, decisions of the Commission and other bodies responding to infringement complaints.

[866] Such as the adoption of scientific opinions or risk assessments.

[867] Such as interpretive guidelines issued by EU institutions or bodies.

[868] For instance, Ombudsman, Case 1800/2016/JAP, *Committee of Regions*.

[869] Ombudsman, Case 904/2014/OV, *Commission*.

[870] Most of them were directed against the European Personnel Selection Office.

[871] Except for those relating to the award of a tender or grant, which, due to the form of an administrative decision, might equally be challenged by means of an action for annulment.

to correspondence, or failures to act in due time were not included in the dataset.[872] Also, specific allegations and parts of case outcomes relating to delays and failures to act or reply in due time were omitted.[873] Neither were a few cases regarding institutional and EU civil service ethics[874] included in the dataset, as it was not possible to link them to specific law-, rule- or decision-making processes affecting private parties, unlike the cases concerning the composition of expert groups which directly participate in law-, rule- and decision-making in specific policy areas.

In this cluster of cases relating to EU law-, rule- or decision-making closed in 2014–18, the Ombudsman found the case settled at least concerning some allegations, including in response to a proposal or recommendation, in 19 per cent of cases. A finding of maladministration was made in 8.4 per cent of cases.[875] No maladministration whatsoever or only 'no grounds for further inquiries' were stated in 73.5 per cent of cases. Overall, the number of cases in which a finding of maladministration was made was much lower than the number of cases in which the EU Courts or the ECHA BoA annulled the impugned acts in the same period. However, the Ombudsman may also positively influence the conduct of EU institutions and bodies through formal or informal proposals and recommendations. Hence, the rate of settled cases should also be considered in this regard.[876]

Figure 6.2 illustrates the evolution of case outcomes in 2014–18. It demonstrates a very significant increase in cases closed by the Ombudsman and, at the

[872] The latter could be likened to the Article 263(5) TFEU actions for failure to act before the EU Courts which are outside the scope of this study.

[873] In some cases, the Ombudsman considered an allegation relating to a failure to reply or act in due time settled by the institution and then continued the inquiry into the substance of the case. Before the EU Courts, excessive length of the decision-making process, in principle, does not lead to annulment of the act. The EU institutions and bodies may be held accountable in this regard within the action for damages or failure to act. The issue of non-contractual liability and unlawful failure to act is, however, outside the scope of this study.

[874] Ombudsman, Joint Case 2077/2012/TN and 1853/2013/TN, *Commission* (the phenomenon of 'revolving door' between the EU civil service and private sector). Joint Case 194/2017/EA, 334/2017/EA, 543/2017/EA, *Commission* (the work of the former Commission President for a private bank). Case 1697/2016/ANA, *ECB* (the participation of the ECB President in a group of private bank heads).

[875] To put these numbers in context, it could be recalled that the EU Courts found an impugned act at least partially unlawful in around 40% of annulment cases and the ECHA BoA in 50% of appeals closed in the same period.

[876] More research is needed into amicable settlement before the EU Courts and the BoAs, as about a quarter of annulment cases before the EU Courts are withdrawn by the applicants, and about half of the cases before the ECHA BoA are discontinued as the impugned decisions are rectified by the ECHA Executive Director.

Figure 6.2 The evolution of outcomes of the Ombudsman's inquiries related to EU law-, rule- and decision-making (%)

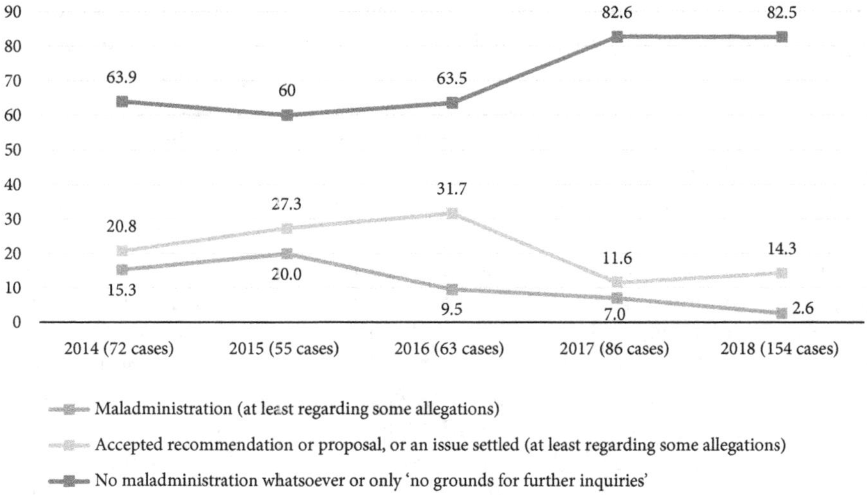

same time, a drop of cases in which the Ombudsman identified an instance of maladministration with regard to at least some allegations or in which she considered an issue settled. However, it should be recalled that these figures only relate to about a quarter of the Ombudsman's work. Still, they may be interpreted as suggesting a decrease of attention to these types of cases, especially under the new procedural rules and practices which entered into force in 2016.[877] They prompt more research into how the Ombudsman allocates her scarce resources to specific types of cases such as regular complaint-based inquiries and high-stakes political interventions concerning institutional ethics.

Whether the Ombudsman is 'taken seriously' can to some extent be inferred from the rate of compliance and constructive follow-ups to her proposals and recommendations, as summarised in the Ombudsman's 'Putting it Rights' reports. According to these reports and annual reports, the yearly overall rate of compliance with the Ombudsman's proposals, recommendations and findings in all types of cases has hovered in recent years at around 83–90 per cent. However, these reports should be considered with a critical eye.[878] The compliance rate is calculated as

[877] The new procedural rules give more discretion to the Ombudsman to decide on which cases to focus her scarce resources. See further, Section IV.

[878] Nonetheless, for research on the compliance rate with the Ombudsman's recommendations based on her own reports (demonstrating a high compliance rate), see Petia Kostadinova, 'Improving the Transparency and Accountability of EU Institutions: The Impact of the Office of the European Ombudsman' (2015) 53 *Journal of Common Market Studies* 1077.

the overall percentage of what the Ombudsman *herself* classifies as a 'satisfactory reply' to her proposals, recommendations, findings of maladministration and more general suggestions for improvement (earlier: 'further remarks') made in the course of inquiry.[879] At times the Ombudsman's suggestions are formally accepted but then twisted by the authorities, which would rather maintain their current practices. The Ombudsman may be quite indulgent in her compliance assessments as she has a vested interest in reporting a high compliance rate.[880] A low compliance rate could engender doubts about the very sense of bearing the Ombudsman institution's costs.

III. A Public Interest Venue

The ombuds-review can enhance the authority of EU law-, rule- and decision-making by bringing to light potential irregularities, information and arguments notified by individual complainants. The Ombudsman may be confronted with a potentially broader range of information and points of view than the EU Courts and the BoAs. The latter are usually requested to adopt economic operators' perspective and protect their private interests, whereas the EU institutions and bodies are assumed to represent the public interest. The liberal access rules clearly distinguish the Ombudsman from other judicial and non-judicial legal avenues at the EU level, which are in principle circumscribed by the *Plaumann* doctrine.

The ombuds-review has turned out to be accessible to, among other actors, public interest organisations and civil society members, which are traditionally barred from judicial review. Such complainants can use the ombuds-review to fulfil their role of watchdogs of EU institutions and bodies. The Ombudsman is frequently called upon to advance public interest claims, which may not easily be presented before the EU Courts or the BoAs. Complainants must fulfil few admissibility requirements to make a complaint. First and foremost, the two-year deadline for making a complaint is much longer than the two- or three-month

[879] See, for instance, Ombudsman, 'Putting it Right?' (December 2018), Table 4 'Rate of overall compliance by institution', 14.

[880] For instance, in Ombudsman, Case 12/2013/MDC, *Commission* (regarding the Commission's lenient approach to pesticide assessment), the Commission at first seemingly accepted the Ombudsman's proposal to limit the use of controversial confirmatory data procedure. But the complainant argued that the Commission was in fact twisting the Ombudsman's proposal. Nonetheless, the Ombudsman stated sufficient reasons to be 'generally satisfied' with the Commission's reaction (para 38) and stated that the proposal has been accepted. Most probably, however, the Commission continues to apply its previous approach. See, Commission, 'Report of the European Commission on the implementation of the European Ombudsman's Decision in case 12/2013/MDC' (14.2.2018).

deadline for lodging an action for annulment or an administrative appeal.[881] Appropriate administrative approaches must precede a complaint to the institutions and bodies concerned. Such 'approaches' are flexibly interpreted. According to internal guidelines, 'the prior approaches must match in scope the complaint made to the Ombudsman'. They can be made by telephone or via social media. As regards complaints brought in the public interest, prior approaches are not required if the institution concerned is clearly aware of the problem.[882]

The Ombudsman has not developed any 'standing' criteria. She does not require a special relationship between the complainant and the contested measure (legal interest in contesting the measure). Quite to the contrary, the Ombudsman has recognised the *actio popularis* character of the complaint[883] and the most liberal interpretation of formal conditions laid down in the Treaties: the condition of residence or legal personhood and registered offices in the EU.[884]

The quantitative analysis of the complainants in the examined period 2014–18 has demonstrated that the ombuds-review is open to certain categories of private parties that would have considerable difficulty meeting the standing criteria for annulment actions. The Ombudsman can receive complaints from industry associations and trade unions against rule- and decision-making leading to measures which could affect the whole industry or profession, but which would be formally addressed to a Member State or adopted as acts of general application. In similar circumstances, private parties could not bring annulment actions as the contested acts would most likely not affect them 'directly and individually', or they would require national implementation.

For instance, in a case brought by the European Dairy Association, the Ombudsman inquired into the Commission's decision not to raise objections against a French draft decree introducing mandatory origin labelling for certain milk and meat products. The decree had raised concerns regarding the access of non-French ingredient suppliers, particularly small and medium-sized enterprises,

[881] According to Article 2(4) of the Ombudsman's Statute, a complaint must be made within two years of the date on which the facts on which it is based came to the attention of the person lodging the complaint.

[882] Ombudsman (n 788), paras, 64–69.

[883] Ombudsman, Case 1917/2005/IP, *Parliament*, para 2.5. Nevertheless, the vast majority of cases brought to the Ombudsman are inadmissible because they concern national bodies. See Ombudsman, 'Annual Report 2017', 37. Precise quantitative data on inadmissible complaints and reasons for their inadmissibility, such as those regarding inadmissibility before the EU Courts, are, however, unavailable. Due to a large number of inadmissible cases and limited resources, the Ombudsman's Office does not keep records of such cases. Ombudsman, 'Annual Report 2016', 34.

[884] Even if the complainant does not fulfil the 'residence' requirement, the Ombudsman may open an own-initiative inquiry. For instance, Ombudsman, Case OI/11/2010/AN, *Commission*. In practice, the question of whether the complainant fulfils the said conditions very rarely gives rise to controversy, as opposed to formal conditions such as prior administrative approaches to the institution concerned or the two-year deadline for making the complaint. Ian Harden, 'Article 43: European Ombudsman' in Steeve Peers, Tamara Hervey, Jeff Kenner and Angela Ward (eds), *The EU Charter of Fundamental Rights: A Commentary* (Hart Publishing 2014), 1129.

to food production and distribution in France.[885] The Commission's decision had not affected any of the Association's *own* rights and obligations. It had not directly and individually affected any of its members. Hence, the Association might not be able to trigger the judicial review of the contested decision.

Likewise, in a case brought by the British Airline Pilots' Association, the Ombudsman inquired into an introductory part of a rule-making procedure by the EASA and the Commission. This procedure could ultimately lead to the adoption of general regulations regarding the EU rules on flight and duty time limitations and rest requirements for commercial airlines. It would probably have been impossible for the Association to trigger the judicial review of the resulting regulation, an act of general application, imposing obligations on the airline companies rather than their employees, and most likely requiring some national implementation.[886]

The Ombudsman received complaints from multiple public interest organisations against both individual decision-making and generally applicable rule-making regarding substantive EU policies.[887] She also received complaints against soft measures which might not be classified as 'acts producing legal effects' that would have been challengeable before the EU Courts, even though they produced tangible, practical effects.[888] In this way, the Ombudsman demonstrated the potential to fill an important gap in the legal protection of private parties at the EU level.

The bilateral structure of judicial review proceedings is not always adapted to the polycentric nature of disputes regarding EU legal acts.[889] The action for annulment functions on the premise that the pursuit of *public* interest falls on the EU authorities. The right to trigger the judicial review is therefore reserved to persons acting in their *private* interest. As the subject matter of most legal acts embodying and enforcing EU policies is the regulation of economic activity, the applicants for judicial review are most often individual economic operators. Even if civil society considers the activities of an EU body to be insufficiently protective of a given public interest, they cannot have recourse to the EU Courts in this respect. In principle, public interest organisations may bring actions for annulment only against administrative decisions addressed directly to them, which usually concern access to documents. Conversely, they cannot trigger judicial review of substantive policy matters, mainly due to the criterion of 'direct concern'. This criterion cannot be satisfied by reference to the organisation's statutory objectives.

[885] Ombudsman, Case 1212/2016/PMC, *Commission*.

[886] Ombudsman, Case 1171/2013/TN, *EASA*. See also a case brought by an association of farmers against a Common Agricultural Policy implementing regulation, Case 417/2015/NF, *Commission*. Interestingly, a similar situation in Case C-50/00 P, *Unión de Pequeños Agricultores v Council*, ECLI:EU:C:2002:462 gave rise to an important chapter of the debate on access to justice at the EU level.

[887] For another case in which the Ombudsman inquired into the process of elaboration of a generally applicable regulation, see Ombudsman, Case 23/2018/SRS, *Commission*.

[888] For instance, Ombudsman, Case 212/2016/JN, *Commission*.

[889] Joana Mendes and Katalin J Cseres, 'Consumers' Access to EU Competition Law Procedures: Outer and Inner Limits' (2014) 51 *Common Market Law Review* 483.

These problems do not occur in the case of ombuds-review. For instance, in the above-mentioned cases against the ECHA's approval of animal tests or the cases relating to the Commission's overly lenient approach to new pesticides, public interest organisations could present before the Ombudsman claims pertaining to the protection of animal welfare, public health and the environment, having considered that the EU bodies do not properly fulfil their tasks as assigned by the co-legislators. In another case, a Welsh pressure group campaigning to keep Wales free of GM crops challenged a process leading to the adoption of an implementing regulation regarding the renewed approval of the herbicide glyphosate.[890]

Figure 6.3 Types of complainants before the Ombudsman in inquiries relating to EU law-, rule- or decision-making closed in 2014–18 (%)

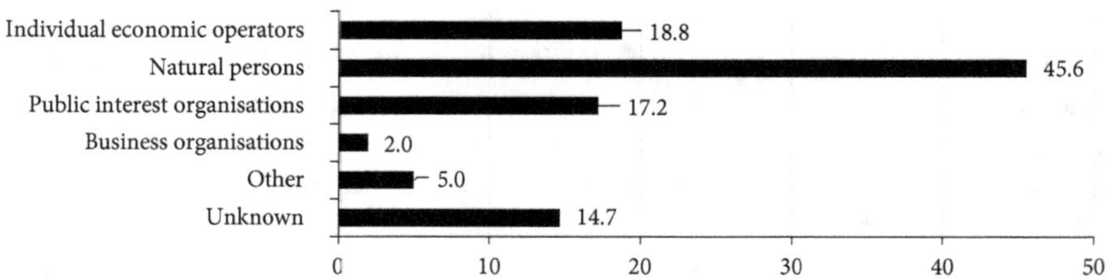

The Ombudsman's potential as a public interest venue has been corroborated by quantitative analysis of Ombudsman's cases closed in 2014–18. A distinctly high number of public interest organisations lodging complaints to the Ombudsman can be observed, as shown in Figure 6.3. This category of complainants brought 17.2 per cent of all examined cases. At the same time, 18.8 per cent of cases were brought by individual economic operators, and 45.6 per cent by natural persons, including members of the Parliament, journalists, researchers and other persons acting in the public interest. Only a few cases were also brought by industry organisations, trade unions and research entities. Importantly, in 14.7 per cent of cases it was not possible to identify the complainant type.

More specifically, about 60 per cent of cases brought by public interest organisations concerned acts directly addressed to them, such as decisions regarding

[890] Ombudsman, Case 952/2014/OV, *EFSA*. See also, Case 1409/2014/MHZ, *Commission* (an NGO challenging the lack of a human rights impact assessment in the negotiations of an EU–Vietnam trade agreement). In brief, The EU Courts are likely to review the ECHA or Commission's rule or decision-making if these institutions *refuse* to authorise a chemical test or a new pesticide, but not when their approach is too lenient and not sufficiently protective of a public interest (unless perhaps the private interests of competitors are at stake). Similar cases were brought in the period under consideration by natural persons, although the Ombudsman's decisions lacked information regarding whether the complainants acted in the public interest or in their own private interest. For instance, a senior lawyer challenged the Commission's established administrative practice of refusing access to the files of State aid cases to the beneficiaries of aid. Ombudsman, Case 1179/2014/LP, *Commission*.

access to documents, an award of grants or tenders, decisions relating to infringement complaint and investigation actions or reports regarding the use of EU funds. The remaining 40 per cent concerned public interest issues such as the composition of expert groups participating in the elaboration of EU legal acts and policies,[891] recurrent decision-making practices,[892] scientific or technical opinions or impact assessments leading to the adoption of regulatory acts[893] or international agreements.[894]

Interestingly, individual economic operators who were the addressees of administrative decisions, or their competitors, who could also have a chance to trigger judicial review at some point, sometimes opted for ombuds-review. Apart from complaints about access to documents and the award of tenders, economic operators complained about competition investigations (for instance, an ongoing investigation of a possible cartel[895]), the Commission's handling of State aid complaints[896] and anti-dumping investigations.[897] Sometimes, economic operators brought to the Ombudsman cases which, arguably, could not have been presented before the EU Courts due to the strict admissibility criteria or because the decision-making process was still ongoing at the moment of making the complaint. In such cases, economic operators sought, among other things, protection of their procedural rights in a regulatory process,[898] review of general scientific guidelines affecting the approval of pharmaceutical products,[899] or a Commission's approval of national measures supporting agriculture.[900]

In 87.2 per cent of examined cases, the Ombudsman dealt with complaints about individual decision-making. About 40 per cent of cases in this cluster concerned access to documents, 17 per cent concerned the award of grants and tenders, and as many as 30.4 per cent concerned decisions pertaining to EU law infringement complaints by the Commission in different policy fields or financial agencies. Such infringement decisions do not constitute challengeable acts before the EU Courts as they are not governed by binding law. A certain number of complaints about general law- or rule-making were also lodged. These cases amounted to 9.3 per cent of all examined cases. On top of that, in 3.5 per cent of cases the Ombudsman inquired directly into recurrent administrative practices[901] which might relate to both individual decision-making and general rule-making.

[891] For instance, Ombudsman, Case 203/2012/MMN, *Commission*. Case 2522/2011/CK, *EFSA*.

[892] For instance, Ombudsman, Case 12/2013/MDC, *Commission*.

[893] For instance, Ombudsman, Case 174/2015/FOR, *EFSA*.

[894] For instance, Ombudsman, Joint Cases 506-509-674-784-927-1381/2016/MHZ, *Commission*. Case 1409/2014/MHZ, *Commission*.

[895] Ombudsman, Case 1021/2014/PD, *Commission*.

[896] Ombudsman, Case 1773/2016/JAP, *Commission*.

[897] Ombudsman, Case 1167/2016/ANA, *Commission*.

[898] Ombudsman, Case 48/2015/ANA, *EFSA*.

[899] Ombudsman, Case 2018/2/KR, *EMA*.

[900] Ombudsman, Case 13/2015/NF, *Commission*.

[901] Such as, for instance, the approach of the ECHA to verifying alternative testing methods to avoid animal testing by chemical registrants wishing to comply with REACH requirements.

A large number of complaints against general law- or rule-making and recurrent practices were brought by public interest organisations and civil society actors. A few cases were also brought against 'soft' measures, such as interpretive guidelines[902] and recommendations or reports.[903] Several complaints were directed against the composition of expert groups participating in the elaboration of EU legal acts and policies.

As regards the policy fields, the Ombudsman was most often involved in access to documents cases (35.3% of examined cases) and the award of grants and tenders (17.7%). Interestingly, in 10.9 per cent of cases, the Ombudsman was involved in matters relating to public health and the environment, many of which raised normative and empirical uncertainty problems.

IV. Towards Greater Procedural Discretion

A. The Ombudsman's Procedural Law

The legitimacy assets delivered by the process of ombuds-review should, in theory, differ from those of judicial or administrative review due to a more 'investigative' character of the Ombudsman's procedure,[904] and an ensuing more active procedural role of the Ombudsman and her case handlers. Can such a procedural setting compensate for some of the shortcomings of partisan fact-finding before the EU Courts or the BoAs, especially in cases involving contentious empirical determinations and appraisals? Be that as it may, the adjudicator's more active procedural role is not incompatible with extensive participation opportunities for the parties to the inquiry process. Moreover, the Ombudsman enjoys more direct access to the EU administration through the inspections of case files and face-to-face meetings with the relevant officials, including in the course of the decision-making process rather than only after its completion. This way, the Ombudsman should be able to put pressure on the EU administration to amend their processes, empirical determinations or normative appraisals, for instance by considering underrated or underrepresented values and interests, for the benefit of the instrumental quality of administrative action and its deliberative credentials alike.

[902] Ombudsman, Case 1581/2013/ANA, *Commission*. Case 1130/2016/JAS, *Commission and ECHA*.

[903] Ombudsman, Case 222/2017/TM, *Commission* (unpublished; on file with the author; the case concerned information published in the Commission's Country Report Bulgaria 2015 on macroeconomic imbalances). Case 2042/2017/AMF, *Commission* (the case concerned the Commission's communication regarding the right to strike encouraging the Member States to adopt certain practices).

[904] Harlow and Rawlings (n 770), 80.

The procedural law governing the ombuds-review consists of primary law provisions,[905] the Statute of the Ombudsman (after the Treaty of Lisbon it should be adopted as a legislative regulation of the Parliament),[906] and the Implementing Provisions (adopted by the Ombudsman herself).[907] The highest in the hierarchy are Article 228 TFEU and Article 43 of the Charter. But these sources lay down only the right to complain, the right of the institution to respond to an alleged instance of maladministration and the Ombudsman's right to report on maladministration to the Parliament. Article 228 TFEU delegates to the Parliament the power to adopt the Ombudsman's Statute. Just as in the case of the EU Courts, there is no indication of the depth with which the Statute should define the Ombudsman's role and the objectives of her inquiries.[908] The current Statute focusses on the Ombudsman's institutional status, measures of investigation and confidentiality. Regarding the rights of the parties, it mentions only the right of the institution to submit an opinion on the draft recommendation and the indeterminate right of the complainant to be informed and comment on the solutions proposed by the Ombudsman.[909]

In early 2019 the Parliament adopted a new Statute,[910] which at the time of writing is still awaiting Council's approval.[911] The new Statute largely repeated the substance of the previous one. The declared goal was to adopt the new Statute in a post-Lisbon form of regulation in lieu of decision. However, the new Statute may reflect to some extent O'Reilly's vision of the Ombudsman's role. The power to initiate strategic inquiries with a view to identifying repeated or particularly serious instances of maladministration, promote best administrative practices and proactively address structural issues of public interest, as well as the power to maintain 'structural and regular dialogue' with EU institutions and bodies are highlighted in the new draft Statute. The Commission opined that these provisions might be misleading as to the goal of the Ombudsman's inquiries and 'might raise public expectations as to the Ombudsman's capacity to initiate new

[905] Article 288 TFEU and Article 41 of the EU Charter.

[906] The Ombudsman's Statute was first adopted in 1994 and last amended in 2008. It is unsure whether the 1994 Statute will be replaced by the one adopted in 2019 due to the reservations made by the Council Legal Service. See Council, 'Mandate for negotiations with the European Parliament' (Council doc. 13579/20). Under Article 228(4) TFEU, introduced by the Treaty of Lisbon, the Statute of the Ombudsman is the only legislative regulation adopted at the initiative of the Parliament, and not the Commission. The Parliament must, however, seek an opinion of the Commission and consent of the Council.

[907] Decision of the European Ombudsman adopting Implementing Provisions [2016] OJ C321/1. For the previous Implementing Provisions, see Decision of the European Ombudsman adopting Implementing Provisions [2002], (last amended by Decision of European Ombudsman of 3.12.2008).

[908] There is also no rule as to which matters should be regulated in the Statute of the EU Courts and which matters can be regulated in their Rules of Procedure, other decisions or internal procedural guidelines.

[909] Article 3(4) of the Statute.

[910] Statute of the European Ombudsman (n 762).

[911] As required by Article 228(4) TFEU.

policies or modify existing ones'.[912] It remains to be seen whether the legislative works on the Statute would involve a more fundamental discussion regarding the Ombudsman's role.

The current Statute delegates the bulk of authority to determine the parties' participatory rights, and the degree of the Ombudsman's procedural activity, to the Ombudsman herself.[913] Therefore, in practice, the so-called Implementing Provisions are the most important source of Ombudsman's procedural law. In 2016 O'Reilly adopted new Implementing Provisions, forming part of broader internal reforms which, according to some interviewees, have given rise to controversy within the Office. According to O'Reilly, the new Implementing Provisions make the procedure for those seeking help more efficient and effective.[914] But procedural efficiency is relative to the general goal of proceedings, O'Reilly's goal moving towards immediate systemic improvement and institutional ethics rather than individual dispute-settlement.

Crucially, the Ombudsman's procedural law leaves the office holder significant leeway in defining the degree of her activity in the course of an inquiry and a narrower or broader objective of her proceedings. By the same token, these procedural law sources enable the Ombudsman to make a discretionary choice as to the distribution of her limited resources. The Implementing Provisions are interpreted and concretised by multiple internal documents, such as the Handbook/Manual on case-handling procedures.[915] According to them, the current procedure is supposed to be less automatic or standardised. Individual proceedings are to be more attuned to the particular needs of a case, allowing the Office to avoid wasting scarce resources. Simultaneously, more resources can be devoted to selected 'star cases' and own-initiative inquiries.

B. Investigatory Approach in Practice and its Limits

A corollary of the lack of binding powers is the lack of procedural formalism. Procedural freedom allows the Ombudsman to assume a more active role in an inquiry and a flexible case-by-case adjustment of procedural rights and duties

[912] 'Commission Opinion on a Draft Regulation of the European Parliament Laying Down the Regulations and General Conditions Governing the Performance of the Ombudsman's Duties' (COM(2019) 553 final/3), 8.

[913] Article 14 of the Statute.

[914] 'The new Ombudsman's implementing provisions make the procedure for those seeking help more efficient and effective. By introducing a more flexible approach to handling complaints, the new procedure aims to ensure a more common sense and results-oriented approach to inquiries.' Ombudsman, 'Annual Report 2016', 30.

[915] Ombudsman, 'Handbook for Legal Officers: Provisional – Internal Use Only – January 2012' (internal procedural guidelines received on 16.1.2019, request Ares(2018)6490466). The new manual replacing the old handbook does not have exactly the same scope. The new Manual is described as a living document which codifies the existing, dynamic practice. Some practices described in the old handbook are still relevant under the new Manual, Ombudsman (n 788).

of the parties. However, the Ombudsman's procedural freedom also results in a study of her procedural practices being necessary to evaluate the activity of the Ombudsman's case handlers and the parties during an inquiry from the perspective of legitimacy assets that this activity might generate.

From the outset, the Ombudsman's procedural care for the complainant is potentially greater than in the case of the EU Courts or the BoAs, even with regard to defining the subject matter of proceedings. The Statute admittedly requires the complaint to state clearly the complaint's subject matter,[916] but not to set out formal pleas in law as before the EU Courts or the BoAs. The previous officeholders developed a practice of proactively identifying in the complaint specific 'allegations' and 'claims' which are functionally similar to 'pleas in law' and 'remedies sought', as operating before the EU Courts and the BoAs. An 'allegation' was 'an accusation that the institution, body, office or agency has failed to act in accordance with a rule or principle which is binding on it'. A 'claim' was 'what the complainant wants: for example, that a tender procedure should be cancelled; access to a document should be given; or that he should receive compensation'. These categories were used as tools to delineate the scope of an inquiry. O'Reilly encourages the case handlers to use simple language in drafting inquiry documents, which may be more appropriate to describe the inquiry's subject matter.[917] Also, according to the current guidelines,

> the scope of the inquiry into a complaint is limited to the issues raised in the complaint. In general inquiries officers should not raise new issues. However, the Ombudsman does not need to simply copy the complainant's framing of the issues. The complainant lays down the framework/scope of the inquiry: within that framework/scope, the Ombudsman may reframe the issues raised.[918]

In any case, the case handlers can always ask the complainant for clarification,[919] which in the case of the EU Courts and the BoAs is limited by formal provisions on regularisations. The 2012 Handbook recalled that

> our main duty is to try to help citizens to achieve their rights. Especially when the complainant is an ordinary citizen, we must make an effort to understand the complaint and its grounds, if they have not been very well expressed.[920]

The Handbook warned against dismissing the case only after a desk inquiry. This possibility should be used 'in very specific and limited number of cases', where the allegations are 'too general' or there is 'not enough supporting evidence supplied'.[921] Formal inquiries should be opened as much as possible, and as a

[916] Article 2(3) of the Statute.
[917] Ombudsman (n 858), para D.1.
[918] Ombudsman (n 788), 128.
[919] Article 3.1. of the 2016 Implementing Provisions.
[920] Ombudsman (n 915), para 3.2.1.
[921] ibid, para 2.3.10.

first step the complainant should be asked to clarify the complaint and supply evidence.[922] The 2020 Manual still emphasises that even though the Ombudsman 'enjoys wide discretion whether to open an inquiry or not', 'recourse to the Ombudsman is a fundamental right'.[923]

> Inquiries officers must make an effort to understand the complaint and its grounds, if they have not been very well expressed, particularly if the complainant is a member of the public with limited knowledge of how the procedures or institutions in question operate.[924]

Nonetheless, the case handler cannot be required 'to study extensive annexes in order to discover the essential elements of the case and the complainant's allegations and claims'.[925] Nor should flexibility in interpreting the complaint lead to a broadening of the scope of inquiry, even though this is in theory possible. Otherwise, the Ombudsman would need to prolong the proceedings to enable additional observations to be filed by the institution concerned.[926] In general, case handlers may be less demanding towards complaints lodged by natural persons and more demanding towards those filed by companies, public interest organisations or other entities which benefit from professional legal assistance.[927]

The Ombudsman is limited by her resources – an office employing only a few dozens of case handlers. The Ombudsman is not always able to assign the case to a case handler with relevant expertise. A distinct issue, particularly relevant in cases involving empirically contentious and uncertain appraisals, is what kind of fact-finding activity the Ombudsman can undertake in practice. From a legal point of view, the Ombudsman has at her disposal a variety of investigatory measures, starting from access to documents, through case file inspections and taking testimony from EU officials to public consultations. The pending amendment of the Ombudsman's Statute even seeks to somewhat broaden the investigatory powers by broadening the Ombudsman's access to secret documents, or hearing individual EU officials without prior authorisation of their superiors, to which the Commission is, however, opposed.[928] But in the overwhelming majority of cases, the Ombudsman confines herself in practice to examining the explanations and specific documents provided by the interested institution and the complainant. In case of contentious empirical determinations, the complainant bears the burden of proof.[929] The Ombudsman usually assumes the explanations provided for by the institution sufficiently accurate and complete.

[922] ibid.
[923] Ombudsman (n 788), para 92.
[924] ibid, para 122.
[925] Ombudsman (n 915), para 3.2.1.
[926] In such a case, the complainant is informed of the possibility of making a new complaint, if the two-year deadline has not yet elapsed. Ibid, para 3.5.
[927] ibid, 123.
[928] 'Commission Opinion' (n 912), 10 and 13–14.
[929] That the complainant is to provide sufficient evidence is emphasised in the current guidelines, Ombudsman (n 915), para 99.

The inspection of files and witness hearings – aimed at identifying specific documents or verifying the information provided by the complainant or the institution[930] – have played a relatively small role in general quantitative terms. From 1995 until 2017 inclusive, over 6,100 inquiries were carried out. Files were inspected in fewer than 160 cases,[931] and oral evidence was taken in around eight.[932] However, requests for specific documents from the institutions are made quite often.[933] It may also seem, however, that file inspections have become more frequent over time.[934] This upward trend may continue as, at present, the Ombudsman has a remote access arrangement with the Commission, which enables rapid 'virtual' inspections.[935]

The study of disclosed case files reveals that face-to-face meetings between the Ombudsman case handlers and EU officials, often coupled with examining case files, may prove crucial in empirically contentious cases. Relevant EU officials may elucidate the meaning of intricate scientific data, methodologies or technical assessments to the Ombudsman's case handlers.[936] But at the same time, it cannot be excluded that the EU officials might leverage the assumption of correctness attributed to their explanations by the Ombudsman's team as the latter is deprived of access to independent scientific or technical expertise. The meetings do not have an adversarial nature as the complainants or their representatives, as confirmed by interviewees, are never present. The complainants only subsequently receive a report from the meeting for written comments. Expert reports are in principle not commissioned even in cases involving complex assessments due to the costs such reports involve and to avoid the impression that the Ombudsman's authority is being delegated.

The Ombudsman's practice of relying on the inspected institutions' and bodies' information was challenged by a complainant in the recent *Staelen* case.[937] The case concerned an action for damages due to errors in factual statements reported to the Ombudsman by the Parliament, which the Ombudsman had not detected. The Ombudsman argued before the ECJ that she must predominantly base her inquiries on the information provided by the institution concerned.

[930] A simple request for a specific document and a file inspection are two different activities under Article 4(3) of the Ombudsman's Implementing Provisions.

[931] Alexandros Tsadiras, 'The Ombudsman' in Paul Craig (ed), *EU Administrative Law* (Oxford University Press 2018), 807. Alexandros Tsadiras, 'Unravelling Ariadne's Thread: The European Ombudsman's Investigative Powers' (2008) 45 *Common Market Law Review* 757.

[932] Ombudsman, 'Instances in which testimonies were taken (September 1995–September 2016)', an annex to 'Guidance for the Implementation of Article 3(2) of the Statute (testify powers)' (internal document received on 16.1.2019, request Ares(2018)6490466).

[933] Case file inspections are distinct from requests for documents. Ombudsman (n 788), 148.

[934] As observed also by Busuioc (n 6), 226.

[935] Ombudsman, 'Inspection Guidelines' (internal document received on 16.1.2019, request Ares(2018)6490466).

[936] Ombudsman (n 788), 150.

[937] Case T-217/11, *Staelen v European Ombudsman*, ECLI:EU:T:2015:238; Case C-337/15 P, *European Ombudsman v Staelen*, ECLI:EU:C:2017:256.

This information must be deemed to enjoy the presumption of truth under the principle of loyal cooperation. If the Ombudsman were to regularly double-check the information by means of file inspections or testimonies, she would have to radically limit the number of inquiries due to scarce resources.[938] It would also most likely increase the duration of Ombudsman's proceedings, which are currently rather short compared to judicial proceedings. In principle, the Ombudsman's proceedings in most complex cases last between 12 and 18 months.[939]

However, the EU Courts awarded damages to the applicant. They held that the Ombudsman should go to great lengths to verify the accuracy of information provided by the institutions, and should use, as much as possible the investigatory powers granted by the Statute. This inevitably brings to the fore the question of the available resources granted to the Ombudsman in order to perform her functions.[940] As noted by Vogiatzis, the ECJ could have supported the Ombudsman by picking up on the point advanced by the AG that the EU authorities should assist the Ombudsman in the investigation implying perhaps a 'duty of truthfulness'.[941]

In cases involving uncertain and intricate empirical appraisals, arguably the only way for the Ombudsman to enhance her ability to scrutinise their correctness or even foster a meaningful deliberation regarding these data among the parties would be to appoint expert witnesses or use the support of specialised staff. By doing so, however, the Ombudsman would encounter the same problems as those considered with regard to why the EU Courts abstain from appointing expert witness or commissioning expert opinions: how to assure that an expert witness or research entity responsible for producing a scientific report for the EU Courts, the Ombudsman or any other review authority would enjoy at least the same, or preferably superior, instrumental and deliberative legitimacy assets to those stemming form first-instance administrative proceedings. The production of regulatory science at the EU level usually involves inputs from many EU-level and domestic experts and administrators, seasoned with a pinch of political legitimacy thanks to these experts and administrators being delegated by national governments or specialised agencies.

C. Tailor-made Inquiries or More Procedural Discretion?

The fact that the Ombudsman is not equipped with binding powers in relation to the EU authorities makes the procedural justice of her inquiries and the

[938] Ombudsman, 'Requête en pourvoi contre l'arrêt du Tribunal du 29 avril 2015 dans l'affaire T-217/11' (received on 14.12.2018, requests Ares(2018)6444829, Ares(2018)6071292), paras 81–85 at 19–20.

[939] Ombudsman, 'Annual Report 2018', 40.

[940] Nikos Vogiatzis, 'The EU's Liability Owing to the Conduct of the European Ombudsman Revisited: *European Ombudsman v. Staelen*' (2018) 55 *Common Market Law Review* 1251, 1269–70.

[941] ibid, 1271.

institutions and bodies' procedural rights particularly important for fostering compliance with the proposals and recommendations. As noted by O'Reilly, 'if the institutions see that you're treating them fairly, that you don't automatically jump and take the violin out and be on the side of the complainant, then they are generally more willing to listen to you ….'[942] How the complainants are treated in the course of procedures may also affect their willingness to bring new cases,[943] which seem to especially concern repeat players such as public interest organisations.

Söderman modelled the ombuds-review proceedings on the court-inspired principle of 'fair procedure', conceptualised as a quasi-adversarial procedure in which the parties enjoy an equal right to comment on each other's submissions and evidence. The Ombudsman could base the final decision only on information that had been discussed by the parties.[944] As a result, several exchanges of written submissions between the parties must occur before the Ombudsman could take a position on the matter. The principle of 'fair procedure' is not explicitly mentioned in the current Statute or Implementing Provisions. It was clearly described in the 2012 guidelines[945] and maintained in 2020 guidelines, which provide for more procedural discretion.[946]

Underlying the principle of 'fair procedure' was the conception of the Ombudsman as, to some extent, a mediator who facilitates and promotes bargaining between the parties, who negotiate the best solution in the concrete case.[947] An inquiry had several fixed stages. First, the complainant was informed about the planned course of the inquiry in a letter declaring the admissibility of the complaint. Second, the complaint was transmitted to the institution concerned with an invitation to submit an opinion within a specified time that was normally no more than three months. The invitation could also specify particular issues that the opinion should address.[948] Third, the institution's opinion was transmitted to the complainant for further observations, to be submitted within one month.[949] Finally, having considered the written submissions, the Ombudsman could either decide to close the case with a reasoned decision or continue the inquiry.

[942] Interview with E. O'Reilly, EU Confidential – Episode 65, available at www.politico.eu/podcast/eu-confidential-episode-65-presented-by-google-emily-oreilly-vestager-vs-german-carmakers-macrons-job-tips/.

[943] A view strongly expressed by one of the interviewees.

[944] 'The Ombudsman's decision on a complaint cannot take into account information contained in documents provided by one party, unless the other party has had the possibility to respond. The institution's opinion on the complaint, its answers to any further inquiries and its responses to any proposal for a friendly solution or draft recommendations are therefore normally forwarded to the complainant, who has the possibility to submit observations. Similarly, the institution must have had the opportunity to comment on any material submitted by the complainant which is taken into account in the Ombudsman's decision', Ombudsman (n 915), para 3.1.2. Similarly, Ombudsman (n 788), paras 115–16.

[945] Ombudsman (n 915), para 3.1.2.

[946] Ombudsman (n 788), 115.

[947] Harden (n 857), 208.

[948] Article 4.3. of 2002 Implementing Provisions.

[949] Article 4.4. of 2002 Implementing Provisions.

She could ask for further information and observations, especially if one of the parties made new allegations or raised new arguments.[950] In any case, the Ombudsman informed the complainant and the institution concerned on the next steps.[951] In particular, at this point the complainant used to be asked informally whether she accepted the Ombudsman's proposal of a friendly solution.[952]

O'Reilly saw this procedure as, occasionally, overly formalistic, with too many procedural burdens which might slow down the inquiries.[953] The new Implementing Provisions and practical arrangements are intended to give the case handlers and legal officers more discretion in deciding whether specific involvement of the complainant or the institution would be instrumental to reaching the inquiry's goal. 'The Ombudsman's intention [is] to be able to choose flexibly in each inquiry the steps that appear best fit to achieve a concrete outcome'.[954] These changes are supposed to speed up proceedings and help the Ombudsman's team concentrate on cases deemed most important.[955]

At the time of writing,

> the primary focus is on ensuring that the inquiry measures used reflect the specific needs of each inquiry. Thus, the Ombudsman should obtain the views of an institution or a complainant where needed … There should be no automatism as regards obtaining such views ….

The inquiries are supposed to be 'tailor-made rather than automatically passing through rigid procedural stages'.[956] However, the other side of this coin is that the procedural rights of the complainants and the issues to which more resources are devoted become more dependent on the case handler's appraisal.

Nowadays, the complainants are perceived as 'vehicles' bringing information about possible instances of maladministration, whereas it is up to the Ombudsman to choose the cases on which she should concentrate her scarce resources.[957] This naturally implies a genuinely political choice between competing substantive values to be pursued. A legal basis for this practice was introduced by the Ombudsman herself in Article 9.1. of the 2016 Implementing Provisions, pursuant to which the Ombudsman may take steps to ensure that a complaint is dealt with as a matter of priority, considering her strategic objectives.[958]

[950] ibid.

[951] Article 4.5. of the 2002 Implementing Provisions.

[952] Harden (n 857), 218.

[953] As described by interviewees.

[954] Letter from the Ombudsman's Secretary General to the European Court of Auditors' Secretary-General of 28.4.2016 (received on 2.4.2019, request Ares(2019)1027373).

[955] The Ombudsman's proceedings last an average of 8.5 months, but some proceedings may last more than 18 months. Ombudsman (n 939), 40.

[956] Ombudsman (n 763), 1.

[957] As put by one of the interviewees.

[958] One of O'Reilly's strategic objectives is transparency. Therefore, she set up a simplified procedure for cases regarding access to documents. Ombudsman, 'Prioritisation of Access to Documents cases: Accelerating the processing of complaints relating to access to documents' (Ref. Ares(2017)4618822 internal document received on 16.1.2019, request Ares(2018)6490466), 1.

The previously mandatory procedural steps have accordingly been made optional. At the time of writing, the Ombudsman *may* ask the institution concerned to provide a reply in relation to the complaint, whereas the right of the complainant to make observations on the reply (previously: 'opinion') is no longer mentioned in the Implementing Provisions. The Ombudsman may arguably shorten the institution's three-month period to provide a reply if the urgency, complexity or public interest character of the inquiry so requires.[959]

The complainant is no longer automatically informed in the admissibility letter about the steps which are to be taken in her inquiry. The internal guidelines leave the case handler a considerable discretion in this respect and instruct them not to tie their own hands.[960] The complainant's view on the proposed solution is not automatically sought before the proposal is made to the institution.[961]

> It is often appropriate to sound out the complainant beforehand. That said, formal solution proposals are normally not communicated to complainants until after the institution's reply has been received. Their views should be sought after the Office has received the institution's reply.[962]

In brief, the complainant's participation in the inquiry may be confined to lodging the complaint, which is subsequently dismissed following a desk inquiry.

The Parliament has expressed doubts with regard to the compliance of the 2016 Implementing Provisions and Ombudsman's practice with the rights of complainants:

> Existing explicit provisions on informing the complainant at each stage of the procedure have been deliberately left out in the draft on the new Implementing Provisions … We understand that this choice was made in order to allow for more flexibility in the handling of complaints and for a better use of existing resources. However, it needs to be ensured that the appropriate provisions of the European Code of Good Administrative Behaviour regarding information of the complainant are observed …[963]

Nor is the complainant automatically provided with the report of an inspection of case files in her case.[964] Such reports normally contain the list of documents inspected so the complainant is informed that the inspection has occurred. Likewise, it is up to the competent head of unit to decide if it is necessary to request that the institution or the complainant provide a view on the separate inspection note or meeting note, which may set out conclusions from the inspection.[965] Internal guidelines instruct that a careful assessment be made in this respect

959 Article 4.4. of the 2016 Implementing Provisions.

960 Ombudsman (n 763), paras D.2, N.3.

961 ibid, para E.1.

962 Ombudsman (n 788), 172.

963 Letter from the Parliament's Secretary-General to the Ombudsman's Secretary General of 8.7.2016 (D313080, received on 2.4.2019, request Ares(2019)1027373).

964 That was the case under the previous practice, as informed by an interviewee.

965 Ombudsman (n 763), paras D.6 and D.7.

and highlight that, if requested, the complainant's observations must bring some instrumental value.[966]

To make up for the lesser procedural guarantees, the complainants obtained a new right to demand review of the Ombudsman's decision. The apparent reason for this was that the complainants often write to the Ombudsman following a decision on their complaint, and this correspondence usually contains comments and questions. The new review procedure implies a procedure for reconsideration of the decision.

However, in her internal guidelines regarding the review procedure the Ombudsman explicitly underlined that this is 'not the EO's preferred way' of addressing a complainant's response to the Ombudsman's decision.[967] The Ombudsman does not conceal the fact that she has little faith in the new procedure's added value, emphasising that it 'involves a potentially cumbersome process, simply repeating work already done'. For this reason, she has laid down admissibility requirements for requests for review, which, not surprisingly, resemble the requirements for annulment actions. The requirements include a two-month deadline and the obligation to set out detailed arguments as to why the decision is incorrect. Moreover, the complainant cannot adduce new evidence in the request for review.[968]

To guarantee an impartial re-examination, the case is assigned to a different head of unit from the one who coordinated the original case but not to a different case handler.[969] The original case handler has the most extensive knowledge of the case. Assigning the case to a different case handler could be seen as wasting resources. The data disclosed by the Ombudsman suggest that the review procedure does not in principle lead to changes of the Ombudsman's original decisions.[970]

The involvement of the institution may also be reduced. There may be cases in which, to save time, the institution's opinion or reply is not sought before a preliminary finding or proposal is made, even one which implies maladministration.[971] This applies particularly in access to documents cases, where a solution can be proposed based on an administrative confirmatory decision provided by the institution to the complainant and the examination of the document sought. In the 'most exceptional circumstances', the Ombudsman can also announce

[966] The guidelines recall the aforementioned *Staelen* case and argue that had the case handlers dealing with that case sent the full inspection note to the complainant, her observations might have helped in avoiding the error in factual assessment for which the Ombudsman ultimately had to pay damages. Ibid, para D.6.

[967] Ombudsman, 'Internal procedures for handling requests for review and service complaints' (document received on 16.1.2019, request Ares(2019)3842629), 1.

[968] ibid, para 5.

[969] ibid, para 9.

[970] Ombudsman, Email to the author of 27.8.2019. The Ombudsman disclosed that, from June 2019, 17 requests for review of decisions closing inquiries were processed and *none* of the decisions was ultimately revised.

[971] Ombudsman (n 763), paras D.3, D.4 and D.5, E.2.

a finding of maladministration in a recommendation – normally published on the Ombudsman's website – before asking the institution for an opinion. Such exceptional circumstances occur if the same institution has provided an opinion on an identical issue in another very recent inquiry or if the institution already rejected a proposed solution in the case at hand.[972]

This practice has raised doubts inside the Office as regards compliance with the Statute, which guarantees the institution's right to submit an opinion.[973] More importantly, it has also raised opposition of EU institutions and bodies that had been given an opportunity to comment on the Ombudsman's 2016 Implementing Provisions. For instance, the Secretary-General of the Commission expressed the following reservation:

> The fact that the Ombudsman could produce a non-binding preliminary assessment *before the institution has been given the opportunity to make its views known on the complaint* would imply that the only information at the disposal of the Ombudsman when producing such a preliminary assessment would be the account of the facts and the allegations made by the complainant. This could result in prejudging the Ombudsman's position and could thus have a negative impact on the institution's possibility to make its views known during the procedure … Both sides should be able to express their views before any analysis or conclusions, even preliminary, are drawn by the Ombudsman.[974]

Likewise, the Director of the Agency for the Cooperation of Energy Regulators expressed the following reservation:

> I am surprised that the Ombudsman suggests a procedure in which a solution can be put forward without the Institution (the Agency, in our case) being given the opportunity to be heard. In this way, the Ombudsman will be able to rely solely on the input of the complainant. I trust that the Ombudsman would only avail themselves of this opportunity for very simple and seemingly straightforward cases, but this approach remains nonetheless somewhat at odds with the duty of the Ombudsman to act independently and neutrally, and with the Institution's/Agency's right to be heard.[975]

Several other institutions and bodies expressed the same reservations.[976] In response, the Ombudsman reassured ACER that where a proposal for a

[972] ibid, para F.2.

[973] As observed by an interviewee.

[974] Letter from the Commission's Secretary-General to the Ombudsman's Secretary General of 21.4.2016 (Ares(2016)1887120, received on 2.4.2019, request Ares(2019)1027373) (italics in original).

[975] Letter from the ACER Director to the Ombudsman's Secretary General of 5.4.2016 (ACER-2016- … -169, received on 2.4.2019, request Ares(2019)1027373).

[976] Parliament (n 963). Letter from the European External Action Service's Secretary-General to the Ombudsman's Secretary General of 10.6.2016 (Ares(2016)SN3341274). Letter from the European Anti-Fraud Office's Director-General to the Ombudsman's Secretary-General of 9.5.2016 (olaf.c.4(2016)2377899). Letter from the EU Publications Office's Executive Director to the Ombudsman's Secretary-General of 21.4.2016 (ARES/2016/2395107). All the documents were received on 2.4.2019, request Ares(2019)1027373.

solution is made without first hearing the view of the authority concerned, this proposal

> will be made without a finding of maladministration … it is only once the Ombudsman has obtained the reply of the institution, and thus safeguarded the institution's right to be heard, that the Ombudsman will share a copy of the proposed solution and the institution's reply with the complainant … The substance of the solution proposal will always be based on the Ombudsman's own understanding of the issue at stake.[977]

V. Conclusion

Overall, does the ombuds-review fill some of the gaps of judicial review at the EU level, overcoming and compensating for the latter's shortcomings? Undoubtedly, the ombuds-review has proven widely open to challenges against a variety of individual decision-making acts and processes, as well as potentially general rule-making, soft law and acts producing weak legal effects – affecting expectations or interests of individuals – which normally fall beyond the concept of 'acts producing legal effects' as applied by the EU Courts. Moreover, the Ombudsman accepts public interest complaints pertaining to recurrent decision-making practices, enabling her to scrutinise administrative action beyond the confines of individual processes or cases. The Ombudsman can thus take a broader view of the compliance of given administrative processes with the normative standards than the EU Courts, whose scrutiny is confined to specifically delineated acts or processes, and whose systemic impact is less direct.

In a few highly complex cases decided between 2014 and 2018 and involving normatively and empirically uncertain appraisals, the Ombudsman has leveraged the legislative mandates of the challenged institutions or agencies to foster a more thorough consideration of potentially underrated or underrepresented public and private interests, such as the protection of public health or the environment, animal welfare or equal treatment. Due to the restrictive admissibility criteria of annulment actions, similar public interest claims are in principle not presented before the EU Courts by private parties. Be that as it may, faced with indeterminate legal mandates, which do not clearly indicate a hierarchy of competing private or public interest, the EU Courts are likely to defer to the political discretion of primary decision-makers. Deprived of binding powers, the Ombudsman may formulate normatively more demanding recommendations. On top of that, the Ombudsman has also proven capable of applying a searching process-oriented review technique, arguably not inferior to that elaborated by the EU Courts.

Conversely, even though the Ombudsman currently reports a higher number of closed inquiries, she seems to identify fewer instances of maladministration

[977] Letter from the Ombudsman's Secretary General to the ACER Director of 28.4.2016 (received on 2.4.2019, request Ares(2019)1027373).

and settled cases. Although the discussed figures are not conclusive in and of themselves, they prompt more investigation into the way the Ombudsman sets her priority cases and allocates her scarce resources. A broader normative question regarding the level of leeway which the Statute leaves to the office holder in redefining the role of the Office should also be asked. At the same time, the Ombudsman regularly reports a high rate of compliance and constructive follow-up to her proposals and recommendations. However, more empirical research should be undertaken into the relations between the Ombudsman and the supervised institutions and bodies, independent of the Ombudsman's self-evaluations, to paint a realistic picture of compliance and her de facto authority. In particular, it remains to be seen whether changes in the strategy and procedural practices introduced by O'Reilly will, in the long run, have an impact on the rate of identified instances of maladministration and compliance.

Crucially, just as in the case of the judicial and administrative review, an important weak point of ombuds-review is access to specialist expertise that could enable an independent verification of potential substantive errors in cases involving empirically uncertain determinations and appraisals. At present, the Ombudsman has no choice but to impose on the complainant the burden of adducing and elucidating enough empirical proof to demonstrate a 'manifest' error of assessment in the challenged decision-making. Changes in this practice would require more resources to be allocated and, arguably, a broader political discussion, among the Parliament and other institutions, on the Ombudsman's specific role within the broad lines of her Treaty mandate. At present, each office holder enjoys significant leeway in defining the strategies and specific priorities and the broader goals of the ombuds-review.

7

Conclusions

I. The Assets and Shortcomings of Extra-judicial Review

The question underlying this book has been whether extra-judicial review mechanisms proliferating at the EU level can remedy shortcomings of EU judicial review, especially concerning its restrained thoroughness in epistemically uncertain cases and limited accessibility for private parties. This book has also revealed the relative authority of these mechanisms by confronting their practical operation. The advantages and disadvantages of such mechanisms better come to light through their comparison. The unique Treaty mandate and acquired de facto authority of the EU Courts among their audiences cannot fully compensate for their institutional and procedural shortcomings. These shortcomings might affect the de facto authority in the long run.

The findings presented in the book prompt more scholarly attention to the extra-judicial review. By leveraging their institutional assets and improving procedural practices, even in the absence of explicit legislative guidance, the examined extra-judicial review mechanisms have indeed managed to delve into detailed empirical and normative appraisals, which the EU Courts tend to subject only to light-touch review. As the ECHA BoA experience shows, the BoAs may compensate for judicial review's generalist character by dint of their mixed and specialised composition, their proximity to the agencies and their expertise, and informal procedural practices. Through the partial specialisation and in-depth written and oral deliberation with the parties on contentious empirical issues, a BoA may achieve highly favourable results in terms of the review thoroughness. Simultaneously, far-reaching administrative arrangements may enhance the BoA's actual independence and public appearance of independence.

The Ombudsman also engages with instances of EU law-, rule- and decision-making. She can contribute to the EU system of justice – paradoxically – through the lack of binding powers. This feature allows her to develop normative standards creatively, prompting the EU institutions and bodies to self-reflect on their normative choices. It has proven useful in cases involving disputable scientific findings and political discretion. Not dependent on binary judgments (lawful or unlawful), the Ombudsman may proactively persuade the primary rule- or decision-makers to take greater account of underrated values and foster a candid reconsideration of contested acts or processes. Consequently, the Ombudsman and other 'soft' mechanisms[978] may instil the deliberative legitimacy assets in EU rule- or decision-making, while avoiding the risk of normative overreach. The practical operation of such mechanism deserves more scholarly attention from lawyers.

The extra-judicial review has also expanded access to the accountability process concerning EU law-, rule- and decision-making, including acts or actions in atypical or non-binding forms. It has proven highly relevant for parties traditionally barred from the EU judicial review such as public interest organisations and social actors. The Ombudsman and the BoAs (with liberal intervention rules) act to some extent as public interest watchdogs of EU institutions and bodies.

However, the examined judicial and extra-judicial review mechanisms suffer from similar shortcomings. As a matter of path dependence or scarce resources, these mechanisms have adopted the dispute-settlement or adversarial procedural model's basic premise. The applicants bear the responsibility for collecting, adducing and elucidating the meaning of evidence to the adjudicators. The adjudicators may demonstrate a hands-on and active approach to clarifying the contentious issues and steering the parties' deliberation to find a sound, acceptable or simply pragmatic solution. However, they do not engage in pro-active fact-finding and comprehensive scrutiny of all potential legal problems, at least without the applicant's initiative and activity.

The EU Courts are clinging to the interpretation of their procedural framework which allows them to eschew independent and proactive scrutiny of the broad legality and empirical bases of impugned legal acts. They confine themselves to assessing the pleas in law and the evidence provided by the applicants. This practice has been taken over by the examined extra-judicial review. It allowed them to develop a meaningful review technique despite scarce resources. The ECHA BoA and other BoAs replicated the deferential review technique in cases involving decision-making faced with inescapable empirical and normative uncertainty, where a decision had to be made despite persisting doubts and data gaps. So did the Ombudsman in cases where she was expected to settle purely scientific matters and in which uncertain empirical and normative appraisals were embroiled at every possible level. In such cases, the BoAs and the Ombudsman did not consider themselves authorised to second-guess contestable assessments of first-instance decision-makers. Such assessments had partly followed from the 'gut feeling' of first-instance experts rather than rigorous, well-established and uncontroversial methodologies.

Further strengthening of the administrative and ombuds-review technique likely hinges upon greater resources, access to necessary expertise, or even wider composition encompassing an array of experts, specialised lawyers, appointed expert witnesses or even representatives of various stakeholders. Only such extended composition and resources could enable the BoAs and the

[978] Such as the Parliament Petitions Committee.

Ombudsman to more readily delve into difficult choices between competing substantive values and evidence.

The outstanding and broader question is whether the dispute-settlement or adversarial procedural model meets the litigants' expectations in cases characterised by highly uncertain empirical and normative appraisals. Litigants frequently present only general evidence and arguments, putting in question the veracity or credibility of the EU institutions' and bodies' empirical findings. They seem to expect the EU Courts, the BoAs or the Ombudsman to autonomously and authoritatively affirm or refute these findings; something that these review bodies are currently ill-equipped to do.

In this context, it is unclear to what extent a broadening of individual access to the EU judicial review, especially for public interest (environmental) organisations – traditionally advocated by the scholarship and practitioners – would serve its actual purpose of enhancing the public accountability of EU institutions and bodies. Public interest organisations are themselves ill-equipped to produce empirical data capable of refuting, with the required degree of certainty, the presumption of accuracy attributed to the EU institutions' and bodies' appraisals. Opening the EU Courts' gates might only decrease the system's efficiency by generating an influx of empirically difficult and politically controversial cases. The EU Courts would have to muddle through such cases, although their current institutional and procedural structure is not entirely adequate to this task. Broader access might, at the same time, increase the risk of judicial errors and normative overreach. The EU judicial review's accessibility should be seen as forming part of a larger discussion on the institutional and procedural legitimacy assets offered by the EU judicial and extra-judicial architecture.

II. The Rule of Law and Epistemic Uncertainty

There is no consensus regarding the scope of judicial or extra-judicial review's responsibility for the rule of law in empirically and normatively uncertain cases. The traditional instrumentalist idea behind the independent judicial review is that it can objectively decode legitimate constitution-makers' or law-makers' directives and apply them based on a neutral consideration of relevant empirical factors.

Nowadays, both premises of this syllogism break down. EU substantive legal frameworks do not indicate the right priority between clashing interests, and empirical data do not lend themselves to unambiguous interpretations. Therefore, more elaborate justifications of judicial review, or complementary extra-judicial review, are needed. Such mechanisms are currently interpreted as contributing to aggregation and balancing of affected interests or an open and reasoned deliberation on public matters. However, these interpretations justify interference with the disputed law-, rule-, or decision-making only to a certain extent. Where this endpoint lies can be subject to serious disagreement.

Arguably, the rule of law implies that legislative or administrative actions should be founded upon 'objective truth'. Even if the latter is ultimately unattainable, public institutions and bodies must still seek to reduce epistemic uncertainty to the greatest possible extent. Mechanisms should be put in place that are capable of reducing empirical and normative uncertainty through aggregation and balancing of different views on the matter or fostering an open and reasoned deliberation among different stakeholders. Nonetheless, we could reasonably argue that this duty lies predominantly with primary law-, rule- and decision-makers. The rule of law does not necessarily imply an utterly exhaustive and widely accessible judicial review or even extra-judicial review mechanism for all-encompassing supervision over law-, rule- and decision-making.

Moreover, the EU judicial and extra-judicial review currently operates within a largely adversarial procedural framework geared towards individual dispute settlement rather than autonomously seeking factual truth and enforcing an objective order of substantive values. But is relying on partisan evidence adequate in cases whose outcomes affect public interest goals, such as the protection of public health and the environment? Most review mechanisms adopt a hands-on approach and reduce uncertainty as much as possible, within their limited institutional and procedural resources.

Their responsibility could be increased by introducing more inquisitorial practices. However, such techniques may require a considerable expenditure of public resources, and there is still no guarantee that they will further reduce the level of empirical or normative uncertainty. The law-, rule- and decision-making at the EU level already involves a myriad of politically representative and accountable institutions, expert committees and consultation forums that may increase or decrease the level of uncertainty. The EU Courts and other review mechanisms, in their limited institutional and procedural structures, surely have difficulty in beating these legitimacy assets and claiming the authority to decide on controversial political or scientific issues.

Therefore, the research agenda and institutional and procedural reform strategy should encompass improved safeguards and new forms of legal protection and accountability at the pre-judicial or pre-review level, as part of primary law-, rule- and decision-making processes. When cognition of convoluted empirical truth is left to the primary law-, rule- and decision-makers, the safeguards of transparency, inclusivity, independence and conflict of interest policies of expert bodies, internal review proceedings involving the firm and visible safeguards of independent verification and candid reconsideration may still deliver potent legitimacy assets. In this scenario, generalist courts should concentrate on polishing and enforcing the said institutional and procedural safeguards, and ombudsman-like bodies on bringing in an underrepresented or underrated public interest perspective.

In other words, a possible reform strategy is to provide more potent legitimacy assets at the root of the problem, rather than by creating or expanding additional stages within the broader governance process. Seeing judicial or extra-judicial review as culminating stages of a broader governance process helps us to see that legislative, administrative and judicial bodies may play on the same team, rather than against each other. The necessary institutional or procedural legitimacy assets may be instilled into a governance process at any stage that seems most appropriate, considering the process's entire design.

III. The Political Design of Judicial and Extra-judicial Architecture

The extra-judicial review has become a firmly established feature of the EU system of justice, which is likely to develop further. The Commission and EU co-legislators support the setting up of new BoAs.[979] Recent debates in the Parliament and the Council regarding the Ombudsman's reappointment and her Statute's revision revealed an opulent offering of ideas, some quite far-reaching, regarding how the Ombudsman's powers could be further expanded – or, quite to the contrary, more precisely circumscribed[980] – to fill gaps in the EU system of justice or prevent an overstepping by the Ombudsman of her role.[981]

The extra-judicial review might never constitute a perfect alternative for judicial review. Some litigants might expect a determination of their rights and obligations with a degree of authoritativeness characterising the EU Courts' rulings. Since the judicial review is a limited good, however, a legal order makes a choice regarding its distribution and priority goals, such as either broad availability or thoroughness. In the EU legal order, this choice has been codetermined by the Member States, as the main Treaty authors, and the EU Courts themselves. The Member States have carried out several significant amendments to the Treaty provisions governing the EU Courts and judicial review. At the same time, the indeterminate Treaty and case-law concepts such as 'legality review' or 'direct and individual concern', as well as 'pleas in law relating to public policy' and the like,

[979] Most recently, the Commission envisaged setting up a new board of appeal in the Body for European Regulators of Electronic Communications. Ultimately, the Body did not receive the powers to issue decisions addressed to private parties and so the envisaged BoA became devoid of purpose. Council, 'Proposal for a Regulation of the European Parliament and of the Council establishing the Body of European Regulators for Electronic Communications – Examination of the Presidency Text' (Council doc. 12512/17), 5.

[980] The Council recently proposed to clarify in the Ombudsman's Statute that the Ombudsman is *not* empowered to inquire into the organisation of the legislative process, Council (n 897).

[981] Members of Parliament proposed, among other things, to confer upon the Ombudsman powers to issue *binding* decisions regarding public access to documents or to intervene, just like other EU institutions and bodies, in the proceedings before the Court. Ultimately, none of these radical proposals was accepted. Some were clearly going beyond the Ombudsman's Treaty mandate. Parliament, 'Opinion of the Committee on Petitions (27.11.2018) for the Committee of Constitutional Affairs on the proposal for amending Parliament's Decision 94/262/ECSC, EC, Euratom of 9 March 1994 on the regulations and general conditions governing the performance of the Ombudsman's duties (2018/2080(INL))'.

have been subject to more-or-less creative interpretive evolution in response to expectations voiced by litigants, practitioners, scholars and even domestic courts.

However, it should be emphasised that the EU co-legislators and the Commission enjoy far-reaching political discretion in determining a detailed design of the judicial and, to an even greater extent, extra-judicial review mechanisms. The Statute of the EU Courts, the Statute of the Ombudsman, and the founding regulations of the BoAs – including rules for their composition, accessibility, procedural principles and strategic objectives – can all be modified via the ordinary legislative procedure by the Parliament and the Council at the initiative of the Commission. The EU law-makers can decide on the inquisitorial or adversarial model, the composition, and access to expertise and resources. These factors might influence the judicial and extra-judicial review to a greater extent than formal review 'criteria', abstractly prescribed by the procedural text. The law-makers should readjust the procedural frameworks and resources of review mechanisms in response to novel challenges.

A logical next step would be to settle the controversies surrounding the availability of review. Admittedly, the basic rules of the accessibility of judicial review are determined by the Treaties. However, the co-legislators have partially succeeded in making the judicial review more accessible to environmental organisations, bestowing upon the latter formally procedural rights to internal review.[982] They could also broaden access to extra-judicial review before the BoAs by amending the founding regulations, thereby indirectly broadening access to the EU Courts against BoA decisions.

The point of these concluding considerations is to accentuate the *political* discretion that the EU law-makers enjoy to shape the EU judicial and extra-judicial architecture. The recent investment into the enlargement of the EGC is just one of the possible options which, at any rate, implies further problems. The enlarged EGC is currently paying a lot of attention to internal measures for consistency of case law, such as the extended composition of chambers and monitoring inconsistencies by its Vice-President.[983] As recently argued by the ECJ, it is still too early to evaluate the EGC enlargement's effects.[984] In the future, nonetheless, more attention should be paid to the role of extra-judicial review – especially the BoAs – in the EU judicial and extra-judicial architecture. If their appearance of independence were reinforced, could they satisfactorily warrant the fundamental right to effective judicial protection? In this scenario, could the EGC better focus on maintaining the consistency of case law across the variegated subfields of EU administrative law?

[982] For instance, see Case T-177/13, *TestBioTech et al v Commission*, ECLI:EU:T:2016:736.
[983] ECJ (n 464).
[984] ibid.

Besides a rationalisation of costs and flexibility, a more deconcentrated system of extra-judicial review by the BoAs might offer benefits in preventing error and normative overreach. Suppose a legal interpretation advocated by private litigants in a specific case is validated by the EU Courts' supreme interpretive authority. This interpretation is likely to stay with us in the long term as it is difficult for the political institutions to overrule the EU Courts. The litigants benefit from reinforced legal certainty, but there is also some risk of judicial error and normative overreach.

These concerns have been addressed by a normative idea of dispersed allocation of the review power across a variety of mechanisms representing different institutional and procedural models. According to this idea, extant and novel review mechanisms, and their interrelations, should be structured in such a way as to maximise the possibilities for dialogue between individual review actors and their input into the multi-stage process of review. The basic intuition behind this proposal was that it could minimise the risk of normative overreach, overload and error by multiplying the sites of review. Before the supreme interpretive authority uses its power of the last word on a controversial matter, the matter has been subjected to the consideration of middle-level authorities.[985]

At the domestic level, a vertical dispersal of review authority is possible by dint of the multiple-tier system of administrative courts and quasi-judicial structures: specialised tribunals, chambers, commissions, ombudsmanry and the like. At the EU level, the vertical dispersal of review authority is relatively limited. At present, the EGC cumulates the review authority over a wide range of legal acts. The ECJ judges have their hands full with an increasing number of preliminary references. They have recently limited the right of appeal from EGC rulings and the filtering device is likely to be extended in the future. Therefore, the responsibility of the EGC for the horizontal consistency of case law increases. But the EGC is at the same time burdened with convoluted empirical appraisals in many policy fields and with routine and technical cases such as those concerning the EUIPO BoA's decisions in trademark disputes.

A clearer articulation by the law-makers of the specific role of each layer and kind of review could help make the system more efficient. The law-makers should take stock of legal experiments with supplementary review mechanisms and consciously decide on their future role. The lack of an explicit prior legislative specification of the tasks and competences of extra-judicial review mechanisms may in the future hamper the building of prospective litigants' trust in this form of justice. Also, a several-tier system of judicial, administrative and ombuds-review, in which different tiers and kinds replicate a similar type of adversarial proceedings, misses the point. So does a widely available review mechanism in which, however, the adjudicator is passive and neither do the applicants have resources

[985] Zurn (n 30), 265.

to produce enough proof to put in question the uncertain empirical basis of impugned measures.

In particular, since the administrative review by the BoAs is strictly interconnected with the judicial review by the EGC, their respective and somehow distinct role should be more clearly articulated to avoid a repetition of essentially the same or similar type of review. Importantly, the law-makers enjoy the broadest discretion with regard to determining the scope and availability of the judicial and administrative review of decision-making by the agencies.[986] Should the added value of administrative review by the BoAs consist only in limiting the number of complex cases reaching the EU Courts? Or should the BoAs be the main review mechanism, with reinforced independence safeguards, for private parties in the areas where uncertain empirical and normative appraisals are enmeshed. In this scenario, the role of the EGC could be limited to maintaining the horizontal consistency of case law. Consequently, the EGC could apply only a light-touch review of BoA appraisals. Going a step further, Article 263(5) TFEU could be interpreted as allowing for introducing a case-filtering device already at the level of the EGC. The BoAs would not have to be transformed into specialised courts.[987] The organisational proximity of a BoA to the agency may also be a valuable asset worth preserving. Due to all the opportunities offered by the model of BoAs, the designers of the EU judicial and extra-judicial architecture should make a well-informed decision as to whether to 'invest' in an expansion of the generalist EGC or specialised BoAs, or similar bodies operating within EU institutions and modelled upon the ECB ABoR.[988]

The Ombudsman and similar mechanisms, such as the Parliament Petitions Committee, could play a greater role in the review of legal acts, including acts of general application, underpinned by controversial normative appraisals. When EU constitutional and legislative frameworks do not specify a choice between competing legally protected private and public interests, the EU Courts – equipped only with the power to give 'binary' judgments – have difficulty in enhancing the authority of EU law-, rule- and decision-making. In such cases, the access-to-justice ambitions of public interest organisations, civil society and other

[986] They may establish the already mentioned 'specific conditions and arrangements' for annulment actions brought by private parties against agency decisions under Article 263(5) TFEU.

[987] As argued in this book, the problem is not the organisational proximity to the agency, in and of itself, but rather specific administrative links to the management board, which can be modified through legislative amendments.

[988] Article 263(5) TFEU does *not* authorise the co-legislators to introduce 'special conditions and arrangements' with regard to the annulment actions directed against institutions. But the EU co-legislators enjoy broad freedom in shaping EU administrative proceedings including by the creation of specialised adjudicatory units inside institutions. Such adjudicatory units may offer formally non-binding but practically highly authoritative opinions on draft decisions. As the example of the ECB ABoR shows these opinions may subsequently facilitate judicial review. Concetta Brescia Morra, René Smits and Andrea Magliari, 'The Administrative Board of Review of the European Central Bank: Experience After 2 Years' (2017) 18 *European Business Organization Law Review* 567.

social actors could be satisfied by the Ombudsman and similar deliberation- and persuasion-oriented mechanisms, which do not foster the risk of judicial normative overreach. The Parliament (subject to the Council's consent) enjoys in this respect power to specify to what extent the Ombudsman's concept of 'maladministration' may relate to the substance of regulatory acts[989] and the course of legislative proceedings. The Parliament may also decide to define by itself, in more concrete terms, the overarching objective of the Ombudsman's inquiries. At present, the Ombudsman's Statute as adopted by the Parliament leaves to individual officeholders the bulk of important decisions as to striking a balance between a narrow dispute-settlement and a broader standard-setting function. However, tectonic shifts in the defining features of the Ombudsman's inquiries may harm the Office's authority and, ultimately, the rate of compliance with Ombudsman's proposals and recommendations.[990]

IV. Protecting the Courts from Uncertainty

A discussion about models of institutional and procedural justice and how they can enhance the authority of law-, rule- and decision-making usually accompany profound changes in the allocation of real power. The power at the EU level is nowadays increasingly dispersed among a myriad of specialist bodies, agencies and offices, which must reach decisions having far-reaching societal impact despite persisting normative and empirical uncertainty.

At the same time, we have found ourselves at, perhaps, the pinnacle of post-modernist deconstruction. We realise that the objectivity of science or 'complex technical appraisals' is often just a gut feeling of experts, even if based in good faith on their acquired experience. EU constitutional and legislative norms must cover increasingly intricate and controversial social relations but, hammered out in a supranational setting constantly requiring vagueness to reach political compromises, they lose their capacity to frame and constrain the exercise of public power. As a result, the judicial pronouncements of rights and obligations, as well as the cogency of underlying science and the balancing of substantive values, expose themselves to growing criticism, public contestation, and even backlash. If nothing is certain anymore, why should judicial rulings enjoy special authority?

The authority of courts is largely relative to their institutional and procedural assets and those can become outdated. Instead of taking refuge against the

[989] At present, the Ombudsman shies away from interfering in what she defines as 'political' matters. It should be emphasised, however, that the concept of 'maladministration' is indeterminate and in some Member States the ombudsmen do assess the substance of political actions.

[990] The draft Ombudsman's Statute proposed by the Parliament in 2019 largely replicates the substance of the previous one and does not add much clarity as to the primary goals of ombuds-review.

hostile reality in the well-established legal concepts and constructs, this book has attempted to explore the degree of their adjustment to the novel challenges, through the emergence, proliferation and evolution of extra-judicial review. In a more lawyerly, solution-oriented spirit, it has also suggested that EU law-makers would enjoy great latitude in a further adjustment and expansion of judicial and extra-judicial review if they only appreciated their interconnectedness and potential.

BIBLIOGRAPHY

Alemanno A and Pech L, 'Thinking Justice Outside the Docket: A Critical Assessment of the Reform of the EU's Court System' (2017) 54 *Common Market Law Review* 129–76

Arnull A, 'Private Applicants and the Action for Annulment since *Codorniu*' (2001) 38 *Common Market Law Review* 7–52

—— *The European Union and its Court of Justice* (Oxford University Press 2006)

—— 'Judicial Review in the European Union' in Chalmers D and Arnull A (eds), *The Oxford Handbook of European Union Law* (Oxford University Press 2015) 377–401

Backes C and Eliantonio M, *Cases, Materials and Text on Judicial Review of Administrative Action* (Hart Publishing 2019)

Barents R, 'EU Procedural Law and Effective Legal Protection' (2014) 51 *Common Market Law Review* 1437–62

—— *EU Remedies and Procedures* (Wolters Kluwer 2016)

Barnes J, 'Towards a Third Generation of Administrative Procedure' in Ackerman S-R and Lindseth P (eds), *Comparative Administrative Law* (Edward Elgar 2010) 336–56

Bartlett O and Macculloch A, 'Evidence and Proportionality in Free Movement Cases: The Impact of the Scotch Whisky Case' (2020) 11 *European Journal of Risk Regulation* 109–30

Bast J, 'Legal Instruments and Judicial Protection' in Bogdandy A von and Bast J (eds), *Principles of European Constitutional Law* (Hart Publishing 2010) 345–85

—— 'New Categories of Acts After the Lisbon Reform: Dynamics of Parliamentarization in EU Law' (2012) 49 *Common Market Law Review* 885–928

Bergkamp L, *The European Union REACH Regulation for Chemicals: Law and Practice* (Oxford University Press 2013)

—— 'Private Party Standing and EU Risk Regulation: Expanded Standing Rights in the Public Interest' (2016) 8 *European Journal of Risk Regulation* 557–568

Bergström M, 'Judicial Protection for Private Parties in European Commission Rule-Making' in Bergström CF (ed), *Rulemaking by the European Commission* (Oxford University Press 2016) 205–32

Berry E and Boyes S, 'Access to Justice in the Community Courts: A Limited Right?' (2005) 24 *Civil Justice Quarterly* 224–45

Bickel A, *The Least Dangerous Branch: The Supreme Court at the Bar of Politics* (Yale University Press 1986)

Binder T, Inglese M and Waarden Fv, *The European Ombudsman: Democratic Empowerment or Democratic Deficit?* (BEUCITIZEN: Barriers Towards EU Citizenship 2017)

Bobek M, 'Quantity or Quality? Reassessing the Role of Supreme Jurisdictions in Central Europe' (2009) 57 *American Journal of Comparative Law* 33–66

Bobek M and Kosař D, 'Global Solutions, Local Damages: A Critical Study in Judicial Councils in Central and Eastern Europe' (2014) 15 *German Law Journal* 1257–1292

Bonnor P, 'The European Ombudsman: A Novel Source of Soft Law in the European Union' (2000) 25 *European Law Review* 39–57

—— 'Institutional Attitudes in Context: A Comment on Rawlings' "Engaged Elites' – Citizen Action and Institutional Attitudes in Commission Enforcement' (2001) 7 *European Law Journal* 114–19

Bramante C, 'Launching and Participating in Proceedings Before the ECHA Board of Appeal: An Industry Perspective' (2018) 1 *International Chemical Regulatory and Law Review* 114–18

Brenninkmeijer A and Gelder Ev, 'The Rule of Law in the European Union: Standards of the Ombudsman, Judge, and Auditor' in Hertogh M and Kirkham R (eds), *Research Handbook on the Ombudsman* (Edward Elgar 2018) 151–65

Brink T van den, 'Danger! Glyphosate may Expose Weaknesses in Institutional Systems: EU Legislation and Comitology in the Face of a Controversial Reauthorisation' (2020) 11 *European Journal of Risk Regulation* 436–49

Brito Bastos F, 'Derivative Illegality in European Composite Administrative Procedures' (2018) 55 *Common Market Law Review* 101–34

—— 'Doctrinal Methodology in EU Administrative Law: Confronting the Touch of Stateness', *German Law Journal* 2021 (forthcoming)

Bronckers M and Gerven Y van, 'Legal Remedies Under the EC's New Chemicals Legislation REACH: Testing a New Model of European Governance' (2009) 46 *Common Market Law Review* 1823–71

Buck T, Kirkham R and Thomson B, *The Ombudsman Enterprise and Administrative Justice* (Routledge 2017)

Burley A-M and Mattili W, 'Europe before the Court: A Political Theory of Legal Integration' (1993) 47 *International Organization* 41–76

Busuioc M, 'Extra-judicial Accountability: The European Ombudsman and "Life Beyond Legality"' in *European Agencies: Law and Practices of Accountability* (Oxford University Press 2013) 221–44

Butler G, 'An Interim Post-mortem: Specialised Courts in the EU Judicial Architecture after the Civil Service Tribunal' (2019) 17 *International Organizations Law Review* 1–47

—— 'Implementing a Complete System of Legal Remedies in EU Foreign Affairs Law' (2018) 24 *Columbia Journal of European Law* 637–76

—— 'Hidden Administrative Review in EU Law: The Boards of Appeal of EU Agencies in the Common Foreign and Security Policy' in Chamon M, Eliantonio M and Volpato A (eds), *Boards of Appeal of EU Agencies: A New Paradigm of Legal Protection?* (Oxford University Press, forthcoming 2021)

Cane P, *Administrative Tribunals and Adjudication* (Hart Publishing 2009)

—— 'Judicial Review and Merits Review: Comparing Administrative Adjudication by Courts and Tribunals' in Ackerman S-R and Lindseth P (eds), *Comparative Administrative Law* (Edward Elgar 2018) 426–48

Carolan E, *The New Separation of Powers: A Theory for the Modern State* (Oxford University Press 2009)

Carolan E and Curtin D, 'In Search of a New Model of Checks and Balances for the EU: Beyond Separation of Powers' in Mendes J and Venzke I (eds), *Allocating Authority: Who Should Do What in European and International Law?* (Hart Publishing 2018) 53–76

Cassatella A, 'Appeals Before the European Aviation Safety Agency' in Marchetti B (ed), *Administrative Remedies in the European Union. The Emergence of a Quasi-judicial Administration* (Giappichelli Editore 2017) 21–54

Castillo de la Torre F and Fournier EG, *Evidence, Proof and Judicial Review in EU Competition Law* (Edward Elgar 2017)

Chamon M and Volpato A, 'Sketching Out the Role and Function of the ECHA Board of Appeal: Germany v ECHA and BASF v ECHA' (2020) 45 *European Law Review* 840.

Chirulli P, 'La denuncia al Mediatore Europeo' in Chirulli P and Lucia L de (eds), *Rimedi amministrativi ed esecuzione diretta del diritto europeo* (Giappichelli Editore 2018) 191–231

Chirulli P and Lucia L de, *Rimedi amministrativi ed esecuzione diretta del diritto europeo* (G. Giappichelli Editore 2018)

Choper J, *Judicial Review and the National Political Process* (University of Chicago Press 1980)

Clausen F, *Les moyens d'ordre public devant la Cour de justice de l'Union européenne* (Bruylant 2018)

Clément M, 'La jurisprudence administrative en droit de l'environnement: Entre technique et acteurs' (2020) *Revue juridique de l'environnement* 51–61

Coutron L, 'The Changes to the General Court' in Guinchard E and Granger M-P (eds), *The New EU Judiciary: An Analysis of Current Judicial Reforms* (Wolters Kluwer 2018) 143–60

Craig P, 'Standing, Rights and the Structure of Legal Argument' (2003) 9 *European Public Law* 493–508
—— 'Courts' in Craig P (ed), *EU Administrative Law* (OUP 2018) 280–310
—— 'The Precautionary Principle' in Craig P (ed), *EU Administrative Law* (Oxford University Press 2018) 694–721
Curtin D, *Executive Power of the European Union: Law, Practices, and the Living Constitution* (Oxford University Press 2009)
—— 'Legal Acts and the Challenges of Democratic Accountability' in Cremona M and Kilpatrick C (eds), *EU Legal Acts: Challenges and Transformations* (Oxford University Press 2018) 9–29
Damaška MR, *The Faces of Justice and State Authority: A Comparative Approach to the Legal Process* (Yale University Press 1986)
Davies G, 'Legislative Control of the European Court of Justice' (2014) 51 *Common Market Law Review* 1579–1608
—— 'Does the Court of Justice Own the Treaties? Interpretative Pluralism as a Solution to Over-constitutionalisation' (2018) 24 *European Law Journal* 1–18
Diamandouros N, *The European Ombudsman: Origins, Establishment, Evolution* (Office for Official Publications of the European Communities 2005)
—— 'The Relationship Between the Principle of Good Administration and Legal Obligations' in Baudenbacher C, Gulmann C, Lenaerts K, Coulon, Emmanuel E and de la Serre B (eds), *Liber Amicorum en l'honneur de/in honour of Bo Vesterdorf* (Bruylant 2007) 315–41
Douglass-Scott S, 'Justice, Injustice and the Rule of Law in the EU' in Kochenov D, Burca G de and Williams A (eds), *Europe's Justice Deficit* (Hart Publishing 2015) 51–66
Dragos DC and Marrani D, 'Administrative Appeals in Comparative European Administrative Law: What Effectiveness?' in Dragos DC and Neamtu B (eds), *Alternative Dispute Resolution in European Administrative Law* (Springer 2014) 539–63
Dumbrovský T, Petkova B and Sluis M van der, 'Judicial appointments: the article 255 TFEU advisory panel and selection procedures in the member states' (2014) 51 *Common Market Law Review* 455–82
Dworkin R, *Law's Empire* (Harvard University Press 1986)
—— *Freedom's Law: The Moral Reading of the American Constitution* (Harvard University Press 1997)
Dyevre A, 'Technocracy and distrust: Revisiting the rationale for constitutional review' (2015) 13 *International Journal of Constitutional Law* 30–60
Eckes C, 'EU Restrictive Measures Against Natural and Legal Persons: From Counterterrorist to Third Country Sanctions' (2014) 51 *Common Market Law Review* 869–906
Eckes C and Abazi V, 'Closed Evidence in EU Courts: Security, Secrets and Access to Justice' (2018) 55 *Common Market Law Review* 753–82
Eliantonio M, *Europeanisation of Administrative Justice? The Influence of the ECJ's Case Law in Italy, Germany and England* (Europa Law Publishing 2009)
—— *Standing Up for Your Right(s) in Europe: A Comparative Study on Legal Standing (Locus Standi) before the EU and Member States' Courts* (Intersentia 2013)
—— 'Information Exchange in European Administrative Law: A Threat to Effective Judicial Protection?' (2016) 3 *Maastricht Journal of Comparative and European Law* 531–49
Eliantonio M and Stefan O, 'Soft Law Before the European Court: Discovering a "Common Pattern"?' (2018) 37 *Yearbook of European Law* 457–69
Ely JH, *Democracy and Distrust: A Theory of Judicial Review* (Harvard University Press 1980)
Forrester I, 'A Bush in Need of Pruning: The Luxuriant Growth of "Light Judicial Review"' in Ehlermann C-D and Marquis M (eds), *European Competition Law Annual: The Evaluation of Evidence and its Judicial Review in Competition Cases* (Hart Publishing 2009) 407–52
Forwood N, 'The Commission's More Economic Approach – Implications for the Role of the EU Courts, the Treatment of Economic Evidence and the Scope of Judicial Review', *European Competition Law Annual: Evaluation of Evidence and Its Judicial Review in Competition Cases* (2009)

Freeman S, 'Constitutional Democracy and the Legitimacy of Judicial Review' (1990–91) 9 *Law and Philosophy* 327–70

Fritzsche A, 'Discretion, Scope of Judicial Review and Institutional Balance in European Law' (2010) 47 *Common Market Law Review* 361–403

Fromont M, 'L'influence du droit français et du droit allemand sur les conditions de recevabilité du recours en annulation devant la Court de justice des Communautés européennes' (1966) *Revue Trimestrielle de Droit Européen* 47–65

Fromont L and Waeyenberge A van, 'La protection juridictionnelle effective en Europe ou l'histoire d'une procession d'Echternach' (2015) 51 *Cahiers de Droit Européen* 113–50

Fuller L, 'The Forms and Limits of Adjudication' (1978) 92 *Harvard Law Review* 353–409

Gaudissart M-A, 'La refonte du règlement de procédure de la Cour de Justice' (2012) 48 *Cahiers de Droit Européen* 603–69

Gentile G, 'Ensuring Effective Judicial Review of EU Soft Law via the Action for Annulment before the EU Courts: A Plea for a Liberal-Constitutional Approach' (2020) 16 *European Constitutional Law Review* 466–92

—— 'The ECJ as the EU Court of Appeal: Some Evidence from the Appeal Case-law on the Non-contractual Liability of the EU' (2020) 13 *Review of European Administrative Law* 73–107

Gonzales CM, 'The Spanish Proposal to the Intergovernmental Conference on Political Union', in European Ombudsman, *The European Ombudsman, Origins, Establishment, Evolution* (Office for Official Publications of the European Communities 2005) 27–37

Gormley L, 'Access to Justice and Public Interest Litigation: Getting Nowhere Quickly?' in Purnhagen K and Rott P (eds), *Varieties of European Economic Law and Regulation: Liber Amicorum for Hans Micklitz* (Springer 2014) 781–92

Granger M-P and Irion K, 'The Court of Justice and the Data Retention Directive in Digital Rights Ireland: Telling Off the EU Legislator and Teaching a Lesson in Privacy and Data Protection' (2014) 39 *European Law Review* 835–50

Green S and Sossin L, 'Administrative Justice and Innovation: Beyond the Adversarial/Inquisitorial Dichotomy' in Jacobs L and Baglay S (eds), *The Nature of Inquisitorial Processes in Administrative Regimes: Global Perspectices* (Ashgate 2013)

Grimm D, 'The Democratic Costs of Constitutionalisation: The European Case' (2015) 21 *European Law Journal* 460–73

Gryllos G, 'Discretion and Judicial Review in EU Competition Law: A Technical Analysis on Sources of Discretion, Judicial Review and Implications for the Litigants' (2016) 4 *Concurrences* 1

Habermas J, *Between Facts and Norms: Contributions to a Discourse Theory of Law and Democracy* (MIT Press 1996)

Harden I, 'Article 43: European Ombudsman' in Peers S, Hervey, T, Kenner, J and Ward, A (eds), *The EU Charter of Fundamental Rights: A Commentary* (Hart Publishing 2014) 1121–50

—— 'The European Ombudsman's role in promoting good governance' in Hofmann HCH and Ziller J (eds), *Accountability in the EU: The Role of the European Ombudsman* (Edward Elgar 2017) 198–216

—— 'The European Ombudsman and Good Administration in the European Union, by Nikos Vogiatzis (Book Review)' (2018) 24 *European Public Law* 365–71

Harding C, 'The Private Interest in Challenging Community Action' (1980) 5 *European Law Review* 354–61

Harel A, *Why Law Matters* (Oxford University Press 2014)

Harel A and Shinar A, 'Between Judicial and Legislative Supremacy: A Cautious Defense of Constrained Judicial Review' (2012) 10 *International Journal of Constitutional Law* 950–75

Harlow C, 'Accountability Through Law' in Harlow C (ed), *Accountability in the European Union* (Oxford University Press 2002) 144–67

—— 'Towards a Theory of Access for the European Court of Justice' (1992) 12 *Yearbook of European Law* 213–48

Harlow C and Rawlings R, 'Firefighting and Fire-watching: Courts and Ombudsmen', *Process and Procedure in EU Administration* (Hart Publishing 2014) 64–92

Hofmann HC, 'Interdependencies between Delegation, Discretion and the Duty of Care Regarding Facts' in Mendes J (ed), *EU Executive Discretion and the Limits of Law* (Oxford University Press 2019) 220–36

Hofmann HCH, 'The Developing Role of the European Ombudsman' in Hofmann HHC and Ziller J (eds), *Accountability in the EU: The Role of the European Ombudsman* (Edward Elgar 2017)

Horeth M, 'The Least Dangerous Branch of European Governance? The European Court of Justice under the Checks and Balances Doctrine' in Witte B de, Muir E and Dawson M (eds), *Judicial Activism at the European Court of Justice* (Edward Elgar 2013) 32–55

Hovell D, *The Power of Process. The Value of Due Process in Security Council Sanctions Decision-Making* (Oxford University Press 2016)

Jaaskinen N and Sikora A, 'The Exclusive Jurisdiction of the Court of Justice of the European Union and the Unity of the EU Legal Order' in Cremona M, Thies A and Wessel RA (eds), *The European Union and International Dispute Settlement* (Oxford University Press 2017) 101–11

Jaeger M, 'The Court of First Instance and the Management of Competition Law Litigation' in Kanninen H, Korjus N and Rosas A (eds), *EU Competition Law in Context* (Hart Publishing 2009) 1–16

—— 'The Standard of Review in Competition Cases Involving Complex Economic Assessments: Towards the Marginalisation of the Marginal Review' (2011) 2 *Journal of European Competition Law & Practice* 295–314

—— '25 Years of the General Court: Looking Back and Forward' in Tomljenović V (ed), *EU Competition and State Aid Rules: Public and Private Enforcement* (Springer 2017) 3–38

Janssen A-MJP and Rosenstock NF, 'Handling Uncertain Risks: An Inconsistent Application of Standards?' (2016) 7 *European Journal of Risk Regulation* 144–54

Jarry J-P, *The European Parliament and the Establishment of a European Ombudsman: Twenty Years of Debate (1974–1995)* (European Parliamentary Research Service 2015)

Kavanagh A, 'Participation and Judicial Review: A Reply to Jeremy Waldron' (2003) 22 *Law and Philosophy* 456–86

—— 'The Constitutional Separation of Powers' in Dyzenhaus D and Thornburn M (eds), *Philosophical Foundations of Constitutional Law* (Oxford University Press 2016) 222–40

Keppenne J-P, 'Les procédures de révision du cadre réglementaire des juridictions de l'Union' (2017) *Cahiers de Droit Européen* 343–70

Kilpatrick C, 'Are the Bailouts Immune to EU Social Challenge Because They Are Not EU Law?' (2014) 10 *European Constitutional Law Review* 393–421

—— 'On the Rule of Law and Economic Emergency: The Degradation of Basic Legal Values in Europe's Bailouts' (2015) 35 *Oxford Journal of Legal Studies* 325–53

Kirkham R, 'Review of Herwig Hofmann and Jacques Ziller (eds.), Accountability in the EU: The Role of the European Ombudsman, Cheltenham: Edward Elgar Publishing 2017' (2018) 11 *Review of European Administrative Law* 84–88

Komarek J, 'Reasoning with Previous Decisions: Beyond the Doctrine of Precedent' (2013) 61 *The American Journal of Comparative Law* 149–72

Kostadinova P, 'Improving the Transparency and Accountability of EU Institutions: The Impact of the Office of the European Ombudsman' (2015) 53 *Journal of Common Market Studies* 1077–93

Krajewski M and Ziółkowski M, 'EU Judicial Independence Dencentralized' (2020) 57 *Common Market Law Review* 1107–38

Krämer L, 'Access to Environmental Justice: The Double Standards of the ECJ' (2017) 14 *Journal for European Environmental & Planning Law* 159–85

Krenn C, 'The European Court of Justice's Financial Accountability: How the European Parliament Incites and Monitors Judicial Reform through the Budgetary Process' (2017) 13 *European Constitutional Law Review* 453–74

Kucsko-Stadlmayer G, *European Ombudsman-Institutions: A Comparative Legal Analysis Regarding the Multifaceted Realisation of an Idea* (Springer 2008)

Kumm M, 'Institutionalising Socratic Contestation: The Rationalists Human Rights Paradigm. Legitimate Authority and the Point of Judicial Review' (2007) 1 *European Journal of Legal Studies* 153–83

—— 'Democracy is Not Enough: Rights, Proportionality and the Point of Judicial Review' in Klatt M (ed), *The Legal Philosophy of Robert Alexy* (Oxford University Press 2009) 201–17

Kyritsis D, *Where Our Protection Lies: Separation of Powers and Judicial Review* (Oxford University Press 2017)

Lafont C, 'Philosophical Foundations of Judicial Review' in Dyzenhaus D and Thornburn M (eds), *Philosophical Foundations of Constitutional Law* (Oxford University Press 2016) 266–80

Lamandini M and Munoz DR, 'Law and Practice of Financial Appeal Bodies (ESAs' Board of Appeal, SRB Appeal Panel): A View from the Inside' (2019) 57 *Common Market Law Review* 119–60

Lasok P, *European Court Practice and Procedure* (Bloomsbury 2017)

Leczykiewicz D, '"Constitutional Justice" and Judicial Review of EU Legislative Acts' in Williams A, Burca G de and Kochenov D (eds), *Europe's Justice Deficit?* (Hart Publishing 2015) 97–108

Lee M, 'Accountability and Co-production beyond Courts: The Role of the European Ombudsman' in Weimer M and de Ruijter A (ed), *Regulating Risks in the European Union: The Co-production of Expert and Executive Power* (Hart Publishing 2017) 217–40

Leino P, 'The Wind is in the North: The First European Ombudsman (1995–2003)' (2005) 10 *European Public Law* 333–65

Lenaerts K, 'De quelques principes généraux du droit de la procédure devant le juge communautaire', *Mélanges en hommage à Jean-Victor Louis* (Editions de l'Université de Bruxelles 2003) 242–61

—— 'The Basic Constitutional Charter of a Community Based on the Rule of Law' in Maduro M and Azoulai L (eds), *The Past and Future of EU Law: The Classics of EU Law Revisited on the 50th Anniversary of the Rome Treaty* (Hart Publishing 2010) 295–315

—— 'The European Court of Justice and Process-Oriented Review' (2012) 31 *Yearbook of European Law* 3–16

Lenaerts K and others, *EU Procedural Law* (Oxford University Press 2014)

Leonelli GC, 'The Fine Line Between Procedural and Substantive Review in Cases Involving Complex Technical-scientific Evaluations: Bilbaína' (2018) 55 *Common Market Law Review* 1217–50

—— 'A Threefold Blow to Environmental Public Interest Litigation: The Urgent Need to Reform the Aarhus Regulation' (2020) 45 *European Law Review* 324–47

Lindseth P, 'Always Embedded Administration: The Historical Evolution of Administrative Justice as an Aspect of Modern Governance' in Joerges C, Stråth B and Wagner P (eds), *The Economy as a Polity: The Political Constitution of Contemporary Capitalism* (UCL Press 2010) 117–35

Lohse EJ, 'Surprise? Surprise! – Case C-115/09 (Kohlekraftwerk Lünen) – A Victory for the Environment and a Loss for Procedural Autonomy of the Member States?' (2012) 18 *European Public Law* 249–68

Lucia L de, 'A Microphysics of European Administrative Law: Administrative Remedies in the EU after Lisbon' (2014) 20 *European Public Law* 277–308

Magliveras KD, 'Best Intentions But Empty Words: The European Ombudsman' (1995) 20 *European Law Review* 401–08

Magnette P, 'The European Ombudsman: Protecting Citizens' Rights and Strengthening Parliamentary Scrutiny' in Diamandouros N (ed), *The European Ombudsman: Origins, Establishment, Evolution* (Office for Official Publications of the European Communities 2005) 106–25

Mahoney P, 'Flogging a Dead Horse: The Appropriate Human Rights Policy for Judicial Treatment of Competition Fines' in Edward D, MacLennan J and Komninos A (eds), *A Scot without Borders – Liber Amicorum Ian S Forrester*, vol I (Concurrences 2015) 225–40

Marchetti B, *Administrative Remedies in the European Union. The Emergence of a Quasi-judicial Administration* (Giappichelli Editore 2017)

Martinsen DS, *An Ever More Powerful Court? The Political Constraints of Legal Integration in the European Union* (Oxford University Press 2015)

Mashaw JL, 'Administrative Due Process: The Quest for a Dignitary Theory' (1981) 61 *Boston University Law Review* 885

—— 'Conflict and Compromise among Models of Administrative Justice' (1981) *Duke Law Journal* 181–212

Mastroianni R, 'New perspectives for the European Ombudsman opened by the Lisbon Treaty' in Hofmann HCH and Ziller J (eds), *Accountability in the EU: The Role of the European Ombudsman* (Edward Elgar 2017) 178–97

Mendes CH, *Constitutional Courts and Deliberative Democracy* (Oxford University Press 2013)

Mendes J, 'Discretion, Care and Public Interest in the EU Administration: Probing the Limits of Law' (2016) 53 *Common Market Law Review* 419–52

—— 'Bounded Discretion in EU Law: A Limited Judicial Paradigm in a Changing EU' (2017) 80 *Modern Law Review* 443–72

—— *EU Executive Discretion and the Limits of Law* (Oxford University Press 2019)

—— 'Executive Discretion in the EU and the Outer Boundaries of Law' in Mendes J (ed), *EU Executive Discretion and the Limits of Law* (Oxford University Press 2019) 3–20

Mendes J and Cseres KJ, 'Consumers' Access to EU Competition Law Procedures: Outer and Inner Limits' (2014) 51 *Common Market Law Review* 483–522

Mendes J and Venzke I, 'The idea of relative authority in European and international law' (2018) 16 *International Journal of Constitutional Law* 75–100

Micklitz H-W, 'The ECJ Between the Individual Citizen and the Member States – A Plea for a Judge-made European Law on Remedies' in Micklitz H-W and Witte B de (eds), *The European Court of Justice and the Autonomy of the Member States* (Intersentia 2012) 349–400

Micklitz H-W and Reich N, *Public Interest Litigation before European Courts* (Nomos 1996)

Moloney N, 'The European Supervisory Authorities and Discretion: Can the Functional and Constitutional Circles be Squared?' in Mendes J (ed), *EU Executive Discretion and the Limits of Law* (Oxford University Press 2019) 85–117

Morra CB, Smits R and Magliari A, 'The Administrative Board of Review of the European Central Bank: Experience After 2 Years' (2017) 18 European Business Organization Law Review 567–89

Muguet-Pullennec PG and Domenicucci DP, 'L'intervention devant le Tribunal après l'entrée en vigueur du nouveau règlement de procédure: entre droit d'ingérence et urgence judiciaire' (2015) *Revue Lamy de La Concurrence* 61–71

Naômé C, *Le pourvoi devant la Cour de justice de l'Union européenne* (Larcier 2016)

Nassis C, *Good Administration in the European Union – The Role of the European Ombudsman and the European Network of Ombudsmen* (Esperia Publications 2009)

Nazzini R, 'Administrative Enforcement, Judicial Review and Fundamental Rights in EU Competition Law: A Comparative Contextual-Functionalist Perspective' (2012) 49 *Common Market Law Review* 971–1006

Nehl HP, 'Judicial Review of Complex Socio-Economic, Technical and Scientific Assessments in the European Union' in Mendes J (ed), *EU Executive Discretion and the Limits of Law* (Oxford University Press 2019) 157–97

Neuhold C and Năstase A, 'Transparency Watchdog: Guarding the Law and Independent from Politics? The Relationship between the European Ombudsman and the European Parliament' (2017) 5 *Politics and Governance* 40–50

Nihoul P, 'La recevabilité des recours en annulation introduits par un particulier à l'encontre d'un acte communautaire de portée générale' (1994) *Revue Trimestrielle de Droit Européen* 171–94

Öberg J, 'The Rise of the Procedural Paradigm: Judicial Review of EU Legislation in Vertical Competence Disputes' (2017) 13 *European Constitutional Law Review* 248–80

O'Brien N and Thompson B, 'Human Rights and Accountability in the UK: Deliberative Democracy and the Role of the Ombudsman' (2010) *European Human Rights Law Review* 504–12

Parfouru AA de, '*Locus standi* of Private Applicants under the Article 230 EC Action for Annulment: Any Lessons to Be Learnt from France?' (2007) 14 *Maastricht Journal of European and Competition Law* 361–402

Pascalev V, 'The Clash of Scientific Assessors: What the Conflict over Glyphosate Carcinogenicity Tells Us About the Relationship between Law and Science' (2020) 11 *European Journal of Risk Regulation* 520–38

Pech L, 'A Union Founded on the Rule of Law': Meaning and Reality of the Rule of Law as a Constitutional Principle of EU Law' (2010) 6 *European Constitutional Law Review* 359–96

Pech L and Ward A, 'Effective Judicial Remedies before the Court of Justice' in Peers S, Hervey, T, Kenner, J and Ward, A (eds), *The EU Charter of Fundamental Rights A Commmentary* (Hart Publishing, CH Beck, Nomos 2014) 1241–50

Popov A, 'La complémentarité entre les recours en annulation formés par des particuliers et les renvois préjudiciels en appréciation de validité avant comme apprès l'entrée en vigueur du Traité de Lisbonne et l'accès au prétoire de l'Union européenne. Est-il (encore) légitime d'évoquer l'existence d'une "tache dans le paysage du drtoi communautaire que constitute la jurisprudence sur la recevabilité"?' (2012) *Cahiers de Droit Européen* 166–94

Prek M and Lefèvre S, '"Administrative Discretion", "Power of Appraisal" and "Margin of Appraisal" in Judicial Review Proceedings Before the General Court' (2019) 56 *Common Market Law Review* 339–80

Rasmussen H, 'Why Is Article 173 Interpreted Against Private Plaintiffs?' (1980) *European Law Review* 112–27

—— *The European Court of Justice* (GadJura 1998)

—— 'The Origins of a Legal Revolution – The Early History of the European Court of Justice' (2008) 2 *Journal of European Integration History* 77–98

Rasquin G and Chevallier R-M, 'L'article 173, alinéa 2 du traité CEE' (1966) *Revue Trimestrielle de Droit Européen* 31–46

Rawlings R, 'Engaged Elites: Citizen Action and Institutional Attitudes in Commission Enforcement' (2000) 6 *European Law Journal* 4–28

Rawls J, *A Theory of Justice* (Harvard University Press 1971)

Redish MH and Marshall LC, 'Adjudicatory Independence and the Values of Procedural Due Process' (1986) 95 *Yale Law Journal* 455–505

Remáč M, *Coordinating Ombudsmen and the Judiciary* (Intersentia 2014)

Ritleng D, 'The Independence and Legitimacy of the European Court of Justice' in Ritleng D (ed), *Independence and Legitimacy in the Institutional System of the European Union* (Oxford University Press 2016) 83–124

—— 'Judicial Review of EU Administative Discretion: How Far Does the Separation of Powers Matter' in Mendes J and Ventzke I (eds), *Allocating Authority: Who Should Do What in European and International Law?* (Hart Publishing 2017) 183–216

Rosas A, 'Oral Hearings Before the European Court of Justice' (2014) 21 *Maastricht Journal of Comparative and European Law* 596–610

Safjan M and Düsterhaus D, 'A Union of Effective Judicial Protection: Addressing a Multi-level Challenge through the Lens of Article 47 CFREU' (2014) 33 *Yearbook of European Law* 3–40

Saphire RB, 'Specifying Due Process Values: Towards a More Responsive Approach to Procedural Protection' (1978) 127 *University of Pennsylvania Law Review* 111–95

Schepel H and Blankenburg E, 'Mobilizing the European Court of Justice' in Weiler J and Búrca G de (eds), *The European Court of Justice* (Oxford University Press 2001) 9–42

Schmidt SK, *The European Court of Justice and the Policy Process: The Shadow of Case Law* (Oxford University Press 2015)

Schwarze J, 'The Legal Protection of the Individual against Regulations in European Union Law' (2004) 10 *European Public Law* 285–303

Scott J and Sturm S, 'Courts as Catalysts: Rethinking the Judicial Role in New Governance' (2007) 13 *Columbia Journal of European Law* 565–94

Serre EB de la and Sibony A-L, 'Expert Evidence Before the EC Courts' (2008) 45 *Common Market Law Review* 941–85

Sharpston E, 'Making the Court of Justice of the European Union More Productive' (2014) 21 *Maastricht Journal of Comparative and European Law* 763–70

Smedt AB de, 'La Cour de Justice dans les négociations du traité de Paris instituant la CECA' (2008) 14 *Journal of European Integration History* 7–34

Solum L, 'Procedural Justice' (2004) 78 *Southern California Law Review* 181–321

Somsen H, 'Scientists Edit Genes, Courts Edit Directives. Is the Court of Justice Fighting Uncertain Scientific Risk with Certain Constitutional Risk?' (2018) 9 *European Journal of Risk Regulation* 701–18

Sordi B, '*Revolution, Rechtstaat* and the Rule of Law: Historical Reflections on the Emergence and Development of Administrative Law' in Ackerman S-R, Lindseth P and Emerson B (eds), *Comparative Administrative Law* (Edward Elgar 2017) 23–25

Stein E and Vining J, 'Citizen Access to Judicial Review of Administrative Action in a Transnational and Federal Context' in Jacobs F (ed), *European Law and the Individual* (North-Holland 1976) 113–43

Stewart RB, 'The Reformation of American Administrative Law' (1975) *Harvard Law Review* 1667–813

Strauss PL, 'Politics and Agencies in the Administrative State: The U.S. Case' in Ackerman S-R, Lindseth PL and Emerson B (eds), *Comparative Administrative Law* (Edward Elgar 2017) 44–59

Tai BYT, 'The Ombudsman and the Rule of Law' in Hertogh M and Kirkham R (eds), *Research Handbook on the Ombudsman* (Edward Elgar 2018) 113–32

Tomkins A, 'Transparency and the Emergence of a European Administrative Law' (1999–2000) 19 *Yearbook of European Law* 217–56

Tridimas T and Gari G, 'Winners and Losers in Luxembourg: A Statistical Analysis of Judicial Review before the European Court of Justice and the Court of First Instance (2001–2005)' (2005) 35 *European Law Review* 131–73

Tridimas T and Poli S, '*Locus standi* of Individuals Under Article 230(4): The Return of Euricide' in Moser P and Sawyer K (eds), *Making Community Law: The Legacy of Advocate General Jacobs at the European Court of Justice* (Edward Elgar 2008) 77–99

Trondal J and Wille A, 'The European Ombudsman: A Resilient Institution in a Turbulent, Evolving Administrative Order' in Hofmann HCH and Ziller J (eds), *Accountability in the EU: The Role of the European Ombudsman* (Edward Elgar 2017) 28–52

Tsadiras A, 'Unravelling Ariadne's Thread: The European Ombudsman's Investigative Powers' (2008) 45 *Common Market Law Review* 757–70

—— 'Of Celestial Motions and Gravitational Attractions: The Institutional Symbiosis between the European Ombudsman and the European Parliament' (2009) 28 *Yearbook of European Law* 435–57

—— 'The European Ombudsman's Remedial Powers: An Empirical Analysis in Context' (2013) 38 *European Law Review* 52–64

—— 'The Ombudsman' in Craig P (ed), *EU Administrative Law* (Oxford University Press 2018)

Türk AH and Xanthoulis N, 'Legal Accountability of European Central Bank in Bank Supervision: A Case Study in Conceptualizing the Legal Effects of Union Acts' (2019) 26 *Maastricht Journal of Comparative and European Law* 151–64

Visser M de, 'A cautionary tale: some insights regarding judicial activism from the national experience' in Muir E, Dawson M and Witte B de (eds), *Judicial Activism at the European Court of Justice* (Edward Elgar 2013) 188–210

—— *Constitutional Review in Europe: A Comparative Analysis* (Bloomsbury 2014)

Vogiatzis N, 'One Ombudsman (EU) or Many (UK)? Interpreting the Singularity of Actors in the EU' (2013) 19 *European Public Law* 739–58

—— 'The EU's Liability Owing to the Conduct of the European Ombudsman Revisited: European Ombudsman v. Staelen' (2018) 55 *Common Market Law Review* 1251–74

—— *The European Ombudsman and Good Administration in the European Union* (Palgrave 2018)

Vos E, 'The European Court of Justice in the Face of Scientific Uncertainty and Complexity' in Dawson M, Witte B de and Muir E (eds), *Judicial Activism at the European Court of Justice* (Edward Elgar 2013) 142–66

Waelbroeck D and Bombois T, 'Des requérants "privilégiés" et des autres … À propos de l'arrêt Inuit et de l'exigence de protection juridictionnelle effective des particuliers en droit européen' (2014) 50 *Cahiers de Droit Européen* 21–75

Waelbroeck D and Slater D, '"Marginal Review" by the European Court of Justice in Competition Cases and its Compatibility with Fundamental Rights' in Merola M and Derenne J (eds), *The Role of the Court of Justice of the European Union in Competition Law Cases* (Bruylant 2012) 277–92

Waelbroeck D and Verheyden A-M, 'Les conditions de recevabilité des recours en annulation des particuliers contre les actes normatifs communautaires' (1995) 31 *Cahiers de Droit Européen* 399–441

Ward A, *Judicial Review and the Rights of Private Parties in EU Law* (Oxford University Press 2007)

—— 'National and EC Remedies under the EU Treaty: Limits and the Role of the ECHR' in Barnard C and Odudu O (eds), *The Outer Limits of European Union Law* (Hart Publishing 2009) 329–61

Warin C, 'Individual Rights and Collective Interests in EU Law: Three Approaches to a Still Volatile Relationship' (2019) 56 *Common Market Law Review* 463–88

Widdershoven R, 'The European Court of Justice and the Standard of Judicial Review' in Poorter J de, Ballin EH and Lavrijssen S (eds), *Judicial Review of Administrative Discretion in the Administrative State* (Springer 2019) 39–62

Wils W, 'The Compatibility with Fundamental Rights of the EU Antitrust Enforcement System in Which the European Commission Acts Both as Investigator and as First-Instance Decision Maker' (2014) 37 *World Competition: Law and Economics Review* 5

Witte A, 'Standing and Judicial Review in the New EU Financial Markets Architecture' (2015) 1 *Journal of Financial Regulation* 226–62

Woehrling J-M, 'Le contrôle juridictionnel de l'administration eu Europe et la distinction entre droit objectif et droits subjectifs' in Schwarze J (ed), *L'état actuel et les perspectives du droit administratif européen Analyses de droit comparé* (Bruylant 2010) 297–322

Wolferen M von and Eliantonio M, 'Access to Justice in Environmental Matters in the EU: The EU's Difficult Road towards Non-Compliance with the Aarhus Convention' in Peeters M and Eliantonio M (eds), *Research Handbook on EU Environmental Law* (Edward Elgar 2020) 148–63

Woodhouse A, 'Process Review as Panacea: A Critique of Process Review Advocacy in the European Union' (2020) 45 *European Law Review* 373–95

Woude M van der, 'Pour une protection juridictionnelle effective: Un rappel des objectifs de 1988' (2014) 4 *Concurrences*

—— 'Towards a European Council of the Judiciary: Some Reflections on the Administration of the EU Courts' in Goudappel FA and Ballin EMH (eds), *Democracy and Rule of Law in the European Union: Essays in Honour of Jaap W de Zwaan* (Springer 2016) 63–79

Zhang AH, 'The Faceless Court' (2016) 38 *University of Pennsylvania Journal of International Law* 71–135

Ziller J, 'Variations Around the O-word: The European Ombudsman from Médiateur to Garante? Some Concluding Remarks' in Ziller J and Hofmann H (eds), *Accountability in the EU: The Role of the European Ombudsman* (Edward Elgar 2018) 259–69

Ziller J and Hofmann H, *Accountability in the EU: The Role of the European Ombudsman* (Edward Elgar 2017)

Zurn C, *Deliberative Democracy and the Institutions of Judicial Review* (Cambridge University Press 2007)

—— 'A Question of Institutionalization: Habermas on the Justification of Court-Based Constitutional Review' in Ungureanu C, Guenther K and Joerges C (eds), *Habermas' Discourse Theory of Law and Democracy: From the Nation-State to Europe and the Postnational Constellation* (Ashgate 2011)

—— 'Judicial Review, Constitutional Juries and Civic Constitutional Fora: Rights, Democracy and Law' (2011) 58 *Theoria: A Journal of Social and Political Theory* 63–94

INDEX

NB – page locators in **bold** refer to information in tables, and those in *italics* refer to information in figures

www.ingramcontent.com/pod-product-compliance
Lightning Source LLC
LaVergne TN
LVHW011802200926
848484LV00003B/758

9781509947294